W9-BKX-700

PE-4-ME

Teaching Lifelong Health and Fitness

LIBRARY
FRANKLIN PIERCE COLLEGE
RINDGE, NH 03461

Cathie Summerford

Human Kinetics

Library of Congress Cataloging-in-Publication Data

Summerford, Cathie, 1957–
    PE-4-ME: teaching lifelong health and fitness / Cathie Summerford.
        p.   cm.
    Includes bibliographical references and index.
    ISBN 0-7360-0165-4
    1. Health education (Middle school)--United States.   2. Health education (Middle
school)--United States--Curricula.   I. Title: PE-for-ME.   II. Title.
LB1587.A3 S87 2000
372.3'7--dc21   99-057431

ISBN: 0-7360-0165-4
Copyright © 2000 by Cathie Summerford

All rights reserved. Except for use in a review, the reproduction or utilization of this work in any form or by any electronic, mechanical, or other means, now known or hereafter invented, including xerography, photocopying, and recording, and in any information storage and retrieval system, is forbidden without the written permission of the publisher.

Notice: Permission to reproduce the following material is granted to instructors and agencies who have purchased *PE-4-ME: Teaching Lifelong Health and Fitness*: pp. 112-253. The reproduction of other parts of this book is expressly forbidden by the above copyright notice. Persons or agencies who have not purchased *PE-4-ME: Teaching Lifelong Health and Fitness* may not reproduce any material.

Acquisitions Editor: Scott Wikgren; **Developmental Editor:** Rebecca Crist; **Assistant Editors:** Chris Enstrom, Laurie Stokoe, and Mark Zulauf; **Copyeditor:** Harbour Hodder; **Proofreader:** Sue Fetters; **Permission Manager:** Heather Munson; **Graphic Designer:** Fred Starbird; **Graphic Artist:** Kathleen Boudreau-Fuoss; **Cover Designer:** Nancy Rasmus; **Illustrators:** Tom Roberts, Mic Greenberg (193), Elizabeth Young (201), and Meghann Bell (pp. 198, 206, 212); **Printer:** Versa

Human Kinetics books are available at special discounts for bulk purchase. Special editions or book excerpts can also be created to specification. For details, contact the Special Sales Manager at Human Kinetics.

Printed in the United States of America   10   9   8   7   6   5   4   3   2   1

Human Kinetics
Web site: http://www.humankinetics.com/

United States: Human Kinetics
P.O. Box 5076
Champaign, IL 61825-5076
1-800-747-4457
e-mail: humank@hkusa.com

Canada: Human Kinetics
475 Devonshire Road Unit 100
Windsor, ON N8Y 2L5
1-800-465-7301 (in Canada only)
e-mail: humank@hkcanada.com

Europe: Human Kinetics, P.O. Box IW14
Leeds LS16 6TR, United Kingdom
+44 (0)113-278 1708
e-mail: humank@hkeurope.com

Australia: Human Kinetics
57A Price Avenue
Lower Mitcham, South Australia 5062
(08) 82771555
e-mail: liahka@senet.com.au

New Zealand: Human Kinetics
P.O. Box 105-231, Auckland Central
09-523-3462
e-mail: humank@hknewz.com

A big thank you to God
for allowing me to be His vehicle
through the PE-4-ME: Radical Wellness Program.
I am truly blessed.

Dedicated

To my loving husband, Bill, for all of your support,
encouragement, and patience.
I treasure our journey through life together,
and I love you more than you could ever know.
You will always be my champion.

To Mom and Daddy, for encouraging me to be "me."
I will always value the opportunities I was given as a child
to create, play, learn, grow, and pursue my dreams.
Thank you for all of your strength and hope. I love you.

And to my sister, Susan,
for teaching me to live each day as if it were my last.

Contents

List of Movement Examples

Movement	Page	Movement	Page

Foreword

Cathie Summerford is a teacher who cares about what children experience in physical education classes. *PE-4-ME* is a book for people who care about children and want them to leave school thinking physical activity is a positive lifetime experience. Writing books is a difficult endeavor. Authors try to convey their philosophies through a sequence of activities and ideas for teachers. It is often difficult to capture the spirit of a program on paper. What looks good in an instructional setting often looks bland in pages. With that in mind, I commend Cathie for being able to explain to readers what it takes to present an exciting and personalized program. When you read the opening pages, it will strike you that Cathie really cares. Her life is filled with emotion and concern for the welfare of others. Teaching is about helping students mature and develop into responsible adults. This text reflects such a caring approach.

PE-4-ME takes a lifetime activity approach to physical education. It is not enough to teach skills and develop fitness if youngsters leave the class with a negative attitude toward physical activity. The text presents wellness topics so that students can learn the fundamentals of nutrition, substance abuse, and antiviolence awareness. A variety of written assignments are included so that teachers can easily implement and discuss the topics.

Physical education is grounded in physical activity. This text is filled with many activities and skills that ensure skill development. Cathie Summerford writes in an easy-to-understand manner and places the activities in a theme setting. Teachers receive a theme for each week and then work with multiple activities that center on the theme. Other teachers have presented many of these activities in the past. However, I find that Cathie is able to present them in an easily understandable manner. When you read the activities, little hints and twists make you think, Why didn't I think of that?

In summary, there is nothing better than an instruction book written by a teacher who cares. One of the key ingredients of a quality program is an author who has passion for the program. Cathie Summerford demonstrates this passion. She believes in children's well-being and the importance of offering a quality physical education program. Want to improve your program? Need some fresh new ideas? Not sure how to cover the cognitive aspect of activity? Need a boost? This book should help. Cathie, I congratulate you. Keep up the good work and thanks for enhancing the lives of your students.

Robert P. Pangrazi
Professor
Arizona State University

Preface

What Is the PE-4-ME: Radical Wellness Program?

The PE-4-ME: Radical Wellness Program originated as my dream and became a reality in 1993 at Apple Valley Middle School, where it is continually utilized today. PE-4-ME blends many powerful concepts and discoveries—including the role of movement, rhythms, emotions, positive thinking, routines, environments, music, authentic assessment, enrichment, novelty, and the absence of intimidation—into a delightful physical education environment that ensures optimal learner success. The program addresses the unique needs of our student population, not only for physical development, but also for personal, social, emotional, and cognitive development. The PE-4-ME: Radical Wellness Program emphasizes prevention as the key to wellness by teaching students the importance of setting personal goals and developing self-efficacy. The overwhelming support of the students and parents is a strong indicator of the program's ongoing success.

The primary goal of the PE-4-ME: Radical Wellness curriculum is to empower students to take responsibility for their own health through a hands-on, theme-based, brain-compatible physical education program. The curriculum follows the National Association for Sport and Physical Education (NASPE) National Standards for Physical Education, and state frameworks regarding National Standards for Physical Education. The PE-4-ME: Radical Wellness Program is also an effective approach to building healthy bodies, schools, and communities as we begin the twenty-first century. In addition, the program stresses substance abuse awareness, nutrition, school safety, social health in personal interactions, and mental health fostered by personal achievement and self-confidence. All of

this is accomplished in a nurturing environment where students can take risks and learn from their mistakes without fear of embarrassment.

The tone is set from the first day of class, when students are greeted by a cheerful voice: "Welcome to PE-4-ME: Radical Wellness Program. Yes! Physical fitness, health, nutrition, learning to prevent substance abuse and violence, and 'being yourself' can be and is *fun!*" Students have been told over and over that fitness is good for them, but for kids, if it's not fun, it's not worth the effort. The PE-4-ME: Radical Wellness Program is a program that motivates students to change the way they have always thought about fitness and learn how movement can make them better learners. With the current brain research showing that movement aids learning, there is even more reason to get kids to move.

In the PE-4-ME: Radical Wellness Program, curricular units are built around themes or concepts rather than around the traditional game skills that students often find so boring. For example, instead of spending two to four weeks on soccer or basketball skills, students may spend two weeks on Cardiovascular Endurance, a week on the concept of Agility and Reaction Time, or a week on the concept of Striking With Implements. In addition, a weekly theme may be interwoven through the yearly game plan that focuses on Fitness Fuel (nutrition) or No Zone (substance/safety awareness). All of the Themes for the Week are reinforced by fun movement activities.

Weekly themes cover all aspects of health and fitness—movement, nutrition, social skills, substance abuse awareness, school safety, and other health issues. A variety of teaching tools bring these themes to life. A daily bulletin board accompanies students to the playing fields, the gym, the courts, the pool, or wherever the activity of the day is centered, reminding them with visual aids that healthy skills are for life. Nontraditional classroom ideas—like a Brain Food Box full of health and fitness tidbits, and a Sport Wows Box full of sports trivia—make "field" learning fun.

The PE-4-ME: Radical Wellness Program allows all students to succeed. Each day offers a menu of class or field activities that enable each student to participate at his or her own level, while at the same time being challenged to stretch toward higher levels of achievement. Smaller units participate in an activity simultaneously, which allows every student to be engaged in the movement activity with the necessary pieces of equipment. The PE-4-ME: Radical Wellness Program is designed to work for every student, including those with special needs. There are neither spectators nor "ball hogs."

Every student is unique and special in the program. Each one is encouraged to achieve his or her personal best and is recognized and acknowledged for personal growth. The students are encouraged to respect and appreciate individual differences. They also learn that they are valued for much more than athletic ability.

Every student keeps a Radical Wellness Book. They bring these notebooks to class daily, allowing them to add weekly homework assignments that correlate with the Theme for the Week. Each Radical Wellness Book includes:

1. Team Rules and Locker Room Guidelines
2. Team Photos
3. Activity Logs: In-Class Journals
4. Activities: PE Homework
5. Fitness Fuel: Nutrition Homework
6. Skills: In-Class Assessments
7. No Zone: Substance and Safety Awareness Homework
8. Fun Stuff: Reading, Puzzles, Brain Teasers, and Word-Search Homework

Along with the weekly homework, the students work on big projects throughout the year—a Skeleton Project, a Muscle Project, a Brain Project, a Letter-Writing Project, and Radi-cal Wellness Poster Projects. The PE-4-ME: Radical Wellness Program takes physical education to an entirely new level. It draws upon multiple intelligences as it integrates math, science, technology, reading, and even language arts into learning about movement, fitness, and health. It is a program in which every student can feel successful, not just the "athlete."

Each day, the class opens with an Instant Activity that gets the kids moving immediately. For example, students will bring their Radical Wellness Books to class and set them in front of the bulletin board on their way to Exercise Stations. At the Instant Activity is a boom box surrounded by at least six Exercise Station cards in a circle. Station cards list exercises such as jumping jacks, push-ups, bicycles, windmills, arm circles, and more. The exercises will vary throughout the year. Students rotate clockwise from one station to the next at their own pace. At the beginning of the year, for example, the students will set goals and complete a certain number of exercises at each station. As the year progresses, the number of exercises completed at each station increases. After they complete the exercises on all of the cards, they go to the bulletin board and fill out personal Activity Logs while the teacher takes roll. More information on Instant Activity is included in chapter 4.

Each day, the class closes with "put-ups"—instead of put-downs—and feedback from the students. The kids comment on what they have learned, what they liked about the day's activities, and how the class may improve. The tone is one of mutual acceptance and encouragement. Many students enjoy reading aloud from the posters on the bulletin board and commenting on the information. In addition, the students present and share the read-aloud materials from the Brain Food and Sport Wows Boxes. Students who prefer may even express themselves in their native language. Spanish can be incorporated into the class bulletin board and may frequently be heard in counting rhythms during an activity.

Through the PE-4-ME: Radical Wellness Program students learn to feel good about themselves while they are learning about their bodies and are actively engaged in health-building activities. As they work together to develop skills, they also discover the importance of teamwork and cooperation. Every student is an active member of the group and is given the opportunity to experience ownership of his or her learning community. A real sense of "family" is fostered as all students become a big part of the team.

Affective outcomes such as increased self-esteem and personal responsibility are a primary goal of the PE-4-ME: Radical Wellness Program. In addition to ongoing in-class skills assessments and weekly homework assignments, essays are assigned on such topics as "What is PE?" to evaluate students' attitude and understanding of the thematic concepts and to make program improvements. One student summed up her feelings this way: "I used to not like PE because I wasn't very athletic and people made fun of me, but now no one makes fun of me, and it doesn't matter if I'm not very athletic because I am who I am and I like me."

The PE-4-ME: Radical Wellness Program continues to make a difference in the lives of the students at Apple Valley Middle School in Apple Valley, California. Improved student behavior and positive parent support are just two indicators of the positive impact the PE-4-ME curriculum is making here.

I know the program will do the same for you. As you read this book, you will be introduced to super motivating ideas on how your PE class can be more student-friendly—a PE class where all kids are winners.

Acknowledgments

I would like to acknowledge and thank the following people:

All of my awesome students at Apple Valley Unified School District. Daily, I learn so much from you.

Ginnie and Jef Chadwick, for your "you can do it" attitude. You are both such an inspiration.

Rocky Speer, for our daily excursion together as educators. Your friendship means the world to me.

Debi Hartzler, for your relentless support and friendship. There have been many days when I have really leaned on you. Thank you. I am truly lucky to be able to call you my friend.

My Adapted Physical Education Fitness Class (PE-5) at Victor Valley College: Kathy, Clayton, Claire, Nancy, Trudy, Kevin, Steve, Sharon, Rick, and the rest of the bunch. All of you are so special.

Mama Munsey, for your never-ending love. You are such an angel.

Tami Marten, for our childhood friendship that continues to grow more and more as the years go by. Thanks for your support.

K.C. Collins, you are such a survivor and I am so proud of you. Thanks for your encouragement.

Valerie Cleveland, for all of your expertise at proofreading and your friendship as well. You are greatly appreciated.

Janet Barnes, for your courage and determination during challenging times. You inspire me. I love having you as my Bloomin' Buddy.

My Munsey family: Marsha, Patty, Chuck, Nelson, Joe, Ted, Laura, and all of the kids. My life has been so much brighter with all of you in it.

Ginjar, for your spirited personality and love for play. You are such a joy.

Linda Canepa, for your incredible artistic ability. You go girl!

Valerie Smith, for the contagious energy you put into kids. You fire me up!

Lynda Williamson, for the support I needed during a very rough time. Thanks.

Meghann Bell, for your impressive creativity. I can't thank you enough.

South PE-HP, thank you for our professional home. All of you have contributed to the PE-4-ME: Radical Wellness Program.

Dr. Terry Rizzo, for sending all of the impressive students from California State University San Bernardino. They truly keep me on my toes.

Pam Bluem, for you and your family. As time goes on, I pray for healing.

Dr. Robert Pangrazi, for taking the time to review materials regarding the PE-4-ME: Radical Wellness Program as it has matured through the years.

Debby Blanchard-Wilson, my Victor Valley College physical education department chairperson, for all of your extraordinary assistance as a wonderful educator and leader.

Eric and Diane Jensen, Carla Hannaford, Rich Allen, and the many other "movers and shakers" in the neuroscience community. Thank you for giving educators the tools to teach.

Sharon Havel, for your upbeat attitude. Each day is a little brighter with you in it.

Jean Blaydes, my neurokinesiologist friend. Thank God there are physical educators like you.

Hope Clack, our PE department is so much better with you as a part of the team.

The Kinesiology Departments at San Diego State, California State University, Fresno, and all of the master teachers and mentors along the way who taught me so much.

Bruce, Irv, and Brian, I love you guys!

Oprah Winfrey, as a public figure, for your continual quest for lifetime wellness and self-renewal. You are such a great role model for kids.

Many thanks to the breakfast club, Judy and Lou-Ann.

Scott Wikgren, for being such a great acquisitions editor at Human Kinetics. You have made this journey so much fun!

Rebecca Crist, my developmental editor at Human Kinetics: there can't possibly be a more thorough, thoughtful, detailed, and supportive developmental editor than you. You're the best!

Introduction

When my sister Susan was killed in a car accident so unexpectedly in 1989, I learned the hard way that life is just too short. My life changed forever that day. In one moment we are here, but the next anything can happen. I remember thinking to myself, "I want to turn this heart-wrenching tragedy into something positive, if that is possible." What could I do in life that would really matter? At that time I was 31 years young, selling insurance and barely making ends meet. I was doing okay, but I wasn't even close to achieving my potential. That year, I promised God, my fiancé Bill, and Susan that I would give everything I could to life, and that I would strive to make a difference in any endeavor I attempted. With Susan's inspiration, Bill's support, my energy, and God's guidance, I knew we could do it. And so, I went back to school.

My first round at higher education had been quite an experience. I was one of those San Diego State University students who would frequently ask, "What's the ocean water temperature?" or "Where's the party?" You could say I wasn't very focused. I used to wonder why people were so worried about grades and fretted about studying. Why? Testing doesn't show what you really know anyway! As you can imagine, my grades were mediocre, to say the least.

When I reentered school at California State University, Fresno, in 1990, I realized for the first time why students studied. My transfer grades were horrific! I practically had to start all over and undo the damage I had done at SDSU. I vividly remember knowing exactly what I wanted to accomplish at FSU. I wanted to become a teacher and teach physical education in a completely different way than I had experienced it. You see, my sister died in a car accident because she made a fatal choice—the choice to drink and drive. I knew I wanted to teach others how alcohol affects everyone, in all walks of life, not just the down and out. I wanted to get this message across to our young people, who naturally think they are invincible. I knew I wanted to integrate this message into physical education, and that is when my own educational journey truly began.

I will never forget sitting in a required course on the first day of the semester waiting for the professor to enter the room. The class was "Introduction to Adapted Physical Education." What the heck was "Adapted PE" anyway? I had no idea what this class was about, but rumor had it that it was extremely cumbersome with tons of homework. I didn't really want to be there. When the professor, Dr. Virginia Foster Chadwick, walked into the room, who would have ever guessed that this instructor would be my mentor for years to come? I was immediately impressed with her organization, her expectations of her students, and her mere presence. I remember thinking, I want to be a teacher and make a difference in the lives of kids like Ginnie is making with her students.

I knew from the get-go exactly what and how I wanted to teach PE. Ginnie was aware of my brain-compatible thematic approach, and continually encouraged me to "go for it." Ginnie and I shared an early distaste for PE when we were kids. I had hated PE. I was one of those kids who never got picked for a team. I was too small to play and didn't enjoy being put-down (what kid does?). Don't get me wrong—I was very athletic in individual fitness skills such as running and swimming. I would exercise at home, but I definitely wasn't encouraged athletically at school. I didn't want to compete against other people for fitness, I only wanted to better myself.

As you probably have figured out by now, I was not your typical Physical Education major. At times it was rough. Most Physical Education majors were successful in PE as kids and continued on to become awesome athletes. Not me. And I truly believe that this has been my greatest asset as a teacher. I can see the "stuff" in a PE class that doesn't work for many students because of my own personal experiences.

During my enrollment at FSU, I took a triathlon class. Jef Chadwick, Ginnie's husband, was enrolled in the class as well. On many runs, Jef and I would share ideas on physical education and health. Jef is a computer wizard and introduced me to technology. Through his guidance and encouragement I got my feet wet and took off surfing on the information superhighway. I would not be where I am today without the guidance of both Jef and Ginnie.

I would often confer with Ginnie about how I wanted to teach the "PE class that I never had." I thought about what children like, such as pictures, posters, birthdays, forts, music, and more—the same types of things we all liked as kids. Children today are still the same in many ways, and different in others. I've found, for example, that their lack of play and creative time has had a big impact on their ability to cooperate in various activities. Many kids only focus on winning, and attempt to do so at any cost. Cheating is common practice. Children today need to learn how to play, long before they begin to compete.

The PE-4-ME: Radical Wellness Program was born during my final student teaching at a local high school in 1992. I approached the Master Teachers at the school and asked them if I could apply some of my ideas and the paradigm shift from a sports-based program to a brain-compatible thematic approach into their current curriculum. No problem! I have many positive memories from that experience. The students had PE notebooks full of all of their assignments and homework. I remember putting stickers on their activity logs, not sure what their "high school" response would be to such an elementary classroom tactic. But the kids would die to get their books back and see what sticker was in their book. It was too funny.

The biggest lesson I learned from student teaching was to be myself, because the kids can see right through you. My last day at the school, there were tears in the eyes of many students. They didn't want me to go. Wow! I *had* made a difference. I knew then that I made the correct choice to be a teacher. I loved it!

For the past seven years, I have been a physical education teacher at Apple Valley Middle School in Apple Valley, California, teaching sixth grade. It's impossible for me to put down on paper all of the different experiences I have had in my classes. And I can't begin to express how rewarding it is for me as a teacher to provide children with the class I never had as a child: a class where all the kids are winners; a class that embraces so many more issues than a typical physical education class; a class that is fun!

Over the years I have frequently called on Ginnie for guidance, feedback, opinions, reflection, and friendship. There have been many times when I wanted to throw up my hands in frustration—not from anything the kids have done, but from the adults, whether in the administration, on the faculty, or among the parents. I don't believe college really prepares student teachers for all of the politics that occur in public education, and I thank God Ginnie takes the time to listen and direct, or I would go crazy! In education, it is never a dull moment.

The PE-4-ME: Radical Wellness Program became a reality because of Ginnie Chadwick's continual support when others were saying I could never do it. Ginnie was willing to look outside the realm of traditional methods and see something in what I was doing. Ginnie is an instructor who asks the question, What if? I truly hope all educators have a Ginnie Chadwick in their lives.

As you read and use this book, I want you to remember that I have created a program that works for me. I am not claiming to be an expert. I'm just a *real* teacher with *real* kids who has created a program that *really* works for me. I hope you will pull from it what works for you. There are many great ideas in the PE-4-ME: Radical Wellness Program, and I am sure you have quite a few of your own. Plug in the suggestions from this book wherever appropriate—that's the beauty of it!

During my daily routine, I usually think about my sister, Susan, knowing she is smiling down with pride. Together, we really are touching children's lives, as I am sure is true of you.

PART

I

Teaching Radical Wellness

1

Radical Wellness:
Learning for the Brain and the Body

For years, research on the benefits of physical fitness have flooded our society. Living longer, experiencing a higher quality of life, enjoying more energy, having leaner and healthier bodies, these are just some of the facts, to name a few. We could go on and on about all of the gains we experience with the physical in fitness, but what about an improvement in academic learning? Does movement actually accelerate cognition? And what effect does this have on education and how kids learn in the classroom?

A recent explosion in brain research is threatening the existing paradigms in learning and education. The new paradigm, known as brain-compatible learning, is a union of many powerful concepts and discoveries in neuroscience that ensures optimal success in learning (Jensen 1995).

As physical educators, we know about all the positive results regarding movement. Now, it is very exciting to learn what scientists are finding out about the role movement plays in cognition. I have found that school board members, superintendents, and administrators think it is great that we have fit kids, but when push comes to shove, how kids learn is their main focus—and the basis for gaining their support. Mention that math or reading test scores go up when kids move, and you will get their attention. I believe that if we tossed out the title physical

education and named it movement education, the educational community might take us more seriously. Welcome to "neural activity class." It's time to get those axons and dendrites to synapse!

Children seem to adjust to physical education as an academic class more quickly than adults do. Adults, whether they're parents, fellow teachers, coaches, or community neighbors, seem to have more trouble letting go of the "old PE" and allowing the "new PE" to take hold. Many adults still associate the PE class for the twenty-first century with the PE class they may have had as kids. Some adults are unaware of the higher standards expected of children in a high-quality physical education class, such as PE-4-ME.

The PE-4-ME: Radical Wellness Program has shifted the paradigm from a sports-based program to teaching physical education in themes or concepts—finally, a program where all kids can experience success! The program provides opportunities for kids to create projects, work together, and learn the importance of movement. The PE-4-ME: Radical Wellness Program creates an emotionally safe, fun, and friendly environment for kids by having visual cues with positive messages, daily exercise music, and "put-ups" (not "put-downs"). The PE-4-ME program exemplifies what "brain-based," or "brain-compatible," learning is all about.

WHAT IS BRAIN-COMPATIBLE LEARNING?

Cognitive scientists are in the process of transforming neurological research findings into principles that suggest new ways of looking at how students learn. This is explained in detail here. Teaching strategies such as thematic instruction, project-based learning, cooperative learning, and authentic assessment draw strong support from these brain-based learning principles. As neuroscience and cognitive science continue to expand our knowledge of "the learning brain," educators will be challenged to find effective and innovative ways to translate these new discoveries into practices that improve teaching and learning in our schools (Castruita, 1998).

The more closely the elaborate interplay of brain and body are explored by neuroscientists, the more clearly one compelling theme emerges: movement is essential to learning. It awakens and activates many of our mental capacities. It integrates and anchors new information and experience into our neural networks. And movement is vital to all the actions by which we embody and express our learning, our understanding, and ourselves (Hannaford 1995).

According to the neurophysiologist Carla Hannaford, every movement is a sensory-motor event that is linked to an intimate understanding of our physical world, the world from which all new learning derives. Every time we move in an organized, graceful manner, full brain activation and integration occurs, and the door to learning opens naturally.

Nearly half of the young people aged 12 to 21 are not vigorously active on a regular basis. In high school, enrollment in daily physical education classes dropped from 42 percent in 1991 to 25 percent in 1995. Only 19 percent of all high school students are physically active for 20 minutes or more in physical education classes every day during the school week (U.S. Department of Health and Human Services 1996). This is bad news.

Let's face it: in education, there are more and more programs being pushed onto the teaching platter today. We are all familiar with the urgent need to raise the standardized test scores, reduce violence, improve reading, implement drug awareness, teach across the curriculum, and more. If education wants to do more with the same amount of time, something has to give. And PE, the Rodney Dangerfield ("I can't get no respect") of education, is usually the first to go. Because some school officials in charge have not kept up with the current Frameworks and National Standards, they still believe physical education is an educational frill. This kind of thinking is misguided.

Linking physical fitness and how we think is actually not a new concept. However, practicing it in education is fairly recent. PE is the "body" stuff, and so-called real academic classes—the "mind stuff"—is what's really important, according to many school administrations. I hope this book will help you put on your "thinking cap" regarding how movement and learning embrace each other, and how movement, in fact, anchors learning.

We, as physical educators, have known for quite some time that kids need at least 30 minutes a day of quality exercise to maintain a healthy body. They also need 30 minutes of daily quality exercise to stimulate the brain, says the President's Council on Fitness and Sports (1979). And as a bonus, if the exercise is aerobic, memory is enhanced as well (Jensen 1997).

Can regular exercise actually make you brighter? A research project done in Canada revealed some powerful information. When kids had their quality physical education time increased to one-third of their school day without changing other academic strategies, their academic test scores went up (Jensen 1997). Fred Gage from the Salk Institute of Neuroscience in La Jolla, California recently overturned the long-standing dogma in neuroscience that we do not gain new brain cells after birth. He has shown that mice raised in what he calls "enriched environments"—which included treadmills, toys, a varied diet, and increased opportunities for social interaction—grew more new brain cells than their litter mates housed in standard laboratory cages. Running doubled the number of brain cells in the mice on the move (Gage 1999). He also pointed out that learning a specific task—any task—might stimulate changes in existing brain cells rather than boost the growth of new cells. So, are the mobile mice smarter? According to Dr. Gage, "It seems reasonable to think they might be—the new cell growth takes place in the part of the

The PE-4-ME program lets all kids participate in a cooperative environment—so every kid can be on our team of winners.

brain called the hippocampus, which has been linked by many studies to learning and memory. And the enriched-environment mice in previous studies performed better on learning tests" (Gage 1999).

When kids discover their world through multiple pathways, better learning occurs (Jensen 1997). A wealth of brain research already supports this theory, and new findings are rapidly emerging. As a physical education teacher, I am not a practitioner of brain research but a translator. I am not qualified to explain the intricacies and complexities of how the brain works, but I urge you as an educator to find out everything you can about the latest explorations on the brain and how children learn. Share the facts about movement and learning with your colleagues. Go to the officials in your district and share the great news with them. You can make a difference!

As educators, our job is to prepare kids so that they can flourish in the real world. Unfortunately, many people mistakenly believe that what is required to be successful in school is the same as what is required to be successful in life. In fact, success in these two arenas requires very different sets of skills. It is true that the ability to read, write, and compute well is important; however, those who get ahead in the world—whatever the criteria—do not do so simply because they read, write, or compute better than others. The people who flourish in

real life do tend to perform well in traditional academic areas, but they also excel because of their ability to understand and work with others, as well as their ability to capitalize on their strengths and compensate for their weaknesses.

The PE-4-ME: Radical Wellness Program plays on these intelligences by promoting children's ability to understand each other and by emphasizing activities where kids need to work together. Of course, throwing in competitive activities now and then is healthy, but to base an entire physical education program on competition can be very damaging to many children. Many kids look at competition as a threat. Threat creates stress, which hinders the learning process. A physical education program for children that begins with an organized sport is analogous to a language arts program beginning with a Shakespearean sonnet. I have had top athletes in my classes who have enjoyed the freedom to work with their peers and felt relieved that they don't have to compete and win. When kids have to win, it can be pretty stressful, and teach the wrong message—you're not okay if you lose. When kids truly work together, magic will happen.

When competitive sports are offered to children, the message to them should be, if you don't win, it *is* okay. The most important competitive concept in the PE-4-ME: Radical Wellness Program is teaching students about personal excellence. If you do your best, that is all you can ask. Strive to be better today than you were yesterday.

As we begin this new millennium, you can create a PE-4-ME: Radical Wellness Program at your school and take your physical education curriculum to the forefront in education. Remember, if you always do what you always did, you will always get what you always got.

For more information and some highly suggested reading materials regarding brain research and movement, I here recommend my favorites. However, there are many, many other books, articles, and reports on the subject that are excellent. A great place to start searching for information is at the The Brain Store, either in person or on the Web:

www.thebrainstore.com

The Brain Store
4202 Sorrento Valley Blvd., Suite B
San Diego, CA 92121

800-325-4769

My favorites include the following books:

Dennison, P. and G. 1994. *Brain Gym.*

Hannaford, C., ed. *Smart Moves.*

Howard, P., ed. *The Owner's Manual for the Brain.*

Jensen, E., ed. *Super Teaching.*

Jensen, E., ed. *Teaching With the Brain in Mind.*

Pert, C., ed. *Molecules of Emotion.*

Sylwester, R., ed. *A Celebration of Neurons.*

USING PE-4-ME FOR ALL GRADE LEVELS

Although this book focuses on upper elementary and middle school grades, the PE-4-ME: Radical Wellness Program can be used from kindergarten through the university level. Instead of basing physical education on sports alone, physical educators teach wellness themes or concepts at an early age and expand on them throughout the school years and well into college. The need for basing physical education on concepts is quite simple. Our children need to learn and understand *why* movement is so critical to learning; the concept becomes the focal point, not the activity. Within the activities, children learn *how* to move and participate, how to cooperate with others, how to strive for common goals, as well as stress-reduction strategies and many other healthy skills for life. The movement activity becomes the vehicle for learning about the Theme for the Week.

The theme can be conveyed using different activities and the depth of the subject can be adjusted for students of all ages. For example, the theme Cardiovascular Endurance provides the students with a great opportunity to learn about their hearts, to engage in activities pertaining to the heart, and more. Let's look at how the theme of Cardiovascular Endurance can be presented at different grade levels.

In the primary grades, children should learn the very basics about the heart. They learn what happens to their hearts when they move their bodies. They discover that they can learn how fast or slow their heart is beating even though they can't see it. This is amazing to youngsters! A stethoscope (even a toy one works) is a great tool to incorporate into an early elementary physical education setting. The children hear the beat of the heart distinctly. The faster they move the faster the beat. Talk to the kids about why their faces turn red when they play. Of course, all the movement activities would be cardio-oriented. Including cross-curricular exercises about the heart, such as drawing a heart, spelling the word, singing a song, or creating a skit, reinforces the theme.

The upper elementary and middle school grades are the areas of instruction emphasized in this book. When the cardiovascular theme is taught, the students are exposed to many aspects of the heart, from how to estimate their target heart rate to calculating the upper and lower limits of their target heart-rate zone. They keep a daily record that tracks their heart rates in their activity logs. Their Radical Wellness Homework revolves around cardiovascular endeavors. Included in the instruction of cardiovascular endurance is the use of high-tech heart-rate monitors. The students are amazed when they actually see the number flashing on the watch, and they love the beeping sound. All activities are fast-paced and high-energy. More information about teaching this theme to this age group may be found in chapter 2, "Teaching in Thematic Units."

The high school years are critical for getting young people to move. Many of them are already settling into very sedentary lives. The PE-4-ME: Radical Wellness Program continues teaching themes instead of sports. You may be wondering, "How do you cover this theme again, knowing they've covered it a dozen times before?" First of all, the themes are taught in much greater depth. In the case of the cardiovascular theme, for example, kids in high school can learn about aerobic exercise in greater detail, then create an aerobic workout with their teammates. They learn the warm-up, the aerobic activity, and the cool-down portions of a workout. I have had the students work in groups five or more, bring music, and put together a portion of a fitness video. After the teacher videotapes the kids' routines, all the classes work out to the fitness videos of all the groups. It's fun stuff! The students learned so much and had such a great time that they want to make more videos.

At the high school age, many students are concerned about having too much body fat. What a great time to teach them how cardiovascular activities can keep their weight down and their energy up. When kids learn the concepts about cardiovascular endurance and then "go run a mile," the fitness recommendations make sense to them. They have learned cardiovascular-intensive exercise is a healthy skill for life, not a punishment.

The high school students can also learn about how cardiovascular movement facilitates cognition. By offering classes such as "Movin' Up Those SATs," "Stress Zappers," and "Sharpening Your Saw," you can teach young people how to participate and compete in the game of life, and win. With teen suicides and drug use on the rise, kids need to know they have a choice. In his international best-seller *The Seven Habits of Highly Effective People*, Stephen Covey includes movement as one of the seven central behaviors for success. Habit number seven, "Sharpen the Saw," discusses the principles of balanced self-renewal and how the physical dimension, including cardiovascular exercise, nutrition, and stress management, are central to the lifestyle that makes people highly effective (Covey 1989). Why aren't we teaching this to our children?

Teaching the PE-4-ME: Radical Wellness Program at the university level continues in much the same fashion as the high school level, but the themes are more involved and the physical activities are more intense. Courses on subjects such as exercise physiology teach us much of the science to incorporate into a cardiovascular theme at the college level. Teacher preparation in university level classes can emphasize *how* to teach in themes. Your creativity is truly unlimited when deciding what to implement into the PE-4-ME: Radical Wellness Program. Because the emphasis is on the concept and not the activity, students have a choice as to how they want to move. When certain sports or activities are more popular than others, there isn't a problem; just adjust your program accordingly.

While the activities and teaching concepts presented here may seem middle-school-specific, be assured that the innovative idea of teaching in themes instead of skills can work for you—no matter what grade level you teach.

PE-4-ME ADDRESSES SCHOOL VIOLENCE PREVENTION

If you walk onto the Apple Valley Middle School campus in Apple Valley, California, you will find that the PE-4-ME: Radical Wellness Program is not only the curriculum for physical education, but also the program servicing student awareness for school violence prevention. Shifting a PE program based on sports to a program where all kids learn to value each other, get along, cooperate, and take the "must" out of winning can make for a very powerful hour of the day. As you will see, the PE-4-ME: Radical Wellness Program can play a vital role in school violence prevention.

In our society, when children enter middle school they may take their first structured, regular physical education class. That is the case in our school district. Some children think of PE as a "giant recess," "park and recreation," or "after-school sports." Whatever their expectations, most of the students assume that PE is all about competition. They have to win—and they will go to any and all lengths to win. In the past five years, I have seen a dramatic increase in cheating, lying, "in-your-face" talking, fighting, crying, threats, and more. It used to take me a couple of weeks to shift the tone from competition to cooperation, but nowadays it takes much longer than that. Kids are being taught at earlier and earlier ages that they will be rewarded if they win—and looked down upon if they lose.

Don't get me wrong—winning has its place. Sports programs and athletics are critical to child development. After-school programs are vital to our communities. Nonetheless, children need to see the other side of the coin as well. It's all about having a healthy balance in their lives. Balance is critical. They need to learn that not all activities are based on competition, and that it's okay if they don't win every time.

The last thing we as educators should be doing is allowing our physical education programs to honor the athlete and neglect the many other students in the PE class. Physical education programs should not be based on sports alone, but on positive movement experiences that encourage social interaction and develop self-esteem for all students. Our school athletic programs should be "after-school" programs. Student-athletes should be applauded, but not in a physical education class. When athletics is taught in PE, the entire class knows who the "jocks" are, and the students in this clique are now set apart from the rest of the class.

What role do cliques play in schools? As the old story goes, it's the frustrated "outcasts" versus the popular kids on campus. With easy access to guns, knives, and drugs, what kind of new problems do we face as children play out their hostilities through violent acts? Cliques come in a variety of guises: preppies, stoners, gang-bangers, skaters, jocks, nerds, "goths," surfers, cowboys, and on and on, depending on where you live. How can schools de-emphasize the separation of students into cliques and bring them together as a team? And is such a coalition possible?

Yes, it is possible. Use the PE-4-ME: Radical Wellness Program to value every child in the class. If a student works with others, participates, cooperates, gives his or her best effort, and completes the Radical Wellness Homework, then that student is celebrated. Every student sets his or her own goals. And every student knows his or her own potential for greatness— that he or she could become the next Michael Jordan, Mia Hamm, or whoever their favorite

role model may be. In the PE-4-ME: Radical Wellness Program, athletic ability does not foster more attention, a better grade, or special treatment. The PE-4-ME class creates the feeling of being a member of one big family. For many kids, this may be the first time in their lives that they have been treated as such.

Any clique can cause trouble, including the cliques that are considered positive in our American society. Without a doubt, most student-athletes are very nice and courteous to their peers. On many school campuses, however, some of the jocks are the instigators. Often it is they that can be abusive. They can be cruel to their less fortunate and less socially prominent peers. Some jocks pick on less popular kids because they think it's just fun to do. And to add insult to injury, some jocks are even exempt from PE class because they are involved in sports. Other extracurricular activity participants such as cheerleaders, band members, and cadet corps participants are often exempt from PE as well. Many administrations think these exemptions are justified because the students get exercise. However, they need to learn social interaction just as much as other students do, if not more. These students need to develop empathy and compassion for all students on the campus, including those who are less popular than they are, and they need to acquire the tools to relate to others mutually.

The socially less fortunate students, or "outcasts," would like the popular kids on campus to interact with them. Most of these students want and need to belong; of course, it may be "uncool" to act like they care. The walls that divide students will continue to rise if these issues are not addressed. The physical education class is a perfect arena in which to unite all kids. It is a tragedy to allow the separation of kids, or what I call "clique development," in our schools. This simply should not be happening to children. Let's teach them the skills to get along.

It is also important to recognize that pop culture can be very violent. Children are bombarded with vicious images on the TV screen and the movie screen, on the Internet and in video games, and even in sporting events. If children are not taught about maintaining an emotional/psychological/social balance with healthy activities, the media can have damaging effects. A student may act out the violence he or she is seeing.

When children go to school everyday and are put-down, made fun of, teased, harassed, and simply treated badly, they will get very frustrated. A quality physical education program will address and discourage negative social behaviors. It's no wonder that there is so much mayhem on our campuses. There isn't enough emphasis on and support for programs like the PE-4-ME: Radical Wellness Program that address cooperation between our students. Many children are not learning these skills at home or in the media. Popular culture at large is not valuing or glorifying such skills, and may even belittle them. More than ever, basic social skills need to be taught at school.

The California State Frameworks for physical education addresses three goals: to teach and develop movement skills, social interaction, and self-esteem. Many states have similar frameworks or guidelines to build curriculums. Social interaction skills and improved self-esteem

might prevent some of students' anger and violence from showing up in school. I can think of no better place to teach school violence prevention than in a physical education class. The PE-4-ME: Radical Wellness Program celebrates all students. It teaches movement skills through cooperative activities where all kids are having fun and all pupils are treated as winners. Social interaction is addressed, taught, and is a central focus of the curriculum. All kids need to belong, and if they can't belong in a positive way at school, they'll find a way to belong in some other way such as joining a gang. Prevention is the key to success.

In conclusion, more support and money should be put into preventing violent disturbances in the schools rather than into fixing the problems after the fact. Cooperative programs like the PE-4-ME: Radical Wellness Program can help. Let's educate our children to create safer, united communities through quality daily physical education programs. Let's say "NO" to school violence and "YES" to PE-4-ME.

2

Teaching in Thematic Units

Why should physical education be taught in themes? Why should physical education integrate into its discipline, in addition to movement, other issues such as nutrition, drug awareness, and school violence prevention? The reasons for teaching physical education in themes is quite clear: children will learn. The main goal of theme-based physical education is to help students develop positive attitudes toward physical activity, grasp the underlying concepts of movement, become skillful movers, and understand wellness skills for life. Thematic teaching creates natural opportunities for progression in education. The students can learn kinesthetically, visually, socially, emotionally, as well as academically through meaningful Themes for the Week.

This chapter presents the different themes and concepts for 36 weeks of the PE-4-ME: Radical Wellness Program, including 26 weeks of physical education concepts, 6 "Fitness Fuel" weeks of nutrition concepts, and 4 "No Zone" weeks of alcohol and substance abuse prevention. This guide is for an entire school year. The Graphic Organizer (page 13) is a quick reference to what is covered through the year in an easy-to-read format. Following the graphic organizer is what I call the Roadmap for the year. This is another quick, user-friendly tool to steer you through the year, but it is more detailed. Finally, this chapter includes the Make It Happen cards, which provide a detailed menu of teaching ideas. Each card shows the theme for the week, the week number, movement examples, and, if

applicable, activities sheets, skill sheets, and fun stuff sheets. There are thirty-six Make It Happen cards, one for each week of school.

ORGANIZING THE THEMES

Your semester will begin with two weeks of physical education orientation, called Locker Room Boot Camp. In these two weeks, students will learn everything they need to know to have a strong foundation for a safe and successful year in PE-4-ME. (A more detailed plan for Locker Room Boot Camp can be found in chapter 4.) Following these introductory sessions, each week introduces a new wellness theme, or expands upon a previous theme—giving your students a continuum of wellness concepts.

Although the weekly themes build on the lessons learned in previous weeks, the PE-4-ME: Radical Wellness Program allows for teachers to integrate new concepts or shift gears whenever they feel the need. There are twenty-six weeks of movement concepts, six weeks of nutrition, and four weeks of substance and safety awareness. For example, if a class is in PE Week 7, you may want to plan the following week with FF (Fitness Fuel) Week 1. No problem! Just continue with PE Week 8 when you return to the movement themes. The Weekly Theme for PE at the end of this chapter is an example of how you might travel through the year.

The possibilities for integrating Fitness Fuel and No Zone weeks are virtually unlimited. However, you need to make sure you keep the weeks in numerical order, as each week builds on the next. For example, you would not teach Fitness Fuel Week 5 before you taught Fitness Fuel Week 3.

I love teaching in themes because it provides much flexibility, yet at the same time is very structured. Because of the rich balance of novelty and ritual, the students and I never get bored. When students aren't bored, learning occurs.

Now, it's time for you to grab a thematic unit card and "make it happen." Enjoy!

PE-4-ME Radical Wellness Program

A BRAIN-FRIENDLY LEARNING APPROACH TO PHYSICAL EDUCATION

Locker room boot camp
What is physical education?
Physical education handbook review
Locks and locker room guidelines
Locker room boot camp
final assessment

Training camp
(Class management)
Rules—safety
Manners—cooperation
Preparing Radical
Wellness Books

Personal excellence
Goal setting

Self-image
Feeling good
about yourself

Fitness fuel
Nutrition

Health-related components of fitness
Cardiovascular endurance
Muscular strength and endurance
Body composition
Flexibility

Skill-related components of fitness
Agility and reaction time
Speed and power

Striking with body parts
Striking with upper body
Striking with lower body

Brain power
Moving-4-learning

No zone
Substance and
safety awareness

Striking with implements
Rackets, bats,
sticks, and more

Moving through space
Moving your body
(coordination and rhythm)
Moving an object

Throwing and catching
Throwing accurately
Catching accurately

Body management
Balance, flight, and
explosive movement

Social skills review
Getting along
Stress-busters

PE-4-ME Radical Wellness Program

A BRAIN-FRIENDLY LEARNING APPROACH TO PHYSICAL EDUCATION

Locker Room Boot Camp

PE Week 1–2

Locker Room Boot Camp

For the first and second week of school, the days are set up as such:

Lesson 1

Super fun intro activities with kids

Movement Examples

Hi, How Are Ya? Gotta Go
Toss-a-Name Game
Birthday Line

Lesson 2

Depending when school starts, Locker Room Boot Camp (everything you need to know to be successful in a locker room). This includes all grade levels.

Locker Room Procedures

#1 What Is Physical Education?
#2 Physical Education Handbook Review
#3 Locks and Locker Room Guidelines
#4 Locker Room Boot Camp Final
Assessment

Movement Examples

Partner Handshakes

Training Camp

The Training Camp is a time to truly train the kids on appropriate behavior. I spend two weeks (very carefully) going over and participating in activities that work on class management.

PE Week 3

Training Camp

(Class Management and Preparing Radical Wellness Books)

• Your rules
• Your divider cover sheets
• Activity log
• Be Fit at Home Checklist

Fun Stuff

#1 Second Chances

Movement Examples

Personal Space
General Space
Scrambled Eggs
Interviews
People to People
Whistle Mixer
Psychic Shake
Match Mates
To the Rescue
Roadway
Aura
Safety Tag

PE Week 4

Training Camp

(Class Management)

Activities

#1 Class Act
#2 Superstars
#3 Symbolizing Movement in Pictures
#4 Symbolizing Movement in Words

Movement Examples

Flag Grab
Toe Tag
Triangle Tag
Group Juggling
Equipment Count
Courtesy Tag

Brain Power

PE Week 5

Moving-4-Learning

Activities

#5 PE . . . Not a No-Brainer?
#6 What's BDNF?
#7 Heart-Brain Buddy System
#8 Sound Body, Sound Mind

Skills

#1   A Peer Evaluation Manners Checklist

Movement Examples

Instant Activity Intro
Crows and Cranes
Rock, Paper, Scissors
Partner Tag
Blob Tag
Brainy Balloon Balance
Shoulder Circles and Massage
Knots
Criss-Crossies

Personal Excellence

PE Week 6

Personal Excellence and Goal Setting

Activities

#9   Personal Excellence
#10 Do I Need an Attitude Adjustment?

Skills

#2   Goal Setting
      (for first semester)

Fun Stuff

#2   Swim With a Buddy
      Don't Be a Fool . . . Follow the Rules!

Movement Examples

Chicken Games
Hog Call
Back-to-Back Dancing
Brainy Barnyard
Warp Speed Group Juggle
Blind Tag

PE Week 7

Personal Excellence and Goal Setting

Activities

#11 How Competitive Am I?
#12 Thinking About Personal Excellence
      in Cooperative Activities
#13 Thinking About Personal Excellence
      in Competitive Activities
#14 Thinking About Personal Excellence
      in Social Activities

Movement Examples

Buckets
British Bulldog

Dog and a Bone
Fun Run Starting Point

Health-Related Components of Fitness

PE Week 8

Cardiovascular Endurance

Activities

#15 Attitude Toward Fitness
      Target Heart Rate Sheet
#16 The Parts of Physical Fitness

Fun Stuff

#3   Skeleton Crossword Puzzle

Movement Examples

Heart Rate Monitors
Rocks
Tennis Ball Relay
Obstacle Course
Circuit Training Stations

PE Week 9

Cardiovascular Endurance

Activities

#17 Components of Physical Fitness
#18 United in Fitness #1

Fun Stuff

#4   Pulse Rate
      The American Sign Language
      Alphabet

Movement Examples

Relays
Aerobic Conga Line
Sweatshop Hop
Mini-Soccer Games
Two-Deep Fitness
Go for It!

PE Week 10

Body Composition

Activities

#19 United in Fitness #2
#20 United in Fitness Challenge Review

Skills

#3   A Group Evaluation Complimenting
      Checklist

Fun Stuff

#5 Swim Hidden Picture
    Math Fractions Boxing

Movement Examples

Aerobic Card Fun
Jump Rope Challenges
Push-Up Wave
Partner Sit-Ups
Hawaiian Banana Ball Mini-Games
Jump Bands
Aquatic Activities

PE Week 11

Muscular Strength and Endurance

Activities

#21 Muscles, Muscles, and More Muscles

Skills

#4 A Group Evaluation High-Five
    Checklist

Fun Stuff

#6 Sports Word-Search
    Wow . . . Double Trouble!
#7 Muscle Magic
    Muscle Word-Search

Movement Examples

Scooter Boards
Tumbling and Gymnastics
Pass the Shoe
Macarena Push-Ups
Math Fitness Fun
Shark Attack

PE Week 12

Flexibility

Activities

#22 Range of Motion

Skills

#5 A Peer and Self-Evaluation NO PUT-
    DOWNS Checklist

Fun Stuff

#8 Sports Fun Puzzle
    Sports Name Game

Movement Examples

Knots
Tarantula

Centipedes
Spiderweb
Slingshots
Chicken Tire Tag
Skin the Snake
Hot Swatter

Skill-Related Components of Fitness

PE Week 13

Speed and Power

Activities

#23 Analyzing Movement
#24 "Checking Out" Locomotor Skills

Skills

#6 A Peer Evaluation Speed and Power
    Checklist

Fun Stuff

#9 Basketball Hidden Picture
    Math Factors Fruit

Movement Examples

Bonus Ball
Three-Legged Races
Across the River
Prediction Run
Power Walk
Inner Tube Relay
Buckets
Jump Rope Challenges

PE Week 14

Agility and Reaction Time

Activities

#25 Agility and Reaction Time

Skills

#7 A Peer Evaluation Agility and
    Reaction Time Checklist
#2 Goal Setting (for second semester)

Movement Examples

Juggling
Swedish Softball
Four-Square
Rocks
Crows and Cranes
British Bulldog

Moving Through Space

PE Week 15

Moving Your Body Through Space
(Coordination and Rhythm)

Skills

#8 Moving a Body Through Space (Dance)

Fun Stuff

#10 Freaky Football Find
Soccer City

Movement Examples

Electric Slide
Surf City
Centerfield
Hand Jive
Elvis Dance
Slap Leather

PE Week 16

Moving an Object Through Space

Skills

#9 Frisbee Fun . . . A Moving-an-Object-
Through-Space Self-Evaluation Checklist

Movement Examples

Spinjammers and Frisbees
Freaking Frisbees
Foxtail Golf
Zwirl Footballs and More
Bocce Ball
Fling-Its
Ribbon Balls
Yo-Yos

Throwing and Catching

PE Week 17

Throwing

Activities

#26 What Games, Sports, or Activities
Use Throwing?
#27 Power Throwing

Skills

#10 A Self-Evaluation Throwing Checklist

Movement Examples

Throw and Run
Star Wars

Big Ball Throw
Swedish Softball
Hawaiian Banana Ball Mini-Games
Mini-Football Games

PE Week 18

Basketballs
(Throwing, Catching, and Dribbling)

Activities

#28 Basketball Fun
#29 Happenin' Hoops

Fun Stuff

#11 Skin Facts: Simple Steps to Protect
Your Skin
Safety First

Movement Examples

Basketball Fun
Mini-Basketball Games
Zone-Passing Basketball
Goal Ball
Sideline Basketball
Basket Bowl
Kickball Basketball

PE Week 19

Catching and Receiving

Activities

#30 Stepping Into It

Skills

#11 A Self-Evaluation Catching Checklist

Movement Examples

Throw and Run
Freaking Frisbees
Swedish Softball
Hawaiian Banana Ball Mini-Games
Mini-Football Games

Body Management

PE Week 20

Balance

Activities

#31 Balance
#32 Principles of Balance

Skills

#12 A Group Evaluation Balancing Act
Checklist

Movement Examples
Partner Balances
Trust Falls
Squat Thrusts
Human Ladders
2 × 4 Quicksand Save
Group Tugs
Pyramid Building

PE Week 21

Flight and Explosive Movement

Activities
#33 Learning About the Principles of Flight
#34 Landing Safely Back to Earth
#35 Body Management

Skills
#13 A Group Evaluation Explosive
    Movement Checklist

Movement Examples
Crows and Cranes
Rock, Paper, Scissors
Partner Tag
Blob Tag
Mini-Basketball Games
Rocks
Hand Jive

Striking With Body Parts

PE Week 22

Striking With Upper Body
  (Bumping, Serving, Setting, and More)

Activities
#36 Striking With Body Parts

Skills
#14 A Peer Evaluation: Striking With
    Upper Body (Arms)

Fun Stuff
#12 Chef Hidden Picture
    Math Fractions Running

Movement Examples
Volleying Drills
Thunder Bumper
Volleyball
Four-Square

Tetherball
Strikeball Basketball

PE Week 23

Striking With Lower Body
  (Kicking and More)

Activities
#37 Fancy Feet

Skills
#15 A Striking-With-Lower-Body
    Self-Evaluation Checklist

Fun Stuff
#13 Brain and Body Fitness
#14 Moving for Learning

Movement Examples
Soccer Drills
Tunnels
Triangle Soccer
Soccer Croquet
Mini-Soccer Games
Hacky Sacks
Takraw
Rounders
Kick and Run

Striking With Implements

PE Week 24

Striking With Implements
  (Rackets, Bats, Sticks, and More)

Activities
#38 Striking and Liking It
#39 Match 'Em

Skills
#16 A Striking-With-Implements
    Self-Evaluation Checklist

Movement Examples
Racket/Paddle Bucket Stations
Triangle Hockey
Four-Square Paddle Tennis
Swedish Softball
Mini-Hockey Games
Hit and Run
Putt-and-Strut Golf
Badminton Fun

Self-Image

PE Week 25

Feeling Good About Yourself

Activities

#40 Fun Time
#41 Hurrah!

Fun Stuff

#15 Basketball Boogie Word Find
    And the Rest Is History. . .

Movement Examples

Heart Rate Monitors
British Bulldog
Dog and a Bone
Fun Run Starting Point
Criss-Crossies

Social Skills Review

PE Week 26

Getting Along
  (Stress-Busters)

Activities

#42 The Blame Game?
#43 Stress-Busters
    What is PE? End of School
    Reply

Movement Examples

Student's Choice, Anything Goes!

Fitness Fuel

FF Week 1

Nutrition

Fitness Fuel

#1   Calorie Graph
#2   Nutrition Puzzle

Movement Examples

Crows and Cranes
Rock, Paper, Scissors
Partner Tag
Blob Tag
Mini-Football Games

FF Week 2

Nutrition

Activities

#3   Energy Expenditure Info
     Let's Do Lunch!
#4   Healthy Hamburger . . . Is It Possible?
#5   Alien Label Connection

Movement Examples

Hog Call
Brainy Barnyard
Brainy Balloon Balance
Chicken Tire Tag
Warp Speed Group Juggle
Blind Tag

FF Week 3

Nutrition

Activities

#6   Eating What's Fit
#7   Balancing Act
#8   All Systems Go!
#9   The "Wild and Crazy" *Chef de Haute*
     Cuisine

Movement Examples

Back-to-Back Dancing
Rocks
Tennis Ball Relay
Obstacle Course
Circuit Training Stations
Mini-Hockey Games

FF Week 4

Nutrition

Activities

#10 Dying of Thirst?
#11 Scrambled Words, Not Eggs
#12 Interview an Athlete
#13 Our Bodies . . . Mean Machines
#14 Answer Sheet (not a worksheet)

Movement Examples

Basketball Fun
Mini-Basketball Games
Zone-Passing Basketball
Goal Ball
Sideline Basketball
Basket Bowl
Kickball Basketball

FF Week 5

Nutrition

Activities

#15 You Choose!
#16 Food Record!
#17 Buiding My Pyramid

Movement Examples

Aerobic Card Fun
Jump Rope Challenges
Hawaiian Banana Ball Mini-Games
Shark Attack
Scooter Boards
Hit and Run

FF Week 6

Nutrition

Activities

#18 How Much Is a Serving?
#19 Where's the Fat?

Movement Examples

Chicken Tire Tag
Hot Swatter
Juggling
Swedish Softball
Electric Slide
Slap Leather

No Zone

NO Week 1

Substance and Safety Awareness

Activities

#1   Substance and Safety Survey

Movement Examples

Four-Square
Yo-Yos
Freaking Frisbees
Surf City
Mini-Soccer Games

NO Week 2

Substance and Safety Awareness

Activities

#2   Dear Ms. Advice
#3   Tobacco Quiz

Movement Examples

Basketball Fun
Mini-Basketball Games
Zone-Passing Basketball
Goal Ball
Sideline Basketball
Basket Bowl
Kickball Basketball

NO Week 3

Substance and Safety Awareness

Activities

#4   Poster Power

Movement Examples

Star Wars
Hawaiian Banana Ball Mini-Games
Mini-Football Games
Four-Square Paddle Tennis
Hit and Run
Fling-Its

NO Week 4

Substance and Safety Awareness

Activities

#5   "Random Acts of Kindness" Survey
#6   Protecting Yourself

Movement Examples

Aerobic Conga Line
Sweatshop Hop
Two-Deep Fitness
Bocce Ball
Big Ball Throw
Mini-Football Games

PE 1-2

PE-4-ME Radical Wellness Program
• • • • • • • • • • • • • • • • Make-It-Happen Card • • • • • • • • • • • • • •

THEME FOR THE WEEK
Locker Room Boot Camp

■ *Locker Room Procedures*

Introduction: Fun Day
1. What Is Physical Education?
2. Physical Education Handbook Review
3. Locks and Locker Room Guidelines
4. Locker Room Boot Camp Final Assessment

■ *Movement Examples*

Hi, How Are Ya? Gotta Go
Toss-a-Name Game
Birthday Line
Partner Handshakes

PE 3

PE-4-ME Radical Wellness Program
• • • • • • • • • • • • • • • • Make-It-Happen Card • • • • • • • • • • • • • •

THEME FOR THE WEEK
Training Camp

■ *Topics*

Class Management
Safety
Manners
Cooperation
Rules
Preparing Radical Wellness Books

■ *Activities*

Activity Log
Be Fit at Home Checklist

■ *Fun Stuff*

1. Second Chances

■ *Movement Examples*

Personal Space	Psychic Shake
General Space	Match Mates
Scrambled Eggs	To the Rescue
Interviews	Roadway
People to People	Aura
Whistle Mixer	Safety Tag

PE-4-ME Radical Wellness Program

Make-It-Happen Card

THEME FOR THE WEEK

Training Camp

■ Activities

1. Class Act
2. Superstars
3. Symbolizing Movement in Pictures
4. Symbolizing Movement in Words

■ Movement Examples

Flag Grab
Courtesy Tag
Toe Tag
Triangle Tag
Group Juggling
Equipment Count

PE-4-ME Radical Wellness Program

Make-It-Happen Card

THEME FOR THE WEEK

Moving-4-Learning

■ Activities

5. PE . . . Not a No-Brainer?
6. What's BDNF?
7. Heart-Brain Buddy System
8. Sound Body, Sound Mind

■ Skills

1. A Peer Evaluation Manners Checklist

■ Movement Examples

Instant Activity Intro
Crows and Cranes
Rock, Paper, Scissors
Partner Tag
Blob Tag
Brainy Balloon Balance
Shoulder Circles and Massage
Knots
Criss-Crossies

PE-4-ME Radical Wellness Program

· · · · · · · · · Make-It-Happen Card · · · · · · · · ·

PE 6

Personal Excellence and Goal Setting

■ **Activities**

9. Personal Excellence
10. Do I Need an Attitude Adjustment?

■ **Skills**

2. Goal Setting (for first semester)

■ **Fun Stuff**

2. Swim With a Buddy
   Don't Be a Fool . . . Follow the Rules!

■ **Movement Examples**

Chicken Games
Hog Call
Back-to-Back Dancing
Brainy Barnyard
Warp Speed Group Juggle
Blind Tag

PE-4-ME Radical Wellness Program

· · · · · · · · · Make-It-Happen Card · · · · · · · · ·

PE 7

THEME FOR THE WEEK

Personal Excellence and Goal Setting

■ **Activities**

11. How Competitive Am I?
12. Thinking About Personal Excellence
    in Cooperative Activities
13. Thinking About Personal Excellence
    in Competitive Activities
14. Thinking About Personal Excellence
    in Social Activities

■ **Movement Examples**

Buckets
British Bulldog
Dog and a Bone
Fun Run Starting Point

PE-4-ME Radical Wellness Program

Make-It-Happen Card

THEME FOR THE WEEK
Cardiovascular Endurance

■ Activities

15. Attitude Toward Fitness
    Target Heart Rate Sheet
16. The Parts of Physical Fitness

■ Fun Stuff

3. Skeleton Crossword Puzzle

■ Movement Examples

Heart Rate Monitors
Rocks
Tennis Ball Relay
Obstacle Course
Circuit Training Stations

PE-4-ME Radical Wellness Program

Make-It-Happen Card

THEME FOR THE WEEK
Cardiovascular Endurance

■ Activities

17. Components of Physical Fitness
18. United in Fitness #1

■ Fun Stuff

4. Pulse Rate
   The American Sign Language
   Alphabet

■ Movement Examples

Relays
Aerobic Conga Line
Sweatshop Hop
Mini-Soccer Games
Two-Deep Fitness
Go for It!

PE-4-ME Radical Wellness Program

······· **Make-It-Happen Card** ·······

THEME FOR THE WEEK
Body Composition

■ **Activities**

19. United in Fitness #2
20. United in Fitness Challenge Review

■ **Skills**

3. A Group Evaluation Complimenting
   Checklist

■ **Fun Stuff**

5. Swim Hidden Picture
   Math Fractions Boxing

■ **Movement Examples**

Aerobic Card Fun
Jump Rope Challenges
Push-Up Wave
Partner Sit-Ups
Hawaiian Banana Ball Mini-Games
Jump Bands
Aquatic Activities

PE-4-ME Radical Wellness Program

······· **Make-It-Happen Card** ·······

THEME FOR THE WEEK
Muscular Strength and Endurance

■ **Activities**

21. Muscles, Muscles, and More Muscles!

■ **Skills**

4. A Group Evaluation High-Five Checklist

■ **Fun Stuff**

6. Sports Word-Search
   Wow . . . Double Trouble!
7. Muscle Magic
   Muscle Word-Search

■ **Movement Examples**

Shark Attack
Math Fitness Fun
Pass the Shoe
Scooter Boards
Tumbling and Gymnastics
Macarena Push-Ups

PE 12 — PE-4-ME *Radical Wellness Program*

Make-It-Happen Card

THEME FOR THE WEEK
Flexibility

■ **Activities**

22. Range of Motion

■ **Skills**

5. A Peer and Self-Evaluation
   NO PUT-DOWNS Checklist

■ **Fun Stuff**

8. Sports Fun Puzzle
   Sports Name Game

■ **Movement Examples**

Knots
Tarantula
Centipedes
Spiderweb
Slingshots
Chicken Tire Tag
Skin the Snake
Hot Swatter

PE 13 — PE-4-ME *Radical Wellness Program*

Make-It-Happen Card

THEME FOR THE WEEK
Speed and Power

■ **Activities**

23. Analyzing Movement
24. "Checking Out" Locomotor Skills

■ **Skills**

6. A Peer Evaluation Speed and Power
   Checklist

■ **Fun Stuff**

9. Basketball Hidden Picture
   Math Factors Fruit

■ **Movement Examples**

Bonus Ball
Three-Legged Races
Across the River
Prediction Run
Power Walk
Inner Tube Relay
Buckets
Jump Rope Challenges

PE-4-ME Radical Wellness Program
Make-It-Happen Card

THEME FOR THE WEEK
Agility and Reaction Time

■ *Activities*

25. Agility and Reaction Time

■ *Skills*

7. A Peer Evaluation Agility and
   Reaction Time Checklist
2. Goal Setting (for second semester)

■ *Movement Examples*

Juggling
Swedish Softball
Four-Square
Rocks
Crows and Cranes
British Bulldog

PE-4-ME Radical Wellness Program
Make-It-Happen Card

THEME FOR THE WEEK
Moving Your Body Through Space

■ *Skills*

8. Moving a Body Through Space
   (Dance)

■ *Fun Stuff*

10. Freaky Football Find
    Soccer City

■ *Movement Examples*

Electric Slide
Surf City
Centerfield
Hand Jive
Elvis Dance
Slap Leather

PE 16

PE-4-ME Radical Wellness Program

· · · · · Make-It-Happen Card · · · · ·

THEME FOR THE WEEK

Moving an Object Through Space

■ **Skills**

9. Frisbee Fun . . . A Moving-an-Object-Through-Space Self-Evaluation Checklist

■ **Movement Examples**

Spinjammers and Frisbees
Freaking Frisbee
Zwirl Footballs and More
Bocce Ball
Foxtail Golf
Fling-Its
Ribbon Balls
Yo-Yos

PE 17

PE-4-ME Radical Wellness Program

· · · · · Make-It-Happen Card · · · · ·

THEME FOR THE WEEK

Throwing

■ **Activities**

26. What Games, Sports, or Activities Use Throwing?
27. Power Throwing

■ **Skills**

10. A Self-Evaluation Throwing Checklist

■ **Movement Examples**

Throw and Run
Star Wars
Big Ball Throw
Swedish Softball
Hawaiian Banana Ball Mini-Games
Mini-Football Games

PE-4-ME Radical Wellness Program

• • • • • • • • • • • • **Make-It-Happen Card** • • • • • • • • • • • •

THEME FOR THE WEEK
Basketball (Throwing, Catching, and Dribbling)

■ *Activities*

28. Basketball Fun
29. Happenin' Hoops

■ *Fun Stuff*

11. Skin Facts: Simple Steps to Protect
    Your Skin
    Safety First

■ *Movement Examples*

Basketball Fun
Mini-Basketball Games
Zone-Passing Basketball
Goal Ball
Sideline Basketball
Basket Bowl
Kickball Basketball

PE 19

PE-4-ME Radical Wellness Program

• • • • • • • • • • • • **Make-It-Happen Card** • • • • • • • • • • • •

THEME FOR THE WEEK
Catching and Receiving

■ *Activities*

30. Stepping Into It

■ *Skills*

11. A Self-Evaluation Catching Checklist

■ *Movement Examples*

Throw and Run
Freaking Frisbees
Swedish Softball
Hawaiian Banana Ball Mini-Games
Mini-Football Games

PE 20

PE-4-ME Radical Wellness Program
Make-It-Happen Card

THEME FOR THE WEEK
Balance

■ **Activities**

31. Balance
32. Principles of Balance

■ **Skills**

12. A Group Evaluation Balancing Act Checklist

■ **Movement Examples**

Partner Balances
Trust Falls
Squat Thrusts
Human Ladders
2×4 Quicksand Save
Group Tugs
Pyramid Building

PE 21

PE-4-ME Radical Wellness Program
Make-It-Happen Card

THEME FOR THE WEEK
Flight and Explosive Movement

■ **Activities**

33. Learning About the Principles of Flight
34. Landing Safely Back to Earth
35. Body Management

■ **Skills**

13. A Group Evaluation Explosive Movement Checklist

■ **Movement Examples**

Crows and Cranes
Rock, Paper, Scissors
Partner Tag
Blob Tag
Mini-Basketball Games
Rocks
Hand Jive

PE 22

PE-4-ME *Radical Wellness Program*

Make-It-Happen Card

THEME FOR THE WEEK
Striking With Upper Body

■ **Activities**

36. Striking with Body Parts

■ **Skills**

14. A Peer Evaluation: Striking With
    Upper Body (Arms)

■ **Fun Stuff**

12. Chef Hidden Picture
    Math Fractions Running

■ **Movement Examples**

Volleying Drills
Thunder Bumper
Volleyball
Four-Square
Tetherball
Strikeball Basketball

PE 23

PE-4-ME *Radical Wellness Program*

Make-It-Happen Card

THEME FOR THE WEEK
Striking With Lower Body

■ **Activities**

37. Fancy Feet

■ **Skills**

15. A Striking-With-Lower-Body
    Self-Evaluation Checklist

■ **Fun Stuff**

13. Brain and Body Fitness
14. Moving for Learning

■ **Movement Examples**

Soccer Drills
Tunnels
Triangle Soccer
Soccer Croquet
Mini-Soccer Games
Hacky Sacks
Takraw
Rounders
Kick and Run

PE-4-ME Radical Wellness Program
Make-It-Happen Card

THEME FOR THE WEEK
Striking With Implements

■ **Activities**

38. Striking and Liking It
39. Match 'Em

■ **Skills**

16. A Striking-With-Implements
    Self-Evaluation Checklist

■ **Movement Examples**

Racket/Paddle Bucket Stations
Triangle Hockey
Four-Square Paddle Tennis
Swedish Softball
Mini-Hockey Games
Hit and Run
Putt-and-Strut Golf
Badminton Fun

PE-4-ME Radical Wellness Program
Make-It-Happen Card

THEME FOR THE WEEK
Feeling Good About Yourself

■ **Activities**

40. Fun Time
41. Hurrah!

■ **Fun Stuff**

15. Basketball Boogie Word Find
    And the Rest Is History . . .

■ **Movement Examples**

Heart Rate Monitors
British Bulldog
Dog and a Bone
Fun Run Starting Point
Criss-Crossies

PE-4-ME Radical Wellness Program

Make-It-Happen Card

THEME FOR THE WEEK
Getting Along (Stress-Busters)

■ **Activities**

42. The Blame Game?
43. Stress-Busters
    What Is PE? End of School Reply

■ **Movement Examples**

Student's Choice, Anything Goes!

PE-4-ME Radical Wellness Program

Make-It-Happen Card

THEME FOR THE WEEK
Nutrition

■ **Activities**

1. Calorie Graph
2. Nutrition Puzzle

■ **Movement Examples**

Crows and Cranes
Rock, Paper, Scissors
Partner Tag
Blob Tag
Mini-Football Games

PE-4-ME Radical Wellness Program

Make-It-Happen Card

THEME FOR THE WEEK
Nutrition

■ **Activities**

3. Energy Expenditure Info
   Let's Do Lunch!
4. Healthy Hamburger . . .
   Is It Possible?
5. Alien Label Connection

■ **Movement Examples**

Hog Call
Brainy Barnyard
Brainy Balloon Balance
Chicken Tire Tag
Warp Speed Group Juggle
Blind Tag

FF 3

PE-4-ME Radical Wellness Program

Make-It-Happen Card

THEME FOR THE WEEK
Nutrition

■ **Activities**

6. Eating What's Fit
7. Balancing Act
8. All Systems Go!
9. The "Wild and Crazy" *Chef de Haute*
   Cuisine

■ **Movement Examples**

Back-to-Back Dancing
Rocks
Tennis Ball Relay
Obstacle Course
Circuit Training Stations
Mini-Hockey Games

 **PE-4-ME** *Radical Wellness Program*

Make-It-Happen Card

THEME FOR THE WEEK
Nutrition

■ *Activities*

10. Dying of Thirst?
11. Scrambled Words, Not Eggs
12. Interview an Athlete
13. Our Bodies . . . Mean Machines
14. Answer Sheet (not a worksheet)

■ **Movement Examples**

Basketball Fun
Mini-Basketball Games
Zone-Passing Basketball
Goal Ball
Sideline Basketball
Basket Bowl
Kickball Basketball

FF 5

 PE-4-ME *Radical Wellness Program*

Make-It-Happen Card

THEME FOR THE WEEK
Nutrition

■ *Activities*

15. You Choose!
16. Food Record!
17. Building My Pyramid

■ **Movement Examples**

Aerobic Card Fun
Jump Rope Challenges
Hawaiian Banana Ball Mini-Games
Shark Attack
Scooter Boards
Hit and Run

PE-4-ME Radical Wellness Program

Make-It-Happen Card

THEME FOR THE WEEK
Nutrition

■ **Activities**

18. How Much Is a Serving?
19. Where's the Fat?

■ **Movement Examples**

Chicken Tire Tag
Hot Swatter
Juggling
Swedish Softball
Electric Slide
Slap Leather

 PE-4-ME Radical Wellness Program

Make-It-Happen Card

THEME FOR THE WEEK
Substance and Safety Awareness

■ **Activities**

1. Substance and Safety Survey

■ **Movement Examples**

Four-Square
Yo-Yos
Freaking Frisbees
Surf City
Mini-Soccer Games

 **Radical Wellness Program**

Make-It-Happen Card

THEME FOR THE WEEK
Substance and Safety Awareness

 Activities

2. Dear Ms. Advice
3. Tobacco Quiz

■ Movement Examples

Basketball Fun
Mini-Basketball Games
Zone-Passing Basketball
Goal Ball
Sideline Basketball
Basket Bowl
Kickball Basketball

Radical Wellness Program

Make-It-Happen Card

THEME FOR THE WEEK
Substance and Safety Awareness

Activities

4. Poster Power

■ Movement Examples

Star Wars
Hawaiian Banana Ball Mini-Games
Mini-Football Games
Four-Square Paddle Tennis
Hit and Run
Fling-Its

Radical Wellness Program

Make-It-Happen Card

THEME FOR THE WEEK
Substance and Safety Awareness

■ Activities

5. "Random Acts of Kindness" Survey
6. Protecting Yourself

■ Movement Examples

Aerobic Conga Line
Sweatshop Hop
Two-Deep Fitness
Bocce Ball
Big Ball Throw
Mini-Football Games

Weekly Themes (Example Schedule)

PE	Week 1–2	Locker room procedures
PE	Week 3–4	Class management
PE	Week 5	Moving-4-learning
PE	Week 6–7	Personal excellence and goal setting
FF	**Week 1**	**Nutrition**
PE	Week 8–9	Cardiovascular endurance
PE	Week 10	Body composition
NO	**Week 1**	**Substance and safety awareness**
PE	Week 11	Muscular strength and endurance
FF	**Week 2**	**Nutrition**
PE	Week 12	Flexibility
PE	Week 13	Speed and power
PE	Week 14	Agility and reaction time
NO	**Week 2**	**Substance and safety awareness**
PE	Week 15	Moving your body through space
FF	**Week 3**	**Nutrition**
PE	Week 16	Moving an object through space
PE	Week 17	Throwing
PE	Week 18	Throwing, catching, and dribbling basketballs
PE	Week 19	Catching and receiving
FF	**Week 4**	**Nutrition**
PE	Week 20	Balance
NO	**Week 3**	**Substance and safety awareness**
PE	Week 21	Flight and explosive movement
PE	Week 22	Striking with upper body
FF	**Week 5**	**Nutrition**
PE	Week 23	Striking with lower body
FF	**Week 6**	**Nutrition**
PE	Week 24	Striking with implements
NO	**Week 4**	**Substance and safety awareness**
PE	Week 25	Feeling good about yourself
PE	Week 26	Getting along

3

Creating the Classroom on the Field

Welcome to Reality 101: a typical PE teacher, with no classroom, no place to go, huge classes . . . sound familiar? It is a common practice at many schools to find physical education instructors who don't have the luxury of ready-made classrooms with chalkboards, dry-erase boards, bulletin boards, chairs, teacher's desks, doors, or anything else that can be found inside four walls.

Before my first year of teaching, I pulled out old pictures of my middle school years and asked myself, "What did I like as a kid?" Some of the first things that came to mind were posters, pictures, and forts. I loved plastering my bedroom with lots of posters, even on the ceiling.

What child doesn't like looking at pictures, especially when he or she is in them? And forts—kids love forts! They are emotionally safe and fun places to go. As a physical education teacher, I combined all of these fond memories and created the majestic "classroom on the field." And you can do the same. Teachers *can* create a brain-compatible learning environment in physical education.

VISUAL CUES

Imagine a typical history classroom. Globes line the cabinets, maps hang suspended over the

Visual cues pull the Classroom on the Field together. On the bulletin board, you'll find such handy references as the Theme for the Week, the Que Pasa? Poster, and the birthdays list, as well as a variety of motivational and informational tidbits.

blackboard, and colorful posters and newspaper clippings put dates and events into a smooth visual presentation. Now picture a typical gym. What's on the walls? Mats, perhaps, and probably a clock. If visual cues add so much to the history classroom, why are they so often overlooked in the physical education arena? Many kids need to "see" what is being discussed. If students aren't clear about what is expected of them, they will tune out.

A great way to get all students in your classes motivated, ready to learn, and able to understand "what is going on" is by the use of visual cues. Not only do the visual cues allow students to see the weekly agenda, monthly birthdays, homework schedule, and cool posters, they create an emotionally safe environment by displaying many positive messages. When the students enter the class, they are excited just to be there.

The following is a breakdown of how to incorporate many different visual cues in the PE-4-ME: Radical Wellness Program.

Bulletin Boards

When I was a kid, I disliked PE for the mere fact that I never knew where the front of the class was. It was disorienting. I can remember thinking to myself, "What is this teacher talking about?" Words flew over my head faster than I could ever run. I promised myself that when I began teaching I would never leave students without a focus.

Use bulletin boards to establish the focal point of your "classroom." These are available in varying sizes: the 4-foot-by-8-foot dimensions work well. On the bulletin board, put the various positive posters and calendars for the week. The kids will know exactly what is happening, which eliminates the never-ending question, "What are we doing in PE today?" Use a dolly to transport the boards easily. Put a piece of plywood behind the board so that it will be heavy enough not to blow around in the wind when your class is outside, yet not too heavy to transport. (The woodshop teacher may be a great resource here!) Drill holes in the top of the board to hang a variety of items, such as a clock, Fitness Jar coupons, desk supplies, and more. Use three-inch binder rings for hooking items on the board through the drilled holes. Leave the board out where the students meet for the entire day (you can tie it to a tree or fence by a bungee cord). This way the children can see the board and know exactly where their class is meeting.

Posters and Signs

The more variety of posters you use, the better. The messages on the posters are constant reminders to the kids. A few examples are: *The hand of friendship has no color; Positive people don't put others down;* and *Smart people ask for help.* I purchase many of my posters in mass quantity at discounted prices from retailers such as Argus posters, health catalogs, and

Let the world be your classroom. Creating a Classroom on the Field will keep everything you need on hand, wherever you are.

teacher supply stores (see Resources, page 255, for contact information). In the past, I have approached my School Site Council committee for funding these posters since our school doesn't provide instructional teaching materials to the Physical Education Department.

Many vendors and organizations give posters away for free. The students will also be making and bringing posters to class for the board. In addition, you can clip articles from newspapers and magazines. (It is important to laminate what you put on the bulletin board so that it won't get torn up.) The students love to read the posters out loud to each other at the closing of each class.

Que Pasa?

On the bulletin board is the weekly calendar, or the Que Pasa? poster (figure 3.1). Each Que Pasa? poster displays the Theme for the Week, the date, and the movement activities. Every day has a different movement activity, all reinforcing the Theme for the Week. The Que Pasa? poster may be made with any bright and colorful graphic software, such as Print Shop Deluxe or Print Master and the design can be tied in with the theme and the seasons.

In the upper left-hand corner of the Que Pasa? poster is the teacher's indicator of the weekly *theme number* that the class is currently centered on. The indicator is a quick reminder to the teacher when looking at the Que Pasa? poster for expeditious planning. For example, the theme Speed and Power would be listed on the Que Pasa? poster, with the daily movement activities. Speed and Power happens to be the PE Week 13 theme. Nowhere on the poster does it mention Week 13 except in the upper left-hand corner. The students don't need to know what number the week is, just as long as they know the theme. Nonetheless, putting that number in the corner provides the teacher with an instant record of where they are on the Roadmap when they're out on the field.

Theme for the Week

In addition to the Que Pasa? poster is the Theme for the Week poster (figure 3.2). This sign displays the theme much more prominently than the Que Pasa? poster. This way, there is no mistaking what your class is focusing on during that week. Again, the teacher's indicator of the week number is in the upper left-hand corner.

Birthdays Sign

Birthdays are very special in the PE-4-ME: Radical Wellness Program. Each month, the students' birthdays will be posted on the bulletin board. The kids love to see their names displayed in front of their peers. For some children, this is the only birthday recognition they will receive. In addition to posting the names, the teacher also mails birthday cards home to the students. What kid doesn't like having a birthday card mailed to them? They love it! The kids are not the only ones who are delighted about their cards; the parents are also happy for the recognition of their child. It truly is a win-win situation.

Homework Calendar

On the bulletin board is the schedule for homework (figure 3.3). Listed on the schedule is the "Week of" and "Homework." Thus there is never any excuse for the students not to know what the homework assignment is.

Dry-Erase Chalkboards

To demonstrate different activities and reminders to the students, use writing boards whenever possible. Diagram what you are saying about an activity. This clears up much confusion that may arise from using verbal communication alone. Again, attach plywood to the dry-erase board for more stability. As for the chalkboard, use a small one for instant activities or reminders.

Cardboard Characters

A great motivational technique is to use giant cardboard characters. This sure does get the kids' attention! What are cardboard characters, you ask? These are the cardboard stand-up figures you might see in department stores or pizza outlets to get your attention to buy something. If you take those stand-ups and attach motivational posters or pictures of the class, you can engage your students before the class has even started.

Many cardboard stand-ups are characters that the kids are very familiar with. Popeye, Bugs Bunny, Taz, Tweety Bird, Sylvester, and Babe Ruth are just a few of the many stand-ups you can acquire. These are so effective because most students already have a positive

Que Pasa?

Cardiovascular Endurance
November 2–6

MONDAY: ROCKS
TUESDAY: MONITOR MADNESS
WEDNESDAY: SWEDISH SOFTBALL
THURSDAY: TENNIS BALL RELAY
FRIDAY: OBSTACLE COURSE

Homework
Due
Thursday

Figure 3.1 Que Pasa? poster.

Figure 3.2 Theme for the Week poster.

2000-2001
Summerford's Homework Schedule

Week of:	Homework:
August 7	Tabs and Binder
August 14	What is PE?
August 21	Activities: 1, 2, 3, and 4
August 28	Activities: 5, 6, 7, and 8
September 4	Activities: 9, 10, and Swim Word Puzzle
September 11	Activities: 11, 12, 13, and 14
September 18	Exercise Your Options
September 25	Drug Survey (2 pages) Bone Puzzle
October 2	Activities: 15, 16, and Skeleton Project
October 23	Exercise Your Options
October 30	Activities: 17 and 18
November 6	Activities: 19 and 20
November 13	Exercise Your Options
November 20	No Homework
November 27	Activities: 21 and 22
December 3	Activities: 23 and 24
December 10	No Homework

Figure 3.3 Homework schedule.

connection with these characters. They are certainly happy to have them in class!

The best place to find these great visual additions to your class is to go to vendors and simply ask for them. Many times, vendors will discard these items after a promotion. In addition, you can purchase cardboard stand-ups from companies such as Advanced Graphics in California (see page 255 for their contact information). They are not cheap, but they are well worth it. If you purchase stand-ups in multiple quantities, the vendor will usually lower their prices. After a while, you will have quite a collection.

Mobiles

When the bulletin board is tied to a tree or fence, it is fun to hang mobiles from the tree or fence to add more interest. For example, when my students are studying the different bones in the body, we hang skeletons in the tree. Or when we are working on Fitness Fuel, we may hang healthy cardboard foods on the fence, such as the promotional items hanging in your local grocery store. The first period class will hang up the items, and the last period will take them down. Again, find motivational tools that make the learning process fun.

Seasonal Teaching Tools

Along with mobiles, a variety of festive materials can be used to tie the seasons of the year into the teaching of different themes. For example, during October, use pumpkins as visual cues, as an example of a healthy vegetable, and as something to incorporate into various activities. In winter, use balls of yarn as snowballs and decorative yard snow figures to liven up the atmosphere. The theme of body composition lends itself nicely to a round snowman, and how the snowman might trim down. The kids really enjoy these associations.

Visual cues should be an integral part of any high-quality physical education program. Whatever attempt you have made to assist the visual learner is one step in the right direction. You will be amazed at the results you will receive in just a short period of time. Whether you incorporate all or some of the ideas from the PE-4-ME: Radical Wellness Program, I know your students will become better learners and you will have much more fun.

MAILBOX HOMEWORK EXPRESS

If there is one piece of equipment that keeps the homework running smoothly in the physical education arena, it would have to be the Mailbox Homework Express. The Mailbox serves many different functions. First of all, if a student is absent when homework is assigned, that student never needs to ask the teacher "Where is the homework?" The homework for the week is always kept in the Mailbox; each assignment is kept in separate manila folders. The Mailbox provides a wonderful barrier against the wind and elements. When teachers have large classes as is the case for many, a routine or ritual needs to be established for PE homework to be successful, and the Mailbox Homework Express provides that. Besides, the kids think the Mailbox is pretty neat.

The students' routine is that homework is given on Mondays, and it is due on Thursdays. The PE-4-ME: Radical Wellness Homework strengthens the Theme for the Week, thus enhancing student learning. At the beginning of the year, collect wellness books every Thursday, grading that Thursday evening, Friday, or during the weekend. Return to students by the following Monday. Positively acknowledge the students who give their best effort and finish their assignments. Once the kids have the routine down, skip a week of collecting the wellness books now and then, to free up more of your own time. Of course, the kids know their work is due every Thursday, no matter what! Next time you collect the books, grade all materials that need grading. Examples of the homework for each week are provided in part III of this book.

THE RADICAL WELLNESS WAGON

The best way to describe the PE-4-ME: Radical Wellness Wagon is by comparing it to an "office on wheels." It's awesome! In fact, it is so useful, it is common practice to find two wagons wheeled out to the Classroom on the Field. The wagons are not your basic red wagon. These wagons have giant balloon tires, wooden sides, and a bright red paint job. More students comment about the cool wagons than anything else, as do the many parents who ask about them. This is just one more way to create an emotionally safe environment. Don't a red wagon and a happy kid go hand-in-hand?

Once the wagons are rolled out to the PE area, be sure to take out the different items such as the Brain Food Box, the Sport Wows Box, the Pencil Box, and the Fitness Jar and set them in front of the bulletin board. Explanations for the various instructional tools that are in the wagon are provided in the following sections.

Depending on your school and facilities, store the wagons and the Classroom on the Field wherever it works for you. Whether you have a gym, an office, locker rooms, or not, you will need to adjust accordingly. If possible, store your rolling classroom in the locker room. There is usually quite a bit of room in the locker room when the students aren't at school. Before the kids enter the locker room in the morning, take the classroom items just outside the locker rooms or onto to the field. At the end of the day when all the kids are through in the locker rooms, roll your classroom items back in. The students love to help set the class up and break it down at the end of the day. This is explained in chapter 5, "Putting It Together: The Teacher's Game Plan."

Read-Aloud Boxes

In education, there is more and more emphasis on getting our youth to read. And so it is in the physical education class. The Brain Food Box, the Sport Wows Box, and the It's Fitting Box are great ways for kids to read aloud to their peers

The Brain Food Box.

and share some valuable information. Because of time constraints, have the students usually pick two out of the three boxes to read. Let the students choose a read-aloud box, pick a card, and read aloud to their classmates.

Brain Food Box

At the close of each class, the students love to read from the Brain Food Box. The box is a recipe box full of fitness, nutrition, and brainy tidbits that the students read. The students are not only reading, but they are also presenting material in front of their peers. Because of the emotionally safe environment, children that might never read in front of a class in another context often take the risk and do so here.

The Brain Food cards should reflect healthy tidbits for students to think about. For example, one of my cards is titled "The Same But Different," and reads like this:

Friendship is not only sharing similar interests with someone but also liking that person for who he or she is. We all share personality traits and hobbies with our friends, but no two of us are exactly the same. We all are unique, special in our own way.

I picked up my original fitness recipe cards at a conference years ago; however, you can create your own. After finding a recipe box, fill it up with fitness, nutrition, and self-esteem goodies and print them out on cards. Include the students in the process and have them bring a recipe card full of tidbits to the class. What you can put in your very own Brain Food Box is unlimited.

Sport Wows Box

The Sport Wows Box is very similar to the Brain Food Box, except that the cards have sports trivia on them. On the card will be a statement followed by a question. The student that reads the card will call on other students for their feedback. This is just another great way to get kids to take ownership in their class.

Here is an example of a Sport Wows card:

Coaches have a great impact on the youth of our country. They are often charged with building a competitive spirit and a sense of discipline. They also teach children sportspersonship and teamwork. Question: If you were a coach, what important lessons would you try to pass on to your players?

It's Fitting Box

The It's Fitting Box is similar to the Brain Food and Sport Wows boxes, except that these cards are more specific to the health- and skill-related components of fitness. Again, be creative when making cards of your own. These cards tie in nicely with the Themes for the Week.

Here is an example of an It's Fitting card:

What is aerobic or cardiovascular training? It is exercise that stimulates heart and lung activity for a time period sufficiently long enough to produce beneficial changes in the body. The main objective is to increase the maximum amount of oxygen that the body can process within a given time. Running, swimming, cycling, jogging—these are typical aerobic or cardiovascular exercises.

Fitness Jar

Fun stuff! The Fitness Jar is a plastic jar that sits in front of the bulletin board. Fitness coupons hang on the board. The students participate in activities outside of class for thirty minutes, have their parents or guardian sign off on the coupon to indicate that they did in fact complete the activity, and place the coupon inside the Fitness Jar.

Approximately once each quarter throughout the year, all the PE classes combined will have a huge drawing during lunchtime for cool prizes, such as basketballs, swim goggles, Frisbees, and so on. The more kids exercise outside of class, the more coupons they fill out; the more coupons a kid completes, the greater his or her chance of being one of the lucky ones whose name is drawn. This is an outstanding approach to get kids to exercise their bodies outside of class, and it's loads of fun! The prizes can be freebies, promotions, donations, or items you may have purchased from local stores. Before buying something, always ask for a "donation for the future of our community" first. Many vendors are more than happy to donate to education, and it is a tax write-off for them as well. You can see an example of the Fitness Jar coupon in chapter five (see page 63).

Ticket Box

This is another neat tool to implement novel surprises at random (approximately once or

The Ticket Box.

twice a month) when your classes are going well. Without telling students in advance, set up a ticket drawing for small surprises. The Ticket Box is an old lunch pail with a slit cut into it for the tickets to be placed. Get a roll of raffle tickets from a school-supply store and instruct your students to rip them in half. The kids place one side of the ticket in the box; the other side goes in their shoe. Introduce the ticket drawing by talking about the importance of honesty, so you know they'll only take one ticket. Lay the tickets on top of the Ticket Box. As students arrive to class, they automatically take a ticket. You can be sure the kids will only take one ticket, because you have repeatedly addressed the issue of trust.

Having the kids get their own ticket saves valuable class time for movement. At the end of class, draw a ticket out of the pail, call out the number—making it very suspenseful, of course. Repeat the drawing three or four times. Prizes may be pencils, Hacky-sacks, or wristbands. You will probably be able to obtain most of the prizes as freebies (refer to chapter 5). What kid doesn't like a ticket drawing?

Pencil Box

The Pencil Box is pretty self-explanatory. Keep a pencil box full of pencils for in-class assessments and the students' daily activity log and journal. More information on how to manage pencils in the PE class is provided in chapter 4, "Managing the Classroom."

Radical Wellness Book Bag

This is a mesh bag that contains any Radical Wellness Books that have been misplaced by the students in the locker rooms or elsewhere. The students know not to ask, "Have you seen my Radical Wellness Book?" It is their responsibility to look in the book bag.

Wireless Microphone

Too cool! Finally, all of the kids can hear what you're saying. You'll really like to use this during the students' Instant Activity and while you are taking roll. Instead of having the kids sitting during roll, they are moving. The kids can also use the microphone when they read tidbits from the Brain Food, Sport Wows, and It's Fitting Boxes.

A highly recommended wireless microphone is called the Apollo. It is very small, yet very powerful. When inquiring about the Apollo, mention priority code 25. They will know you are a physical educator and will service your needs. For more information, write to Learning for Living, P.O. Box 279, Meadow Vista, CA 95722, or call 800-874-1100.

Boom Box

Obviously, this is the instrument that allows you to incorporate music into physical education. I highly recommend that teachers use music. Music is a universal language.

Cones and Wristbands

It is advantageous to have twenty or so miniature cones in your wagon for using at any given moment. Who knows? There may be situations where you need to adjust an activity at the last minute.

Having plenty of wristbands available (in two different colors) is handy for designating teams. Most of the time, you will want to use colored jerseys or belts for teams, but keep wristbands in the wagon as well. They don't take up too much space, and you never know when you might need them. You can never be too prepared.

The Everything Else Bag

The Everything Else Bag is another mesh bag full of items for maintaining the class: plenty of bungee cords for tying items down; duct tape for taping; dry-erase markers or chalk for demonstrating activities; and various items such as a stapler, staples, rubber bands, and a hall pass.

Rainy Day Kit

In my Rainy Day Kit I have two editions of the game *Brain Quest*. When it rains at my school, sometimes the only place we can go is under an overhang or a patio shelter. No problem—it's *Brain Quest* to the rescue! Although the game of *Brain Quest* involves little movement, it is an excellent activity. A description of this game may be found in chapter 5, "Putting It Together: The Teacher's Game Plan."

Info Tin

Collect drug, alcohol, tobacco, and safety awareness flyers and bookmarks and put them inside of a tin, which sits at the front of the class. Punch a hole in the materials so that the kids can put them in their Radical Wellness Books. Some of these positive reminders are hanging on the bulletin board as well. I get all of this type of information from the Drug Alcohol Tobacco Education (DATE) coordinator on our campus.

Sticker Box

You just never know when you might have a "sticker attack." Sometimes I will surprise the kids by sticking stickers on them while they are participating in an activity. The students love the spontaneity and acknowledgment for a job well done. "Sticker attacks" happen at random, whenever the moment strikes.

Clock

Make sure you have a clock with a second hand so that the students can check their heart rates.

Past Homework

Each semester, keep all the homework that you handed out that semester in file folders inside a crate within the wagon. This way everything you need is at your fingertips.

The PE-4-ME: Radical Wellness Wagon is a convenient and fun tool for organizing all of the daily equipment needed to run an awesome physical education class. Everything you need is in one convenient, mobile package. So roll out that wagon and make it happen!

Managing the Classroom

The classroom management system in the PE-4-ME: Radical Wellness Program is based on two principles: having predictable rituals and routines, and assigning weekly homework that makes sense to the students. If you do not have a management system established in your physical education classroom, all havoc will break loose. In this chapter you will find super ideas to succeed in managing your class.

This chapter describes the rituals and routines that are part of the PE-4-ME: Radical Wellness Program. Of course, if your routine is working for you, there's no need to change it— why reinvent the wheel? On the other hand, many teachers have asked about the following issues and how to deal with them. I hope that you will find a few good ideas that may work for you.

LAYING THE GROUND RULES

The semester starts with two weeks of Locker Room Boot Camp. This is your chance to set a strong foundation to build your classroom rituals on. The goal of Locker Room Boot Camp is to provide students with everything they will need to be successful in the locker room, and to establish the basics of the physical education class. This eliminates a lot of the confusion and frustration that can occur when locker room issues are not addressed up front. The schedule will depend on when your school starts. For instance, if you begin the school year mid-week,

you will need to adjust Locker Room Boot Camp to last one and one-half weeks, not the full two weeks.

Locker Room Boot Camp requires coordinating classes with the other teachers in your physical education department. Each day during Locker Room Boot Camp, students should meet their instructor at a designated place for roll call. After lesson 1, the girls will go with a female instructor and the boys will go with a male instructor. At my school, for example, there are two sixth-grade teachers, two seventh-grade teachers, and two eighth-grade teachers, one female and one male per grade level. I'm a sixth-grade teacher. After lesson 1 has been completed, the following days will require each teacher to take roll with his or her class, collect any letters sent home to parents, and touch base with students. After that, I will take all of the sixth-grade girls for that period, and the male sixth-grade teacher will take all of the boys. The same is true for all grade levels.

Lesson 1: Acquaintances, Activities, Roll Call

Meet with teacher . . . Acquaintances, activities, roll call. Let students know they will need a pencil for Locker Room Boot Camp for the next week and a half. At this time, hand out the "letter home to the parent" explaining the PE-4-ME: Radical Wellness Program. This letter is explained on pages 55-57. During the following days, take roll and send all the girls to one location, and all the boys to another.

Lesson 2: Test—What Is PE?

In the second lesson, give students the What Is PE? test. Distribute PE handbooks and health forms. Review the health forms, and set a deadline for their return—usually the next day, or as soon as possible.

Lesson 3: Test—PE Handbook Review

Review the tests in lesson 3, making sure students know the correct answers. Show students the map of fields, courts, pools, and classrooms, to orient them with the facilities. Explain the daily information board located in locker rooms.

Lesson 4: Test—Locks/Locker Rooms

During lesson 4, prepare students for the locker room test. After giving and reviewing the test, explain to the students how to open a lock. Be sure to use visual cues while you describe working the combination. Review all rules regarding locks.

Lesson 5: Practice Day

For lesson 5, let students practice opening locks. Many students have never had a lock before, and may fear looking foolish if they can't get it worked out. Let them practice so they feel comfortable. Of course, if you do not use combination locks, you won't need this lesson.

Lesson 6: Issue Locks

Issue the locks during lesson 6. If your locks are not built into the locker, issue lockers as well.

Lesson 7: First Day of Dressing in PE Clothes

This is the final day of Locker Room Boot Camp. Students should have their gym clothes in hand, with their names on them. They should know their locker number and combination, and be able to work the lock. They should understand all the procedures of your class. At this point, students should complete the final test. Then, hooray—you are ready for PE!

RITUALS AND ROUTINES

Children thrive on predictability. Make sure that your class follows ritual and routine procedures, and you will provide them with that necessary stability—as well as make things run much more smoothly for you. What is a ritual or routine? Routines are a number of rituals put together. For example, changing clothes in the locker room is a daily ritual, part of the routine of getting to PE class. For many kids, the rituals and routines they experience at school may be the most consistent part of their day.

Homework

When you assign homework, it is very important that the work is meaningful and relevant to learning. The work should be short, to the point, realistic, and fun. Avoid busywork. Radical Wellness Homework reinforces the Theme for the Week and anchors the students' understanding of the concepts. This is a critical part of the learning process.

Because of the nature of physical education with its emphasis on movement, it is very difficult to give in-class assignments. Time is of the essence. Homework can be a valuable way to explore the themes without cutting into your class's movement time.

Homework falls into the daily routine of the PE-4-ME: Radical Wellness Program. The students begin the school year with an empty plastic binder, in which they proceed to build their personal Radical Wellness Books. They end the year with a notebook that reminds them of many experiences. The Radical Wellness Book could almost be thought of as a PE diary: a place for the special ritual of documenting accomplishments and understanding pertaining to movement, nutrition, and drug safety awareness. This homework routine allows the students to have a tangible book that they have created to reflect on and share.

Locker Room Directions on Dry-Erase Board

Place a giant white dry-erase board at the entrance of both the girls and boys locker rooms. On each board is the teacher's name, and where their class is meeting. For example:

Teacher 1   Field 4

Teacher 2   Volleyball Courts

Teacher 3   Fields 1 and 2

Teacher 4   Basketball Courts

Teacher 5   Track

Teacher 6   Field 6

Usually, each teacher is at a specific location for the entire week or longer. The students know to check the board daily just in case. For example, assemblies, bad weather, and other last-minute changes could alter the schedule in a hurry.

During Locker Room Boot Camp, students are introduced to the school maps showing where each field or court is. The maps are posted in each locker room. The teachers sign up for the various locations via a field sign-up system, which will be explained in chapter 5, "Putting It Together: The Teacher's Game Plan."

If you are at a school where all physical education classes converge at one place for roll call, then the dry-erase board is not needed for class meeting directions. However, to instantly create a more emotionally safe environment, I truly believe that having your class meet for roll call away from all of the other classes helps produce more of a family atmosphere. (Of course, that is only my opinion; many of my colleagues beg to differ.)

Instant Activity

Once the students have entered the locker room, checked the daily information board, changed into their PE clothes, and exited the locker rooms, they proceed to their class meeting location. The students bring their Radical Wellness Books out to class every day, and set them in front of the bulletin board close to their

Setting up stations in advance of class allows students to get moving immediately. In my class, we use exercise station cards set up in a circle around a boombox; some kids are doing push-ups, others are doing jumping jacks, and everybody's active.

roll-call-order spot (more about this in the up-coming pages), on their way to their Instant Activity. The Instant Activity is a way to get kids to move immediately when they come out to class, instead of sitting for roll call, as is the usual procedure.

I thought about using some sort of immedi-ate activity to start the class for a few years, but I was afraid I might lose control of what was going on. You see, with fifty-plus kids in a class, a fear of chaos emerges. With Instant Activity, you do lose the comfort of having all of your students in one spot and not-moving for roll call. It looks very orderly and efficient to an outsider looking on and observing your class. But we are in this business to get kids to move, and to teach them why physical fitness is so important. So instant movement is the way to go, especially since the students have usually been sitting in classrooms with little physical activity.

As I mentioned in the preface, the Instant Ac-tivity is a boom box surrounded by at least six Exercise Station cards in a circle. The Exercise Station cards list exercises such as jumping jacks, push-ups, bicycles, windmills, arm circles, and more. The exercises will vary throughout the year. Students rotate clockwise from one station card to the next, at their own pace. For example, at the beginning of the year the stu-dents set goals to complete a certain number of exercises at each station. As the year progresses, the number of repetitions at each station increases because their goals have changed. After they complete the exercises on all of the cards for that day, they then go to the bulletin board and fill out personal activity logs while the teacher takes roll. Be creative in mak-ing your own station cards, and involve the stu-dents in the process—they love it.

It is very effective to use the Instant Activity to review the prior day's concepts. For example, if the Theme for the Week is Throwing, then in-clude throwing activities in the Instant Activity. This way, the students can practice the move-ment that is being emphasized.

Roll-Call Order

If anyone out there has a roll-call system that is problem-free, more power to you! Roll call can be one of those chores in a PE class that can really waste time. Because of the notes coming and going, you do need a time to handle all of the housekeeping issues. Therefore, I take roll in a semi-structured format and attempt to go at "warp speed."

As students complete the instant activity, they walk over to the bulletin board where they pick up their Radical Wellness Books and settle into their personal spot to fill out their activity log. Their personal spot is a "roll-call" order place and serves a dual purpose. First, it pro-vides an organized means of passing papers and pencils, and second, it provides a quick refer-ence area for guest instructors.

Actually, roll is not taken while the students are in their personal spots. Instead, it is taken while they are completing their instant activity, but the personal spot is where they receive di-rections for the day's movement activity. There is not an exact spot marked on the floor that each student must go to. Instead the students are arranged alphabetically in rows of five run-ning from front to back and left to right.

During the Training Camp week, seat the kids in front of the board. Explain to them that it is important that they have their own "personal spot" for roll. In a single day, the kids are intro-duced to where their spot is, and the class pro-ceeds to practice it. For instance, after the chil-dren know their place, you can run to another location and pretend to be the bulletin board. Call all the kids over and have them sit in roll-call order in front of you, the pretend board. Do this a few times that day, and the kids won't for-get their spot. If a student is absent, leave a blank spot for them, reminding the other stu-dents that when their teammate returns, they need to tell him or her where to sit.

As the year progresses, update the roll-call order approximately once per quarter, or four times a year. When students add or drop the class, plug students in somewhere and don't worry about it being just right until the next quarter.

The roll-call order can also be a highly effi-cient management tool when handing out pa-pers or collecting pencils. It makes the process much more expedient.

Activity Log

The Activity Log is the first page in the activity section of the student's Radical Wellness Book, which is reproduced in part III of this book. Every day, the students fill out what activity they will participate in, the date, how long they will participate, their resting heart rate, and any comments they might have about the activity. The main purpose of recording a resting heart rate daily is learning how to count six seconds while still keeping track of the pulse beat. Many students find this difficult. During movement activities, an active heart rate will be taken. The students are not required to record this information in their activity logs. The log comments section is filled out referring to the previous day's activity as the students reflect on that experience. Students have no problem remembering yesterday's activity. While the kids are finishing up their instant activity and filling out their Activity Logs, take roll.

Homework Hand-Out and Turn-In

Homework can be a real pain if you don't have a structured system in place. Every Monday, the students receive their homework for the week. Depending on your caseload of students, make enough copies of each assignment, three-hole punched, and place the copies in a manila folder, ready to go. If there are two sheets, double-sided, there would be two manila folders, and so on. Hand out a quick mini-stack (approximately ten sheets) to the first person in roll call, who will take one and pass the stack back; re-

peat with each row. Tell the students that when you say "High in the sky," it means that you want them to hold the leftover assignments up in the air so that you can pick them up.

Classes enjoy challenging themselves by seeing how fast they can pass out the papers. They don't let one paper touch the ground, and put them "High in the sky" when the assignment reaches the back row. Use a stopwatch and make it fun! The papers aren't allowed to touch the ground, because you don't want them getting mixed up with the next worksheet.

If a student is absent on a Monday, they know to check the Mailbox Homework Express when they return. Keep only the current week's homework in the Mailbox.

All homework is due on Thursdays at the beginning of class after completing Activity Logs. Explain up front that they place their completed homework in their books. They put the sheets in the books as soon as they get them, and complete them there as well. When the students turn in their work, they continue with their normal routine such as the Instant Activity and filling out their Activity Logs. On their way to the activity for the day, the kids will drop their entire Radical Wellness Book—including their completed assignment—into a duffel bag placed at the back of the class. Remember, they turn in their entire Radical Wellness Books, not just the

Students gather at the board to fill in their activity logs. Others may still be finishing up the Instant Activity.

assignment. When you review their PE homework, check their organizational skills as well.

Pencil Pass-Up

Something as simple as a pencil may seem too trivial to address in a physical education class. But if you don't address it, the pencils can be a nightmare in a hurry. Do you provide pencils for your students? How do you provide them? What happens if the kids don't put them back where they got them? Do your students bring their own pencils? What if they forgot them? What happens if the kids throw the pencils, or stab the grass? As you can see, running successful in-class work may be unproductive if pencil management is not addressed.

The PE-4-ME: Radical Wellness kids keep their pencils collected in a metal tin. When they finish their Instant Activity, they grab a pencil, take their book, get in roll-call order, and proceed to fill out their Activity Logs.

When you say "Pencil pass-up," the kids have ten seconds to pass the pencils up to the front person in their row without ever throwing a pencil. Someone always jumps up to collect them all by grabbing the tin, allowing for the front row students to place them there. There should be fifty pencils at the end of class.

During the Training Camp week, emphasize to the students that they shouldn't stab the grass with pencils, run with pencils, throw the pencils, and so forth. Bombard the kids with the fact that pencils are part of our PE equipment and that they need to take care of them.

Book Stack

Where I live, it is frequently very windy during the year. Because of the wind, the Radical Wellness Books are subject to being thrashed about. Therefore, after the kids hand in their pencils, they pass their Radical Wellness Books to the front of the class, where that person will stack the five or so books so the wind cannot blow them open. This has worked quite nicely in our efforts to protect the books. During Training Camp, I even tell the kids how to face the three-ring edge against the wind so that it won't blow the book open quite so easily. I have learned not to assume anything.

At your school, you may have other elements to contend with. Each situation is different and needs to be dealt with accordingly. Whether you are teaching inside or outside, book stacking is important for getting the books out of the way of the activities, for keeping them in one place, and for keeping them from getting torn up.

You may think that pencil passing and stacking books are very insignificant management techniques in a physical education class, but these are the little things that make the big difference. If you don't have a routine established for the kids, it can get crazy. Kids like structure and continuity.

Non-Stop Activity

After roll call and any demonstration or explanation of the day's activity, the kids will move during the entire period. Make an attempt to have the kids involved in activities where everyone is moving all or most of the time instead of standing in line. Many of the activities in the PE-4-ME: Radical Wellness Program are explained in chapter 2, "Teaching in Thematic Units."

Ten Seconds

When you blow a whistle to signal the end of a movement activity, the students have about 10 seconds to get back to the bulletin board and drop off any equipment in the appropriate pile behind where the students sit and approximately 30 feet in front of the bulletin board. If you need to talk to the kids during an activity, blow the whistle to signal that they need to meet you in 10 seconds. In other words, use the 10-second requirement for everything: pencil pass-up, book stack, calling all kids, and more. Drill the 10-second rule into the students during Training Camp. Of course, there may be times when it is impossible for the kids to come within the 10 seconds, but aim for it, and have them aim for it.

Closure

To help your students make sense of the Theme for the Week and the daily activity, and to give them a feeling of coming together as a class, you definitely need to make a daily ritual out of providing closure. The students need to pull together all that has happened and make sense of it. Feedback brings meaning to the whole lesson. Because of limited time, the need for closure at the end of a PE class can be overlooked. The following sections provide suggestions about creating closure for your students.

Put-Ups

When the whistle is blown to finish the movement activity, the students come to the bulletin board in as close to 10 seconds as they can and get ready for "put-ups." This is a time for students to share with their teammates some of the neat stuff that happened during class time. "Put-ups" is such a rewarding time of the day, because some of the students will say the most precious, kind statements. Kids are really cool. Examples of a "put-up" include, "My partner was really helpful today," or "I like the way no one made fun of me when I didn't catch the ball," or "My teammates didn't yell at me when I fell down."

Introduce "put-ups" during Training Camp to establish guidelines for positive, constructive criticism. If there is something that went wrong during an activity, the kids know not to use names. They should say what happened so we can improve next time. During your Training Camp at the beginning of the year, be sure "put-ups" are incorporated into your regimen. This is a very valuable learning time and only takes a minute or two out of the class time.

Reading From the Read-Aloud Boxes

The kids love to read tidbits from the Brain Food, Sport Wows, and It's Fitting Boxes. Chapter 3, "Creating the Classroom on the Field," explains how these boxes pertain to fitness, nutrition, self-esteem, brainy-tidbits, sports trivia, and physical education facts. After "put-ups" and comments about the activities of the day, the kids volunteer to read from the boxes into the wireless microphone in front of their peers. They think this is pretty neat.

Equipment Count

Every day in every class, the students count equipment after their activity to make sure you have the same amount of stuff at the end of each class session. When the whistle is blown to end the day's activity, all kids should be in front of the bulletin board in ten seconds, dropping off equipment as they come in. As they approach, some will ask you if they can count the equipment—no problem. This takes a minimal amount of time while the rest of the class is

beginning "put-ups." During "put-ups," someone else will be counting pencils. I don't pick student monitors for each duty, but allow the kids to figure out what needs to be done when. The kids will automatically jump in when they realize something needs to be taken care of. They truly take ownership of their class.

If you are strict about counting equipment, you will have the same number of football flags, the same number of koosh balls, and the same number of yo-yos that you started with at the beginning of the school year. During Training Camp, spend an enormous amount of time explaining to the students the importance of being responsible for their equipment. This works and really pays off.

Undoubtedly, establishing strong rituals and routines is vital to creating a class that is manageable, brain-compatible, and fun—not only for the students, but for the teacher as well. When so much time has been taken in planning and preparation for classroom management, you truly will have time to enjoy the kids. Thank you, PE-4-ME!

BUILDING RADICAL WELLNESS BOOKS

If you are teaching at a school where there are no indoor facilities, as many of you are, you are quite aware that homework in a physical education class doesn't just happen. Even if you have facilities, you know you really have to work at making homework run smoothly. This section will explain what to do to make the homework routine successful in the PE-4-ME: Radical Wellness Program.

Letters to Parents

On the first day of school, send home a welcome letter to the parents of your students. This letter explains who you are, what the PE-4-ME: Radical Wellness Program is all about, and what the students need to prepare for class. There is no mention of PE clothes at this time, only that the kids need to get a plastic three-ring binder with five index-tab dividers. Notifying parents on the first day of school gives the students plenty of time to get their binders, which they should have by the third week of class. During Locker Room Boot Camp the issue of PE clothes

PE-4-ME: Radical Wellness Program

A Brain-Friendly Learning Approach to Physical Education

Dear Parents/Guardians:

As your child's physical education teacher, I look forward to an exciting year working with both you and your child.

Our physical education class will follow the curriculum of the PE-4-ME: Radical Wellness Program, a unique program designed to educate your child on the fundamentals and enjoyment of movement, fitness, and health. We will experience a wide variety of activities, including the social and intellectual as well as the physical.

The PE-4-ME: Radical Wellness Program includes a Radical Wellness Book, which is part of your child's daily PE requirements. Your child is responsible for bringing a plastic three-ring binder with five index-tab dividers. (If there is a problem in purchasing a notebook, please feel free to contact me so that we can make other arrangements.) Your child will bring home activity sheets (as homework) in his or her Radical Wellness Book. The homework worksheets will be handed out every Monday, and they are due every Thursday. The students are responsible for bringing their radical Wellness Books to PE class daily. In addition, "team photos" will be taken during the course of the year so that each student will have their own photo in their Radical Wellness Book.

During the school year, I will present wellness concepts and provide activities and projects to encourage your child to learn and apply these concepts to his or her own health program. Your child will be encouraged to do fitness activities at home and at play to improve his or her fitness level.

This effort needs your support. I encourage you to take part in this program whenever possible. Your commitment to wellness and a healthy lifestyle will be beneficial to both you and your child. Feel free to contact me at school if you have any questions or comments, if you want more information, or if you would like to visit our class. I'm looking forward to a rewarding year with you and your child!

Sincerely,

Ms. Summerford
Physical Education Teacher

Student's Name _____   Period _____

Parent's Signature _____   Date _____

Figure 4.1 Example of the first-day letter.

is addressed. See figure 4.1 for an example of the first-day letter.

Plastic Three-Ring Binders

The plastic three-ring binders I prefer that students use are the one-inch, flexible plastic type. The one-inch ring (versus the half-inch ring) has plenty of room for the PE-4-ME worksheets, and the plastic is waterproof. These Radical Wellness Books will last the entire year.

Book Nametags

When the students turn in their first homework assignment in their binders, apply an adhesive name badge to the front, upper, right-hand corner of their books. The sticker badge you use should have your own personal Radical Wellness Book logo, which is different and unique from the other PE teachers. Inform your entire staff of your logo, so that if a book comes up missing, they know it belongs in your class. This will save you from much confusion.

Index Tabs

The index tabs are basic three-hole dividers that have tabs to label each section. The different sections are Activities, Fitness Fuel, Skills, No Zone, and Fun Stuff. As the year progresses, students fill up the different sections with the worksheets that are handed out on Mondays, ending the year with a complete, organized Radical Wellness Book. It is critical that the students put each new assignment behind the last one, in order to maintain numerical order. If this is not done, the books will be one giant mess. I would suggest that if a student does not put a worksheet under the proper index tab or in the proper order, the student does not get credit. This will save you a lot of headaches down the line.

Most of what goes into each section of the Radical Wellness Book is the copied worksheets, completed by the students. However, use reading materials as well. For example, get plenty of brochures on smoking and drug and safety awareness from your Drug Alcohol Tobacco Education (DATE) coordinator on your campus. Three-hole-punch the pamphlets, and give them to the kids to put in the appropriate section of their book. You may notice that the Fitness Fuel and No Zone sections of the Radical Wellness

Book (see part III) appear to be much smaller than the other sections. That is because all of the reading material I normally include in my classes could not be included due to copyright restrictions. In general, whatever I can get for the kids to read, I include.

First Day Start-Up

The first day that you load up the students' notebooks with PE-4-ME: Radical Wellness Program worksheets will take an entire lesson. Don't assume that kids know where to put papers even when the sections are labeled. Many students entering middle school have spent their elementary years turning in one paper at a time and have never learned how to organize materials.

In preparation for the Radical Wellness Book start-up lesson, set ten big buckets along a fence, about ten feet apart. Once class has started, line the students up single file. Instruct them to proceed from one bucket to the next, retrieving one sheet out of each bucket and putting each worksheet behind the previous one. They should end up with ten different worksheets.

Prepare the following sheets for the homework start-up day, in the following order:

1. Your rules
2. Tabbed divider or cover sheet for activities
3. Activity Log
4. Be Fit at Home Checklist
5. Locker Room Procedures #1, What Is Physical Education?
6. Tabbed divider or cover sheet for Fitness Fuel
7. Tabbed divider or cover sheet for Skills
8. Tabbed divider or cover sheet for No Zone
9. Tabbed divider or cover sheet for Fun Stuff
10. Fun Stuff # 1, Second Chances

Then, sheet by sheet, the class will put the worksheets in the proper order in their Radical Wellness Books. Reiterate the importance of worksheets being put in the proper place. Since you, as the teacher, have a large number of students, you need to know where their work is. Once again, if you can't find a worksheet in its proper place, they do not receive credit.

Weekly Homework Procedures

The students' normal routine is to receive homework on Mondays (or the first day of your school week) and turn in homework on Thursdays. When the students turn in their homework, they turn in their entire Radical Wellness Book, and their work has to be in the proper section of their binder—no exceptions. When my students turn in their wellness books, it takes only seconds to find their work. If I had to hunt for it, I would probably be completely overwhelmed. Do not accept single sheets of paper.

The only time handouts are distributed on a day besides Monday is when you use the Skills Sheets. The Skills Sheets are in-class assessments involving social skills, locomotor skills, and object control skills. They are not homework, but part of the Radical Wellness book. The Skills Sheets should be given to the students on a Tuesday, Wednesday, or Thursday. By giving out Skills Sheets on a different day from Radical Wellness Homework, the students feel less overwhelmed about many papers coming at them all at once. The Skills Sheets are in-class assessment tools, not homework assignments.

Organizational Skills

As I mentioned earlier, many students have not been taught organizational skills. Be very strict about the kids staying organized, or you will end up with student materials put every which way. Each new sheet that is handed out goes to the back of the appropriate section, creating a book from the beginning to the end. Because of the many papers and potential for messy books, organization is the only way a program such as PE-4-ME can be successful. The students need to be organized and take responsibility for their own actions and for their work.

Team Photos

During the holiday season, give the students a team photo of the class. Take the photo a couple of months before Christmas, and have it developed at a wholesale warehouse facility. You can ask your school to pay for it, or pay yourself. Either way, it is well worth it. The students can put their team photo on the first index tab of their Radical Wellness Book. This is very special, as some kids have never been on a "team."

They love this so much that I have taken both fall and spring photos for the kids so that they have another team photo in their book. Many students have turned their team photo page into a work of art. I remember when I was a kid walking into the locker rooms with the pictures of the athletes pictures all over the place. I felt like a second-class citizen and wished that I could be on a team too. There are many kids in your classes today that feel the same way. The team photo helps them fulfill that desire.

The day you give the kids their photos, make sure they tape it into their Radical Wellness Books. If you don't follow up on this, the pictures will most likely not make it into their books. Consequently, have plenty of tape dispensers ready for that day.

Be Fit at Home Checklist

The Be Fit at Home Checklist is located in the activity section of the students' Radical Wellness Books. The checklist (page 114) is a great way to get kids to exercise away from their physical education class. If a student exercises continuously for 30 minutes, they will earn 3 points. On the back side of the page are numbers that they continually add up by circling the points they have earned. Once they reach 100 points, they have their parents sign the form, and they can get another Be Fit at Home Checklist. The students challenge themselves to see how many checklists they can complete during the course of the year.

If you want to incorporate Radical Wellness Books into your program, you have to be very strict about homework completion and emphasize the importance of their work, especially at the beginning of the year. A *routine* must be established and followed. If not, homework in PE (or any class) can be very chaotic if students do not know what is expected of them. Acknowledge and make a big deal about students who are organized and do their work. The rest of the class usually catches on and does the same.

The Radical Wellness Books are awesome. The books provide the students with the opportunity to learn about movement, health, safety, nutrition, skills, reading, solving problems, and being creative—all in one organized complete booklet. I have had many former students come back to visit me and say, "I still have my Radical Wellness Book. It's cool."

5

Putting It Together:
The Teacher's Game Plan

In physical education, more than in other disciplines, it is critical to combine and organize materials so that children can tie together the concepts they have learned in other classes with what they learn in your class. I want my students to understand the connection between wellness concepts and many situations in real life, and to grasp how movement can make them better learners.

The last thing I want my students to think is that PE is a frill and doesn't link with or isn't as important as their other classes. Tunnel vision is not allowed in the PE-4-ME: Radical Wellness Program. In this chapter, I'll explain how to make more sense out of the concepts in a physical education class—and how to make the concepts really fun to boot.

PROVIDING CONTINUITY AND STRUCTURE FOR YOUR STUDENTS

Because the PE-4-ME: Radical Wellness Program teaches in themes or concepts, it is easy to pull together a variety of materials and activities into one cohesive lesson. All movement activities in the class reinforce the Theme for the Week. In addition to physical education and movement, the themes include nutrition (Fitness Fuel) and substance and safety awareness (No Zone) weeks. During each of these weeks, integrate the students' homework, bulletin board, activities, and whatever else you can with the Theme for the Week.

One of the great things about teaching in theme units is that you can draw from the students' everyday lives. Plug in themes that make sense to kids by using what is already happening in their world. During the course of a school year, there are many opportunities for such connections. For example, Red Ribbon Week or Tobacco-Free Week are great opportunities to tie in a No Zone week. Thanksgiving is a great time to plug in Fitness Fuel and talk about moderation. Valentine's Day lends itself nicely to heart and muscle projects. When kids see these connections, greater learning occurs. And best of all, inexpensive teaching tools are easy to find—if you know where to look.

Conference Materials

If you attend workshops and conferences, you know how much stuff you can accumulate—stuff you're really not sure what to do with. Frequently, these great ideas are either put on a shelf and forgotten about, or implemented all at once without any rhyme or reason.

My advice is this: without delay, weave what you take away from conferences and workshops into your program in a way that will make sense to the kids. You may not use it for awhile, but plan now so some forethought will go into what you are teaching. Arrange file folders by the Themes for the Week. Whenever you pick up anything of interest, file it into that folder. When you reach that Theme for the Week during the course of the year, review the file folder and update your program. Sometimes material you've picked up can be filed under different themes; just pick the Theme of the Week that fits best for you. This works quite well for me, and I'm sure it will work for you, too.

Freebies

Take advantage of freebies anywhere and everywhere you can. If I walk into a retail store and see something that would be a cool addition to my class, I ask the store manager if he or she would like to donate the item to the kids in this community. This creates a win-win situation. The store gets recognition from your thank you letter, from an announcement in your school newspaper, and from your school board of trustees. In addition, the store receives a tax write-off, and students get exposure to equipment and items that they otherwise might not get to experience.

Remember, all you have to do is ask. If you come across something in the mail that is free, jump on it; or sign up for freebies you come across on the Internet that would make a positive difference for kids. And, wow, there are a lot of freebies out there!

During my student teaching in 1992, I wrote letters to all of the exhibitors at the American Alliance of Health, Physical Education, Recreation and Dance National Convention and Exposition in San Francisco. I asked them if they would donate materials for kids in a day and age when cutbacks were all too common. I received many responses and ended up with an enormous amount of neat equipment and instructional materials for kids. My motto is, "If you don't ask, you'll never know."

Authentic Assessment Projects

When we as educators talk about "assessment," tests are probably the first things that come to mind. You know, tests—those subjective tools that ask questions formatted in a certain way in an attempt to assess what the learner has learned. Many students don't reveal any "real learning" when participating in this method of evaluation. Test-taking is a skill in itself.

A better way to evaluate student learning is through the use of project-based assessment strategies, or authentic assessment. This sort of assessment gives students a choice in what they work on, and how they will share it. Giving students a choice allows them to feel ownership of their assessment. When students are emotionally attached to a project, they will learn more.

When I first made an effort to assign projects to the students with very few instructions or guidelines, I was completely blown away with what the kids came up with—feature films, puppet shows, posters, skits, you name it. For a long time, I had controlled what would be assigned and how the students were supposed to complete it. Putting the students in control of their own assignments has changed that. I have learned so much from my students in the process.

With authentic assessment projects, the kids are given a topic. They are then asked to share with the class everything and anything they can find out about that topic, in any format they choose. For example, during October, the students are assigned a skeleton crossword puzzle in the Fun Stuff section of their Radical Wellness Books. The next week I assign, above and beyond their regular weekly homework, a Skeleton Project, where they are asked to show me and the class what they have learned about the skeleton. I hang a poster on the bulletin board announcing the upcoming "Skeleton Project." The poster includes some idea prompts—such as a skit, video, poster, or story—and the due date for the project. The students might ask, "What *is* the Skeleton Project?" My response: "You tell me. What can you find out about the skeleton? Share that information with the class however you like. Remember, the crossword puzzle you did last week could be a good starting point. You choose what you want to cover and how you want to show us. And remember, have fun!"

I usually give the students a couple of weeks to work on their projects. An example of what I tell the kids can be found in figure 5.1.

Other authentic assessment projects besides the Skeleton Project include the Muscle Project, the Brain Project, the Radical Wellness Poster Project, and the Letter Writing Project. If you haven't included authentic assessment in your program, I highly recommend it. The kids will come up with phenomenal ways to share what they have learned—much more than I could ever assign.

Structured, Yet Flexible

The PE-4-ME: Radical Wellness Program is very structured, yet flexible. That's why it is so successful and fun. When kids are exposed to a variety of different activities, visual cues, music, and concepts, they become more involved in their class and enjoy it more, too. The students, on the whole, will be more willing to get

SKELETON PROJECT

What is it? A creative project where you go out to the World Wide Web, a library, a relative, or a friend and find out what you can about the human skeleton. Your starting point is the skeleton crossword puzzle. Find out what you can! You can present your findings anyway you choose. The following are examples of projects in the past:

- a video
- a puppet show
- a board game
- a book
- a game show
- a commercial
- a poster
- whatever you want!

You are allowed to work by yourself or with a partner, whichever you choose. If you work with a partner, both partners need to contribute equal amounts of work to the project.

Project is due October 28.

Have fun, and good luck!!!

Note: For anyone concerned regarding religious beliefs, this assignment is not a Halloween assignment.

WOW . . .
I have a great idea!!!

Figure 5.1   Example of what to tell the kids about an upcoming project.

that homework assignment completed because they want to. They know what is expected of them, and they like it.

As a teacher, I really enjoy the freedom to shift gears when I need to. For example, if I know it is going to rain for a solid week, I might adjust the schedule and substitute with Fitness Fuel, a theme that doesn't require as much movement to get the point across (although I always try to incorporate movement everyday).

The Kids Love It!

With the PE-4-ME: Radical Wellness Program, it's pretty obvious that the kids are enjoying their PE class. Teachers know this not only from all of the smiles on their students' faces, but also from the many notes sent by students and parents alike. Kids love having different activities during the week, instead of participating in only one sport.

Of course, there will always be a few kids who will complain or gripe about anything you do as a teacher. Try to "nip it in the bud" as soon as one negative remark or gesture is made. Make

it very clear to the kids that they really don't have to be here; they can switch classes if they deem it necessary, but only after a discussion with their parent or guardian. (Of course, our class really needs them to complete our team.) To this day, I have never had a kid change classes, and I have been able to prevent any snowball effect that their negativity might have created.

Teachers Love It!

There are so many curriculums and programs out there in "teachersville" that it is next to impossible to stick to any kind of a game plan. I think many educational agendas are catering to the perfect scenario—awesome facilities, plenty of money, small class sizes, and sufficient class time with the students. Get real! Very few, if any, physical education teachers are so fortunate.

The PE-4-ME: Radical Wellness Program is remarkable for the mere fact that you can switch gears without losing the continuity or momentum you have built with your students. It doesn't matter if it rains, if you have no place to go, or if you have huge class sizes, the program still marches on. And, yes, teachers love it! I always teach with this thought in mind: be firm, but fun. I truly am having as much fun as the kids.

In conclusion, giving careful thought and planning to each theme and tying it into what's happening in students' lives will create magic in your class. The little bit of extra energy you put into planning will pay off enormously. The rewards I get from my students makes all of the extra planning worthwhile.

EXAMPLES OF TEACHER PREPARATIONS

The only place success comes before sweat is in the dictionary. Successful classroom management requires careful planning. The following sections describe the PE-4-ME: Radical Wellness Program planning devices and strategies that I use to make it all happen.

Semester Game Plan

When I approach a brand new school year, I usually break it down into two semesters. This way, I feel less overwhelmed. At our school, we sign up for the places we will be meeting with our students for that semester. All teachers participate in this process, realizing that we need to stay flexible if any changes need to be made.

Map Sign-Ups

Map out your school, showing all athletic facilities. Divide all physical education facilities into sections or numbers—for example, fields one through ten, courts one through six. When the teachers sign up for map locations, draw numbers to decide who will sign up first, second, third, and so on. The next semester, reverse the order to be fair to all teachers. This system works well for us at our school. If teachers need to make any changes in their locations during a semester, they can approach another teacher who may be signed-up for a place they would like to use. They can then arrange a change individually with that teacher.

Cutting, Copying, and Laminating Materials

Complete big copying or laminating projects a full semester ahead of when you will need the materials. Inevitably, if you wait until the last minute, the copy machine will break; there will

be no more paper; the line for the copy machine will be a mile long; the laminating machine will have disappeared; or there will be no more laminating material. I think you get my drift. Don't do that to yourself. You're busy enough as it is.

Copy the Fitness Jar Coupons and Activity Logs a semester ahead of time. Have student assistants cut out the coupons, punch holes in them, and hang them on three-inch binder rings so that you never run out. The whole Fitness Jar Program could flop if you don't have coupons always available for the kids. As for Activity Logs, if you run out of those, the kids will quit filling them out. I make it a common practice to stay ahead of the game. The Activity Logs are actually in the Kids' Radical Wellness Book in part III for you to copy; furthermore, The Fitness Jar coupons are also included on page 63 to copy for your convenience.

Purchase posters in bulk to cut the price in half. Laminate these posters in the early spring for the fall semester, and have student helpers cut them out of the roll of laminating film. Because there are quite a few posters, this is a great project for the kids. Having the kids help saves me a lot of time and ensures that you'll have them ready to go in the fall. During the course of the year, laminate smaller items such as newspaper articles, student handmade posters, and bits of information that would be neat on the bulletin board.

Mailing labels are also useful for teacher preparation. At the beginning of the school year, once most of the students' schedule changes have been made, have your computer staff person create mailing labels for all of your students. Use these labels when you send students' birthday cards. More information on birthdays is found in the next section, the monthly game plan.

Monthly Game Plan

I love birthdays! Every month, I make sure that each student in my class is valued on his or her special day. What kid doesn't like his or her birthday?

Birthday Cards

Every student in my class receives a birthday card in the mail. I have had many students run up to me at school and thank me for their card. The kids love it, and so do the parents. From an administrative standpoint, treat this as a form of parent contact. Hence, I have 100 percent

Fitness Jar Coupons

This Fitness Coupon verifies that _____
student's name

has participated in _____ for at least thirty minutes on
activity

their way to becoming *HEALTHY FOR LIFE!*

_____
parent signature / date

PE-4-ME: Radical Wellness Program

This Fitness Coupon verifies that _____
student's name

has participated in _____ for at least thirty minutes on
activity

their way to becoming *HEALTHY FOR LIFE!*

_____
parent signature / date

PE-4-ME: Radical Wellness Program

This Fitness Coupon verifies that _____
student's name

has participated in _____ for at least thirty minutes on
activity

their way to becoming *HEALTHY FOR LIFE!*

_____
parent signature / date

PE-4-ME: Radical Wellness Program

parent contact with the parents or guardians of my students in all of my classes. Two weeks before the end of school, send cards to students with summer birthdays. That way, all kids are valued on their special days, and you can receive feedback from all students.

The birthday cards I send are actually postcards that cost me approximately $.08 apiece—and they are well worth it. I purchase the postcards from the same company where I purchase most of my posters. When you buy in bulk, it is much less expensive.

If you aren't presently celebrating your students' birthdays in one way or another, I highly recommend that you do. It is difficult for a child to be very defiant when he or she has just received a card from you. It really is a great classroom management tool.

At my school, we have a computer and technology staff person in charge of the technical side of teaching. Every month, I ask her to run off a list of all the birthdays for the next month for the students in my classes. Once I get the list, I make a poster for the bulletin board and post it at the beginning of the month to display the students who will be having birthdays. I also put the mailing labels on the cards, write a comment to the kids on how they're doing in PE, and wish them a great day. As I mentioned earlier, it is well worth the extra time and energy.

Weekly Game Plan

Plot out your game plan a week at a time. This includes what movement activities the students will be participating in, what the Theme for the Week will be, where you are meeting, bulletin board preparations, and more. This sounds as if it is very time-consuming and burdensome, but it isn't. The weekly posters I print out for the bulletin board keep the class running smoothly. The following are descriptions of my weekly preparations.

Prepare Visual Cues

Every week the bulletin board's posters and signs change—and you can bet it doesn't just happen. One day a week, usually on Monday, I arrive at school earlier than normal. I take off all of the prior week's posters and put new ones on the board, correlating with the current Theme for the Week. This really doesn't take too much time. If you really want to prepare ahead, you could pull off the week's posters on Friday,

so you'll be ready Monday morning. Later in the day, I have student helpers pull out the staples from the prior week's laminated posters.

I print the Que Pasa?, Theme for the Week, and Homework Calendar before the week begins, using basic graphics software. These signs are described in the section on "Visual Cues" in chapter 3, "Creating the Classroom on the Field." Remember, prepare the birthday list once a month.

Copy Work for the Following Week

If you want to run a successful homework program in your classes, particularly if you have a high number of students, it's critical to keep one week ahead. For example, during your preparation period at the beginning of the week, copy the worksheets for the following week. This way student helpers can punch holes in them and prepare them for the week ahead.

Share Your Schedules

Each week, I copy enough of the homework schedules and worksheets so that my students' other teachers know what the kids are doing in PE. Student helpers staple the schedules to the worksheets for the week. This is especially beneficial for the special day classes, Resource Specialist Personnel classes, and bilingual classes. Those teachers have been a tremendous help in working with the kids and supporting them with their PE homework. Giving the classroom teachers my homework materials is instrumental, as they have at their fingertips what is expected of each student. This is very convenient for parent conferences, as many times the classroom teachers meet during their preparation periods, usually during PE time.

By providing the homework schedules on what we are teaching in PE, I am educating the staff. The more I can spread the word about what the students are learning in their PE-4-ME: Radical Wellness Class, the more beneficial it is to our discipline. Most of the staff welcomes any information involving their students. However, I have also had teachers say to me, "Why do you waste paper? Don't give me a copy. I'm going to throw it away anyway." Go figure.

Daily Game Plan

I can't think of a situation where a teacher wouldn't have some sort of routine for getting their equipment for the day out where it belongs

Student helpers can provide time-saving assistance with preparing your visual cues. Let students tack up, take down, and remove staples from your posters and other visual aids.

and brought in when necessary. The Classroom on the Field for the PE-4-ME: Radical Wellness Program is no different. The following is a way to expedite this process.

Set-Up

Each day, I do one of two things. Either the students in period one will set-up the class or I will. The bulletin board, dry-erase board, Radical Wellness Wagon, and equipment will be set out by the locker rooms. When the first period students see our PE-4-ME equipment on their way to our meeting place, they will take it out and set up the class. The kids love having ownership in their class and are more than happy to help. Some days I really enjoy setting up the class myself, as it gives me time to reflect on the upcoming days' events.

The Classroom on the Field stays out the entire day, from set-up to take-down. During training camp, emphasize to the students that this Classroom on the Field is *their* class, and that they need to take care of it. If the Classroom on the Field is located in a high-traffic area on campus, put the boom box, station cards, and other equipment closer to the boards or in the wagon before excusing the students from each class. This is called *tightening up* the class. Instruct the students to report anyone they see messing around with our PE-4-ME equipment between classes or during lunches to school officials. I have never had problems with students getting into the supplies, tearing off posters, or taking the wagons. Because the students genuinely *like* their class, they have an underlying respect for it. Current and former PE-4-ME students have a genuine desire to protect the program.

Take-Down

The students in the last period class are in charge of the take-down of the Classroom on the Field. When you have a student who can't participate due to some medical reason, have them supervise the "taking in" of all the pieces that make the class work so well. Teach the kids to take all supplies beside the locker room in a designated spot. After school, pull everything into the locker room.

Grading Procedures: How Often?

Evaluating students is never an easy process, especially when we think about what a quality physical education program entails. Movement, social proficiency, participation, and cognitive competence are some of the criteria to assess. In addition, grading procedures are going to depend on what your district and school have mandated. You might be on a semester or trimester schedule. In either case, report card grades have to be attended to at certain times of the year.

Students should be graded on their own accomplishments; not on comparisons with other students. How fast they can run, how high they can jump, or how many free-throws they can make in a basketball game are not criteria for assessment. Self-improvement is essential for individual student learning. Knowledge of subject matter and daily participation in movement are fundamental for self-efficacy and success of each student.

The students begin each quarter with 75 points, with the possibility of earning 100 points total. The breakdown for the grades is a standard format:

97 - 100+ A+	80 - 82 B-	67 - 69 D+
93 - 96 A	77 - 79 C+	63 - 66 D
90 - 92 A-	73 - 76 C	60 - 62 D-
87 - 89 B+	70 - 72 C-	0 - 59 F
83 - 86 B		

To earn an A, students must complete their Radical Wellness Homework and participate daily in movement activities. The issue here is that they *earn* an A. The cognitive work is worth 25 points or 25% of their grade. The other 75 points or 75% comes from daily participation in movement. Each student starts out with 75 points each quarter, which represent their participation points. All students should participate daily, so there is no need to continually add up participation points for every child every day.

Students are expected to dress in PE clothes and to be actively involved in movement activities. Failure to dress-out for PE will not affect the academic grade, but will be treated as a discipline issue and it will influence their citizenship grade. The first non-dress: parent warning. The second non-dress: counselor consultation.

The third and subsequent non-dresses: administration consultation and detention. If a student is non-dress in class, they will participate in an alternative movement activity. If a student flat-out refuses to participate, the student loses 2 points, takes responsibility for his or her own actions, and can't make it up. PE-4-ME students should understand the consequences of bad choices very clearly early in the school year.

Students on medical excuses are still required to dress in PE clothes unless it is impossible. If they can't dress, send them to an alternative classroom or library for time to work on Radical Wellness Homework. *All* students in the PE-4-ME program should be dressed in PE clothes when they are at the Classroom on the Field. If a student with a medical excuse is in PE clothes, he or she can be an awesome little helper. When parents send students to school with notes pertaining to an illness and asking for their child to be inactive, the student still dresses out.

If a student is absent, the nonattendance does not count against their grade; however, they need to make-up the movement time because of the non-participation. The student can do one of three things. He or she can (1) participate in 30 minutes of a movement activity outside of class, signed off by a parent or guardian, (2) make up movement time during lunch or after school on a designated day of the week, or (3) do nothing at all. If a student does nothing, he or she loses 2 points.

The point value of each homework worksheet depends on the number of worksheets assigned per quarter (or semester). If you want to figure out the point values ahead of time, coordinate the Make It Happen Cards with your own school calendar early in the year. Otherwise, you can add it up later by making each Radical Wellness Worksheet count as one completion. Then, when you know the total number of worksheets you've assigned for the quarter, you can divide the points evenly across the worksheets. For example, say that students were assigned 19 worksheets during the first quarter. There are 25 points for the quarter's homework; 25 divided by 19 equals 1.31 points per worksheet. If Johnny only completed 12 out of the 19, his cognitive work is worth 15.72 points. Add 75 plus 15.72 to equal 90.72 points, or an A minus. On the other hand, if Johnny made a bad choice during the quarter and did not participate one day, he only has 73 participation points; add that to his 15.72 cognitive points and he has earned 88.72 points, or a B plus.

The Radical Wellness Program homework is due every Thursday. At the beginning of the year, collect the work every single Thursday and provide feedback and affirmations for the students who do their work. As the year goes on, you can skip a week here and there, and grade two weeks' work at a time. However, the kids need to know their assignments are due every Thursday of each week.

Each completed page of homework receives a star. Either they did their work or they didn't. Most of the assignments are provided for more awareness of a concept, not for a right or wrong answer. For example, a question on a Radical Wellness worksheet might ask, "How did you feel about this activity?" They either answered it or not, and if they didn't, their work is not complete. If they don't answer every single question, it's not complete and they don't get a star.

Put stickers in their Activity Logs when they turn in their Radical Wellness Books to let them know you appreciate the way they are keeping their logs up-to-date. They really like stickers as feedback!

When the students have worked on a big project such as the Skeleton Project, Muscle Project, or Brain Project, try to make that project worth approximately 10 points, or a number that will make your grading easier. For example, if 19 worksheets were assigned during the quarter, make the project worth less than 10 points (6 points) that quarter, so the sum is an easy 25 for grading. If the students attempt to do a project, they'll get all of the points. They did the project or they didn't. Never compare one project to another; the results may be varied, but each student may have turned in his or her best attempt.

When assigning projects, instruct the students to give their best efforts. I once had a student who presented his project, and it was apparent that the child put no effort into it. After class, I looked him straight in the eyes and asked him, "Did you give your best effort?" He quietly said he had not. I then asked, "What are you going to do about it?" He said, "Do it again." That was the only time I have had to address a student about his or her effort. Most kids get totally into it, and some kids just don't do it at all.

Acknowledging Kids

When kids are behaving appropriately, I like to acknowledge them. I give random surprises to the kids just to let them know I am very proud of them.

Some of the acknowledgments I give out are award coupons for free stuff from local vendors. For example, fast food restaurants (such as Carls Jr., Jack in the Box, In-N-Out), miniature golf courses, bowling alleys, and other retailers have coupons for students who are doing well in school. I will give the kids who have done their Radical Wellness Homework award coupons that tie in with the lesson of eating so-called "junk food" in moderation. The last thing I want to do is promote unhealthy food. However, in this culture, you can't hide fast food from kids. So I ask my students, "Should you eat this for breakfast, lunch, and dinner?" They will say "No," and I'll ask "Why?" They answer, "Because there is too much fat."

Because of the tight budgets in education, I believe you have to take advantage of freebies anywhere you can to acknowledge the kids. Corporate America has money, so I try to benefit from it for the good of children. Other, more fitness-orientated ideas include miniature golf coupons, community center coupons, and after-school sports coupons.

The kids love the Ticket Box drawings as well (see chapter 3, "Creating the Classroom on the Field"). I have all sorts of goodies that can be won from a winning ticket.

During Training Camp at the beginning of the year, I make it very clear to the kids that if anyone asks for a surprise, we won't have any. This is a special treat. I try to emphasize to the kids that positive behavior on a daily basis for the mere sake of being a cool person is more important than a gift.

For the winter holidays, I give the students a team photo of the class that they can tape onto the first index tab of their Radical Wellness Book. This is really special, as some kids have never been on a "team." All the students in my classes are important members of the "class team." For some, seeing themselves in the picture really gives them a boost.

There are so many great ideas to acknowledge kids, and add novelty to their PE-4-ME routines. I say, "Just do it!"

PART II

Movement Activities

It's not easy planning movement activities for physical education classes. Are the activities developmentally appropriate? Do the activities involve plenty of movement? Are the activities safe? Are the activities challenging to the students? Will the activities work at your facilities? Does your class size affect the activity? As you well know, much thought goes into planning quality movement time.

This part of *PE-4-ME: Teaching Lifelong Heath and Fitness* provides examples of some excellent movement activities for your students. Each week, there will be movement suggestions on the Make It Happen cards. These are highly recommended. The movement examples are described step-by-step in this section, for your convenience. Plug into the Theme of the Week any activity that you feel applies. If you have an activity of your own that is not in the examples, go for it. Just be sure there is a tie-in to the theme.

Some activities are more mellow than others, and some are riskier. Some activities are more cooperative, and some are more competitive. When planning it is important to think about the *balance* of experiences for children. Kids need to encounter a wide variety of activities. That is part of the educational process.

The critical component before beginning any movement activity in class is to set the *tone* of the class. The only way a "dodgeball-type" game is acceptable in a quality physical education program such as PE-4-ME is when the requirement for mutual respect between all players has been addressed early on and throughout the year. When an emotionally safe environment has been established, a *riskier* kind of activity, such as throwing at "human targets," is fun and challenging for the kids. It's all in how you deliver the activities to the students, emphasizing courteous behavior and safety first.

Middle-schoolers love challenge when they feel safe. Because of the processing time (the time to debrief the importance of safety, fairness, and teamwork) before, during, and after the activity in a PE-4-ME class, kids learn. They learn that it is never appropriate to throw things in other people's faces. For example, purposely throwing a yarn ball at a teammate's head is inappropriate. They learn about honesty by confessing when a yarn ball does hit them. And, of course, they learn that something as soft as a yarn ball, as opposed to a baseball, is okay for a "human target" game.

When I think of a "human target" in fun activities, I think fondly of playing out in the snow as a child with my dad. We would make these big, fluffy snowballs and then proceed to try to tag each other with them. I loved it when the snowball would explode into a big cloud on me. I remember falling in the snow and laughing so hard. Of course, the snowballs weren't hard, like a stone or rock. That's the difference. I was taught what kind of a snowball is appropriate, as I was taught the force with which to throw it. I felt safe and had fun because I was in an emotionally safe environment. Students need to be taught emotional intelligence skills—like how to get along with each other—repeatedly, so that the positive behavior becomes second nature.

Students need to experience a wide range of movement activities. Along with moving for the physical benefits, movement can be an important component of motivation and learning. When kids become motivated and excited, adrenaline is released from the adrenal gland into the bloodstream. Adrenaline acts as a memory fixative, locking up memories of exciting events (Jensen 1998). If you get students to release some adrenaline and other neurotransmitters during their physical education class, they just might have some better brain activity later on in the day and remember just a little bit more.

The PE-4-ME: Radical Wellness Program is so successful because of the blending of many powerful concepts within a huge variety of activities. If the entire year was based on the same type of activities, the students would get bored. All kinds of activities, no matter what the basis become a cooperative experience. The students are challenged, they are learning, and they love it!

When you ask your students to participate in more athletic-type activities, be careful. Throwing in a little competition is positive for some, but negative for others. Either way, kids need to learn about it. Some kids get their adrenaline going, while other kids can look at it as a stressor. Set the tone. Teach appropriate behaviors. This is not about winning; it's about doing your personal best. Teach kids how to respect everyone on the team and everyone in their PE-4-ME class.

Water activities are always a lot of fun, especially if you live in hot areas. Be sure to ask the students questions before you involve the water. "Do you think it would be appropriate to splash someone with water? Would it be okay to stick your head in the bucket of water? What should be the consequence if someone can't restrain from it?" After you have addressed these issues, have fun!

Because there are so many differing views on what *are* and *are not* appropriate physical education activities in our discipline, you need to decide. What will work for you? Are you going to set the tone in your class? Are you going to create an emotionally safe environment for your students? Do you want your students to learn about a healthy *balance* of movement activities? Create *balance* for student learning.

Enough talking, let's get moving!

Hi, How Are Ya? Gotta Go

Equipment: None

Students walk up to fellow classmates, shake their hands, looking at them, and introduce themselves. Next, students can give the "way cool" introduction to their new classmates. They walk up to a classmate, shake hands regularly, then wrap fingers around the base of the partner's thumb, leaving thumbs interlocked; then, without disconnecting thumbs, wave goodbye. While they are doing this they say "Hi" (with regular handshake), "How are ya?" (with interlocked thumbs), and "Gotta go" (with thumbs connected and waving goodbye). This is a very fun introductory activity.

General Space

Equipment: None

General space is when all of the students are filling up their personal spaces—that is, everyone's personal spaces make up one general space. Tell the kids that there are invisible cones all around the general area. This prevents kids from taking off too far and eliminates the need to set up cones as frequently.

Birthday Line

Equipment: None

Have students line up in a single line according to their birthdays, that is a January 1 birthday is first and a December 31 birthday is last. Explain that they have to do this without saying a word or lip synching (mouthing silently) to each other. The kids can flash fingers to indicate what month and day, but they can't say anything. Then "bend" the line to make a circle. Going around the circle, have the students say their names and when their birthdays are. They should be right next to someone who has the same or a close birthday—already something in common with fellow classmates!

Partner Handshakes

Equipment: None

Students go around shaking hands with fellow students and introducing themselves and sharing one item of information learned from Locker Room Boot Camp that day. Students should introduce themselves to another person, shake hands, and share an item of information. Then, at the next new person, they will introduce themselves, and also introduce the last person they shook hands with and his or her piece of information. Do this throughout Locker Room Boot Camp to get the kids to move and remember.

Personal Space

Equipment: None

Personal space is an area around you where you will not invade anybody else's personal space and you are in your own safety zone. Instructing students to get "personal space" is the same as telling them to "spread out" for a safe place to move without endangering other students. Practice getting into personal space so you can make sure kids have a clear concept of how much space they need.

Toss-a-Name Game

Equipment: 6 Koosh Balls

Form a circle. A student steps forward one step and says his or her name. The entire group, in unison, says the name of that person. Go around the circle. Now add a ball that is tossed to another person. To toss, call the name of the person, make eye contact, then easy toss. The receiver says "Thank you" and the person's name. Add more balls and keep tossing and calling names. Finish by putting the balls away. Go around and have each student step forward silently while the group calls out his or her name.

Match Mates

Equipment: Boom Box

Players are in a scattered formation. When the music starts, the students begin walking around in the general space. When the music stops, the players freeze and listen to the teacher or student leader, who tells how the groups will be formed. For example, "Show us how quickly you can form groups by the color of your eyes." After the groups are formed, players greet each other. Players repeat the activity, performing other locomotor movements (running, skipping, jumping) and using other criteria for group formation (birthday month, first vowel in last name, color of shoes, etc.). The teacher may give examples of criteria at the beginning of activity.

Scrambled Eggs

Equipment: Boom Box

Tell students to get into their personal space. When the music starts, students move (any movement you decide) among each other without touching another person. Have the students walk, race-walk, run, skip, crawl, and so on. This is a great activity to check whether there are any rowdies in your class who are not moving safely. Positively reinforce the kids that are doing a great job, and the rowdies will usually settle down.

People to People

Equipment: None

Each student stands back to back with a partner. The teacher calls out body parts and the students respond by touching that part of their partner (elbow to knee, foot to head, side to side, hand to quadricep, bicep to toe, etc.). The students are laughing so hard that they are comfortable with the activity and don't realize they are touching anyone else. On the signal "people to people" new partners must be formed. Make sure the students figure out how to get a partner quickly. Group discussion on partnering, learning body parts, or the game as a whole is part of the lesson.

Interviews

Equipment: None

Give pairs of students five minutes to interview each other. You can give some questions as prompts or just leave it open. Tell them at the outset that they're going to introduce their partner to the class when done. At the end of the time, have each partner introduce the other partner to the class, based on the interview.

Whistle Mixer

Equipment: Boom Box

Students are moving in scrambled-egg formation. The teacher blows the whistle a certain number of times, and kids position themselves back to back depending on the number of whistles. For example, a group of four whistles means four kids get together, a group of three whistles means three kids get together, and so on. This is a great activity for getting students into groups quickly. Group discussion on this activity is part of the lesson.

Psychic Shake

Equipment: Boom Box

Students pick number one, two, or three in their heads. It's a secret! When the music starts, students shake hands with each other according to the number in their head, without saying or "mouthing" the number. If a student has the secret number one and shakes hands with a student who shakes three times, the student with the number one knows to continue on and look for someone who shakes only once. The class should end up in three groups, the ones, the twos, and the threes. This is a fun activity.

Roadway

Equipment: Boom Box

Students partner up back to back in general space. One partner then stands behind the other. The front partner is the "car" who places his or her hands in front with arms extended as bumpers and closes his or her eyes. The back partner is the "driver" who places his or her hands on the partner's shoulders. When the teacher says, "Go," they move around across the general space. The driver guides the car safely (without bumping any others) by gently turning the partner's shoulders in the direction in which he or she must go to avoid a collision. This can continue for a couple of minutes before the teacher says, "Switch."

Variations: combine cars to make minivans, combine minivans to make limousines, and so forth. The group discussion should be centered around trust.

Aura

Equipment: Boom Box

Have students pair up. Stand facing your partner at arm's length. Touch palms and close your eyes. Keeping your eyes closed, drop your hands and both turn around in place three times. Without opening your eyes, try to relocate your partner's energy bodies by touching palms again. This is very fun and challenging.

Safety Tag

Equipment: Boom Box

All students are in their personal spaces. Everybody is "it." Students safety-tag fellow students on the knee (stress safety) to freeze them. A safe tag is a gentle tap; unsafe tags include slaps, punches, or karate chops. When students are frozen, they stand with hands at their hips. To unfreeze them, touch their elbows gently. This is very fun and active. You can add many variations to this basic tag game, such as High-Fives, Compliments, Put-ups, and so on. For example, instead of touching elbows, students can unfreeze fellow teammates by giving them a high-five. Same goes for compliments and put-ups.

Flag Grab

Equipment: Flag Football Belts and Flags

All students are in their personal spaces wearing flags (one on each hip). Teacher says, "Go." Students pull as many flags as they can, without having their flags pulled. Each flag still on their hip is worth two points, pulled flags in their hands are worth one each. Each round should last about three minutes. Repeat several times. Kids love this game.

To the Rescue

Equipment: Boom Box and Bean Bags

All students have a bean bag that they put on their heads in their personal spaces. Students then *gently nudge* fellow classmates, trying to bump the bean bags off of their heads. If a bean bag falls off, students cannot touch their own bean bag. Another student needs to come "to the rescue" and put the bean bag on the head of the student who dropped the bag.

Group Juggling

Equipment: Kooshy-Type Balls

Groups of six or eight students each form a circle. Provide one fewer ball than the number of members in the group. The leader has all of the balls at his or her feet. Toss one ball gently to someone across the circle. Keep tossing the one ball, across the circle, to anyone who hasn't received the ball. Remember whom you tossed to and who tossed to you. Once you have a pattern that includes everyone in your group, start adding balls until all the balls are in play.

•••••••• Instant Activity Intro ••••••••

Equipment: Boom Box and Exercise Station Cards

After the general routine of the class is set, introduce Instant Activity. The kids immediately start moving after leaving the locker rooms. Start this with Exercise Station cards. The kids warm up to music and later "touch base" in front of the bulletin board before they start the day's activity. As the year progresses, new Instant Activities are added (reinforcing the previous day's main activity and the Theme of the Week). See chapter 4 for more information.

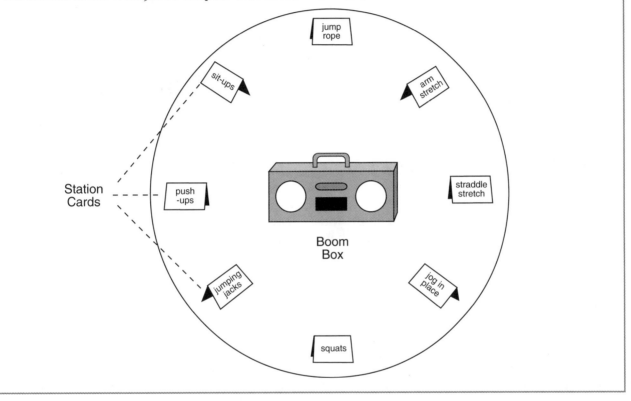

•••••• Triangle Tag ••••••

Equipment: Boom Box

Blow a whistle four times. Because the students learned from the previous activity, "Whistle Mixer," they know to get into groups of four. Three of the members put their hands on their shoulders or hold hands, all facing to the center. The other member is "it" and chases one of the members of the triangle. The other two try to protect their person from the person who's "it" by moving. The "it" cannot go under, over, or through the group. Rotate the "its" when they tag or are exhausted.

•••••• Courtesy Tag ••••••

Equipment: Flag Football Belts and Flags

All students are in their personal spaces wearing flags. Object of the game: to pull another student's flag without losing your own. If a student loses a flag, that student kneels down and waits for another student to bring him or her a flag. The only way you can pull other peoples' flags once you have one in your hand is to be courteous and give it away to someone in need and kneeling. The kneeling position is a safe position (1) to put flags back on teammates, and (2) to be safe from getting your own flags pulled. A student can't kneel for safety if they are not being courteous and putting a flag on another student's belt.

Equipment Count

Equipment: Tons of Stuff

The object of this activity is to have kids practice counting a variety of equipment quickly. For example, kids will throw Koosh balls, or kick hackey-sacks in the general space. When you give the signal to come in, they have 10 seconds to drop equipment in the appropriate spot designated by the teacher and be ready in front of the bulletin board. The kids take turns automatically staying at the equipment pile to count the equipment. (A big part of the lesson is making it happen quickly.) This is a great training activity that eliminates a lot of headaches later in the year.

Crows and Cranes

Equipment: Football Flags

This is a super fun game. "Grow this up" for middle school by talking about the center line as the "line of scrimmage." Students are about a foot off the centerline facing each other. The yellow flags are "crows" on one side, and the red flags are "cranes" on the other. There are end boundaries about 50 feet or so from the centerline. The object of the game is *not* to get points. The teacher says "Croooowwwwwssss," and the yellow-flagged "crows" run to the end zone as fast as they can before the "cranes" pull their flags. The teacher says "Crraaannneeesss," and the red-flagged "cranes" run to the end zone as fast as they can before the "crows" pull their flags. When a flag is pulled, the student puts it back on, and now has a point. I say "bak, bak, bak" like a chicken when the kids don't want to go up to the line of scrimmage—they love it!

Variations include integrating subject matter into the activity. Instead of "crows" or "cranes," the groups could be "odd" or "even" numbers. For example, the teacher calls out, "Nine times five equals?" If the answer is odd, the odd group chases the even group, and vice-versa. The groups could be "nouns" or "verbs." Be creative—it is virtually unlimited what you can do with this.

Rock, Paper, Scissors

Equipment: Football Flags

This game is the same as Crows and Cranes except that students get a partner who faces them across the scrimmage line (it doesn't matter if they have the same or different colored flags). The teacher says, "Ready, set, go." The students then play Rock, Paper, Scissors. Whoever wins that round chases the other student. It's fun to watch the kids process this info quickly.

Partner Tag

Equipment: Boom Box

Students partner up back to back in the general space. One of the partners is "it." All "its" spin around slowly 10 times while their partners are moving scrambled-egg in the general space. The "its" open their eyes and try to find their partners and safety tag them. Then the partner is "it." All students must keep moving during this activity.

Blob Tag

Equipment: Boom Box

Students are in the general space. Two students start the game as the Blobs. When they safety tag other students, they connect by grasping wrists. When they link up to four people, the Blob divides by two, so now there are more Blobs. All students need to keep moving. This continues until all students are Blobs.

Hog Call

Equipment: Blindfolds

Partners create names that go together, such as peanut and butter, salt and pepper, black and white, and so on. One partner is one name, and the other partner is the other name. Partners must split into two groups about 30 yards apart. Everyone blindfolds him- or herself. The teacher says, "Go," and all the students call out their partners' matching names. Once they find their partners, they "high-five" each other and watch the remaining students find their partners. Oink, oink!

Brainy Barnyard

Equipment: Blindfolds

This game is the same as Hog Call, except that students are scattered in the general space. Students have a choice of being a sheep, cow, horse, pig, dog, or rooster (or any five or so animals that you choose), but they decide what they are going to be secretly. Once blindfolded, the teacher says, "Go," and all the students act out what they are with sound only (i.e., a cow says "moo," etc.). Students should end up in groups of the same animals.

Knots

Equipment: Boom Box

Students get in groups of eight. They then join hands with two different people across the circle. After all students have joined hands, try to undo the giant knot without letting go. Have the kids try it a couple of times in their groups, then combine the groups.

Brainy Balloon Balance

Equipment: Balloons for Each Student

Students partner up in the general space. One partner blows up a balloon, and the other partner hangs on to his or hers. First, have the kids bounce it back and forth between them (this gets the ants out of their pants). Then have the students challenge themselves by putting the balloon between their two heads and doing push-ups, or between their backs while they go up and down (as in squats), and so on. They could also do a sit-up balloon pass, or anything else they can come up with. For example, can they move to a destination with the balloon between them? How about forming a circle and having the balloon pass from one student to another without using their hands? If a balloon pops, blow up another one. Challenge the students—maybe a group balance by placing a balloon between the people next to you. Everyone squats at the same time. Loads of fun!

Shoulder Circles and Massage

Equipment: Boom Box

The entire class gets into one big circle, facing the back of the person in front. Students put their hands on the shoulders of the person in front of them. The students massage the back of that person's shoulders. Then they make circles with their hands on the right side of the back, circles on the left side of the back, then figure eights. (This is an excellent activity for stimulation of the brain.) Of course, some students may be more uncomfortable with touching each other than others are. Emphasize the fun of the activity and deemphasize the negative feelings of touching. Most kids truly enjoy it. Next, the kids make "doodles" (moving back and forth with both hands) from top of the back to the bottom. Let the kids know that they are exercising their brains by the movements going cross laterally across their backs. They love it!

Buckets

Equipment: 8 Giant Buckets and a Boom Box

Bucket stations are wonderful because you can change what kind of equipment you put in them. Once the students have the routine down, it's a cake walk! Put at least 6 of one kind of equipment in each bucket, using 8 buckets, totaling 48 pieces of equipment. If you have more students, add more equipment. The buckets are set up similarly to station cards in that they are around a boom box in circular fashion. To begin, students are to sit in the center of the buckets without touching the boom box while the teacher demonstrates how to use the equipment at each bucket station. Next, students are to report to a bucket without touching anything. The teacher needs to make sure that there are not more than six people at each bucket so that each student has a piece of equipment. Then, when the whistle blows, the students participate at that station. In a few minutes, the students rotate clockwise from one bucket to the next, remembering to put their equipment in the bucket before doing so. They truly love this because they always have a piece of equipment. This is a great way to utilize equipment that you may only have a few of, but enough to fill up one bucket. Once the kids learn the routine, this is a wonderful lesson to use throughout the year.

Back-to-Back Dancing

Equipment: Boom Box

Two partners stand back to back with their arms entwined. When the music starts, they must move towards another pair and then switch partners, keeping one arm still entwined with the original partner, and then entwine the other. Next, find another pair to switch partners with; then another, and another. At the middle school level, it is common to see the girls stay around the girls, and the boys stay around the boys. That's fine, just as long as the students are acting appropriately. Usually, they are laughing so hard that they'll do fine. Beware: the upper middle school students may need more supervision regarding inappropriate body gestures than the younger grades.

Warp Speed Group Juggle

Equipment: 24 Koosh Balls, Stopwatch

Form the same circle and same sequence as used in Group Juggling. A group of six or eight students forms a circle. Provide one fewer ball than the number of members in the group. The leader has all of the balls at his or her feet. Toss one ball gently to someone across the circle. Keep tossing the one ball, across the circle, to anyone who hasn't received the ball. Remember whom you tossed to and who tossed to you. Once you have a pattern that includes everyone in your group, start adding balls until all the balls are in play. Now prepare for warp speed! The object is to have a Koosh ball contact each group member in record time. Challenge the groups to lower their times on each trial by timing them with a stopwatch. Ask, "If you could cut the time in half, how would you do it?" Can they get it down to two seconds or less?

Chicken Games

Equipment: Rubber Chickens

You can substitute these crazy chicken games for different tag and relay games. They really are a lot of fun. A couple of favorites are Chicken Catch-A-Tori and Chicken A-La-King. Chicken Catch-A-Tori is an updated version of the old tag game of "Touch and Go." You are "it" if you have the chicken. To get rid of the chicken, you must tag a person with your free hand (not with the chicken). When you tag someone, they are "it," and you drop the chicken and go. Chicken A-La-King is a game where approximately six students are "chicken hawks." Another six students will carry chickens; these are the "rulers" of the barnyard. The rest of the students are "clucks." The chicken hawks tag the clucks, and when they are tagged, the clucks have to freeze in a frozen chicken position. Creativity takes over here, because everyone's idea of what a frozen chicken looks like is different. The rulers of the barnyard can give the frozen little clucks a chicken to free them, and then they become a ruler and the rulers become little clucks. The rulers can then try to save other frozen clucks.

British Bulldog

Equipment: Football Flags and Megaphone

Mark out the play area with a safe zone at each end. Select one player to be "it," who stands in the middle of the play area. Have all other players wear flags. When the teacher shouts through the megaphone, "British Bulldog, one, two, three!" all the players try to run to the safe zone at the opposite end of the play area before "it" can pull their flag. Tagged players become "its" and join the other bulldogs in the middle of the play area. Remind them to return flags to the teacher. Players may change ends only when the "British Bulldog" signal is called. Now the teacher repeats "British Bulldog, one, two, three!" and the players again try to run to the opposite safe zone. Continue until there are more Bulldogs than runners. Stress safety in this game and the importance of watching where you are going. It is suggested that spinning 360° is not allowed. When students spin in a tag game, they lose their direction and accidents can happen. Safety is of the utmost importance when kids are moving fast.

Criss-Crossies

Equipment: None

Also called Hook-Ups, this game is another super-great brain activator and perfect as a closing activity. While standing, students cross legs, cross one arm across the other clasping their hands with fingers interlocked, turn clasped hands under toward the chest (a hook-up), put their tongue on the roof of their mouths, and breathe deeply. Wow . . . this is incredibly relaxing. This activates many parts of the brain because of the many crossovers across the midline of the body. Pressing the tongue to the roof of the mouth adds another dimension to brain stimulation.

Blind Tag

Equipment: Blindfolds and Rubber Chickens

In pairs, one student is sighted and one is not. The non-sighted member of the pair is "it" and carries a rubber chicken to denote this. Sighted partners stand with the non-sighted partners and lead with voice commands only—no physical contact! Teams avoid being tagged by another of the non-sighted "its" with the chicken. After a while, switch sighted and non-sighted people. Before doing so, partners should discuss what things were done positively and what things could be changed.

• • • • Aerobic Conga Line • • • •

Equipment: Boom Box

Students line up in groups of six. When the music starts, the person in the front of the line moves in a "wild and crazy" aerobic kind of way (the kids will come up with some goofy moves). The others follow the moving pattern of the leader. After a few moves, another leader takes over. When the music stops, students join another group, and so on, until the entire class is following one leader.

• • • • • Sweatshop Hop • • • • •

Equipment: Boom Box and Exercise Station Cards

This is an aerobic routine consisting of a set of exercises that repeats itself for a desired number of times. Station cards to use: Jog in Place, Jumping Crossovers, Twist Hops, Elbow-to-Knee Touches, Rocker Steps, Side Kicks, and Sprinter. This is a very good workout and fun.

• • • • • • • • • • Two-Deep Fitness • • • • • • • • • •

Equipment: 20 Cones and Boom Box

Pair up students. Set the cones up to create two circles with equal numbers of students, one small circle inside the big circle. One partner is in the outside circle, and his or her partner is standing in front of them in the inside circle. There is a leader in the middle. The inside circle follows the movements of the leader who creates any kind of movement, such as push-ups. At the same time, the outside circle jogs one lap around the outside circle of cones, without passing another student. Once a person gets back to their partner they stop, jogging in place. On the signal to switch, they switch places. Now there is a new inside circle following the leader's movements and a new outside circle jogging! Continue the activity.

Rocks

Equipment: 30 Frisbees, 2 Large Hoops, Jerseys, 20 Cones

Set up the field by using cones to mark out a large rectangular field, divided in half by a midline. Place a hoop at the end of each half to serve as a goal area. Place half of your Frisbees (the "rocks") in each hoop. Divide the students into two teams. The object of the game is for the students to capture the opponents' rocks while protecting their own. Start the game with a whistle. Players are "safe" on their own side of the field. Once they cross into the opponents' field, they are liable to be safety tagged. Inside the hoop on the opponents' side is safe. If tagged, a player must "freeze" by putting hands on hips. A teammate can be "unfrozen" by a player tapping elbows. The unfrozen player must check in across the midline to his or her side before doing anything else (going to the rock pile or unfreezing anyone else). Players try to get into the opponents' circle, grab a rock, and return to their own circle without being tagged. If a player is tagged with a rock in hand, the tagged player will give the rock to the other team and go back to their home side (they are not frozen). If a player puts one foot over the centerline or one foot into the hoop, he or she is safe. The players guarding the rock pile must stay six feet from the rock pile. The game is over when one team has all the rocks in their circle. Encourage students to take risks, rescue teammates, and play honestly! After a few games, the students come up with some very interesting strategies.

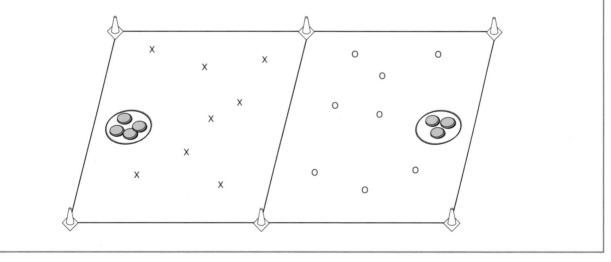

Math Fitness Fun

Equipment: 20 Numbered and Dotted Dice

This is a great warm-up. In small groups, players will take turns rolling dice, adding the dots, and then performing an exercise. Put a giant poster on a bulletin board that gives them great ideas for exercises. Here is one variation: have students add or multiply two dice, and exercise to that number. For example, if the dice are rolled with two "sixes" showing, the students could add them together and do 12 push-ups or 12 jumping jacks. If the students multiply the dice together, then 36 would be the amount of that exercise. There are unlimited kinds of exercise you could do.

Pass the Shoe

Equipment: Boom Box

Students form a shoulder-to-shoulder circle and then sit down in a sit-up position. The students remove their right shoes. The students lie back and touch their shoes to the ground, beside their ears, and say "one" in unison. As they sit up, they tap their shoes in front of them and say "two." Then they say, "Pass the shoe" and pass the shoes from their right hands to their left hands, under their legs, and to the partner next to them. Now everyone has a new shoe and the entire sequence is repeated until everyone has his or her own shoe back! The kids are fascinated with this activity.

Obstacle Course

Equipment: Varied Items

The obstacle course is a simple course that gives students an opportunity to improve all areas of their fitness while having fun. The following is a description of one obstacle course. There are many possible variations, depending upon the available facilities and equipment. The event starts with a quarter-mile run around the track. This run ends where jump ropes are set up, and students complete 50 jumps. Next, students proceed to accuracy throwing, and throw balls into trash cans. They try to make 10 shots. Next, students log-roll down a slight hill. Next, students must weave back and forth through hula-hoops until they get to the end. The students then go around the track another quarter of a mile. To avoid congestion and making slower students feel self-conscious, always stagger the start of the event.

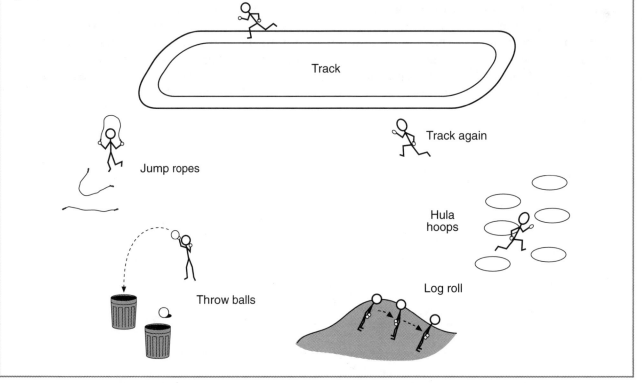

Tarantula

Equipment: Boom Box

Mark out a starting point and a finishing line. Form groups of three players and have them get into the general space. Each group creates a knot. While they are in this position, have them half-squat down and spread their legs: now they are "tarantulas." Have them move around while maintaining their grip. Line up all tarantulas and have them race across to the finish line. Create giant tarantulas!

Chicken Tire Tag

Equipment: Bicycle Inner Tubes, Rubber Chickens, and Boom Box

Students partner up inside an inner tube. Six pairs are "its" holding the rubber chickens. When the music starts, all inner-tubed partners run, trying to get away from the "its." If they are tagged, they take the chicken and are now "it." Your kids will be laughing so hard it will be difficult for them to run.

• • • • • Dog and a Bone • • • • •

Equipment: 10 Towels

Form equal teams of six players. Have the teams line up behind the opposite end lines, about 10 meters (30 feet) apart, facing each other. Number the players in each line, one, two, three, four, five, and six, with the number ones at opposite ends. Place a "bone" (a towel) midway between the two lines. When the teacher calls a number, such as "two," both number twos leap forward and attempt to snatch the bone and return to their home line without being tagged by their opponent. If successful, they earn one point for their team. If their opponent tags them, the tagger's team gets the point. Players may trick and jockey for a position before making the snatch for the towel. One player needs to keep score for their team. Continue until each player's number has been called at least once. Have five or six games going on at once.

• • • Mini-Soccer Games • • •

Equipment: 20 Cones, 5 Soccer Balls, Jerseys

It is advantageous to incorporate mini-games throughout the year. The kids really enjoy them, and it satisfies their need to play traditional games. Everything is in threes. For example, at least three people are on a team; keep the ball for three seconds and get rid of it; three points per goal; and three different people have to touch the ball before a goal is made. There are no boundaries. Set up five mini-fields (depending on your class size), which creates a lot of action. Emphasize safety regarding keeping the ball on the ground, no heading, and so on. At this point, there has been no mention of dribbling, trapping, kicking, and so on, but emphasize that the object of the game is to get personal space so the ball can be passed to you. This is all about kids moving for the entire period. Fun stuff!

• • • • • • • • Fun Run • • • • • • • • •
Starting Point

Equipment: Stopwatch

In this running activity, encourage the kids to work on improvement, not on being first. I always start the year off by determining a starting point for each student that they can improve on. I try to get them to compete against themselves and not anyone else. I stagger when the kids take off, so you don't end up with the really slow kids coming in last. Whatever distance you have the kids run or race-walk, this self-improvement approach really helps the kids. Students record their personal times in their activity logs.

• • • • • • • • Go for It! • • • • • • • •

Equipment: Yarn Balls, Hula Hoops, Tennis Balls, Bean Bags, and Rubber Playground Balls

Divide the class into two teams. Each team has a designated team line at the end of the playing area. All of the different equipment is in the center of the area. There are five different types of equipment, each representing one factor contributing to a healthy lifestyle. The following list gives the equipment used, how it must be manipulated, the number of points it's worth, and what factor it represents:

Yarn Balls. Carry in between knees for 30 points; represents exercise.

Hula Hoop. Use like a jump rope for 25 points; represents proper nutrition.

Bean Bags. Carry on top of head for 20 points; represents drug-free life.

Rubber Balls. Dribble for 15 points; represents adequate sleep.

Tennis Balls. Carry for 10 points; represents stress management.

On the starting signal of "Go for it," both teams run up to the equipment and pick one piece of equipment to take back to their team. They must carry the equipment back in the designated way; if they drop it, they start over. Add up which team is the healthiest once all the equipment has disappeared from the center of play area. Repeat several times.

Centipedes

Equipment: Boom Box

With starting and finishing lines, have players find partners and assume the all-fours position, one behind the other. The front partner supports his or her feet on the back partner's shoulders and takes his or her weight on the hands. The back partner should take his or her weight on feet and hands. Together they should move forward. Have them change places and repeat. Have a centipede race. Create a giant centipede. How about a monster centipede with the whole class!

Slingshots

Equipment: Bicycle Inner Tubes and Balls

Students make sling shots with bicycle inner tubes by using their feet to hold tube, pull back, and let the balls fly. Aim for a target. See how far they can shoot a ball. This takes a lot of strength to do, and the kids love it.

Spiderweb

Equipment: Bungee Cords or Line

Spiderweb is a very challenging activity whereby the students transport their teammates from one side of the "spiderweb" to the other without touching the web. Web bungee cords and rope to create a giant spiderweb on a couple of the goals, being very careful that the ropes are safely attached. If the web is touched, it may wake up the spiders, so the class needs to start over. The students need to problem-solve and figure out how can they do this. Should their teammates lift them? Should they climb through on their own? Problem-solving time should be allotted before any physical action. To make spiderwebs, find giant soccer goals or something similar. This is an awesome cooperative and problem-solving activity. When the students become proficient, this can be a timed event.

Relays

Equipment: Depends on the Relay

Relays should be fun for the kids. It is a serious mistake to encourage children to compete with one another in activities that involve new or unfamiliar skills. In addition, to save kids from standing in lines, make teams very small. During equipment shuttles, students move from one side of the area to the other doing a skill, which varies with the different equipment. In Soccer Shuttle, have each player dribble a soccer ball across to the first player on the other side. In Skipping Shuttle, each player jumps rope across to the first player in the opposite side. In Hockey Shuttle, each player stick-handles a puck across to the first player on the opposite side. In Obstacle Shuttle, set up cone markers, chairs, or pins between the two shuttle lines and have each player zigzag through the objects, using the equipment, to the opposite line.

Tennis Ball Relay

Equipment: 20 Tennis Balls

The tennis ball relay is an activity designed to give students a great aerobic workout in an enjoyable atmosphere. A cone is needed as a starting point for each three-person team. Everyone in class is on a three-person team. To start the race, place two players from each team at their starting marker with the tennis ball on the ground in front of the first player. Place the third player on the team at the far end of the field. Instruct the students that when the race starts, the first player on the team is to kick the tennis ball "soccer style" so that the ball flies to the end of the field. The person who kicked the ball chases it. When he or she arrives at the other end of the field, his or her teammate kicks the ball back to the player who remained at the starting point. This player in turn, when the ball gets there, kicks it all the way back to runner number one, who is waiting at the far end of the field. The runners continue this pattern for 10 minutes or so, counting how many times they completed a cycle.

Heart Rate Monitors

Equipment: Heart Rate Monitors, Bucket of Water

Set up the lesson as "Show me what you can find out about the monitor." If you haven't had the glorious experience of working with heart rate monitors, you are in for a treat. There are various styles and different models. Many have an electrode chest strap and a watch. Instruct students on how to put the chest strap on, and explain how water from a bucket put on the monitor helps conduct the heart beat, and note the configurations on the watch. The kids love experimenting with them, and they really learn this way. For more information and great lessons on heart rate monitors see Beth Kirkpatrick and Burton Birnbaum's *Lessons from the Heart* (1997). Everything you need to know is in there. The students who are not currently using the monitors work on checking their pulse rates the "old-fashioned way."

Circuit Training Stations

Equipment: Buckets, Cardio Equipment, and Boom Box

Same as Buckets, but change the equipment and use exercises that work on aerobic conditioning. Use your imagination about what you can use. Put at least 6 of one kind of equipment in each bucket, using 8 buckets and totaling 48 pieces of equipment. If you have more students, add more equipment. The buckets are set up similarly to Station cards in that they are around a boom box in a circular fashion. To begin, students are to sit in the center of the buckets without touching the boom box while the teacher demonstrates what is at each bucket station. Next, students are to report to a bucket without touching anything. The teacher needs to make sure that there are not more than six people at each bucket so that each student has a piece of equipment. Then, when the whistle blows, the students participate at that station. In a few minutes, the students rotate clockwise from one bucket to the next, remembering to put their equipment in the bucket before doing so. This is a great workout! The kids really enjoy this when you use the music.

Shark Attack

Equipment: Parachute, Life Jackets, Boom Box, and *Jaws* music

This game is outrageous! My students have turned this fun, cooperative game into a feature movie. Students sit in a circle around the parachute with their legs stretched underneath. They grasp the parachute in both hands and pull it up to their waist, shaking the parachute. One or two students are "jaws," and they are crawling around underneath the parachute while the other students start the "waves" across the parachute (of course, all of this is to *Jaws* music). Three students walk around the parachute as lifeguards, wearing life jackets. The shark attacks by gently pulling on whatever pair of legs looks appealing and tries to pull the victim under the water. The lifeguards try to make a rescue by gently pulling under the arms of the victim so the shark doesn't take them under the parachute. The lifeguards are careful not to pull by the arms, as that could be unsafe for the joints. If the shark is successful, the entire class hums a sad song.

Macarena Push-Ups

Equipment: Boom Box and Macarena Music

Have kids perform a Macarena dance for one round, push-ups for the next round, and continuing on throughout the song; for example:

1. Right arm out, palm down.
2. Left arm out, palm down.
3. Turn right palm up.
4. Turn left palm up.
5. Cross right hand to left shoulder.
6. Cross left hand to right shoulder.
7. Move right hand to right side of head.
8. Move left hand to left side of head.
9. Cross right hand to left front hip.
10. Cross left hand to right front hip.
11. Move right hand to right hip.
12. Move left hand to left hip.
13. Hip circle, jump quarter turn.
14. Next sequence, do push-ups.

Tumbling and Gymnastics

Equipment: Boom Box

Only teach tumbling if you feel comfortable with it and have had experience. Be sure you have the proper equipment, such as mats. Teach just the basic skills—forward roll, backward roll, straddle roll, and a cartwheel—so that the kids can create a pop-up routine. Students start in a push-up position. (1) Pop-up tuck: the students push their arms against the ground, causing their seats to pop up and their legs to land under them (squat position). (2) Pop-out: the students place their weight on their hands and push their legs backward to the "up" position of a push-up. (3) Pop-straddle: the students will pop their legs into a straddle while their hands remain on the floor. (4) Pop-pike: students are in a standing pike position with hands on the floor and the legs straight (warm up hamstrings prior to this). (5) Shoot-through: students squat both legs through the hands and finish in a sitting (pike) position with both legs straight. This pop-up is very difficult.

Here is an example of a pop-up routine:

1. Standing, fall forward to a momentary push-up position.
2. Pop-tuck.
3. Forward roll to a stand.
4. Fall forward to a push-up position.
5. Pop-straddle.
6. Straddle stand.
7. Cartwheel to stand, quarter turn jump to.
8. Fall forward to a push-up position.
9. Pop-pike.
10. Backward roll to stand.
11. Fall forward to push-up position.
12. Pop-shoot through to sitting pike position.
13. Roll backward to straddle pike roll.
14. Finish in straddle position and slide one foot in to close the straddle.

•••••••••••• Swedish Softball ••••••••••••

Equipment: 2 Tennis Rackets, 2 Bats, 2 Foxtails, and 2 Tennis Balls

Set up two softball playing areas so two games can be going on at once. Divide your class into four teams; send two teams out to field and two teams to bat. Teams and players do not pitch to each other. Each batter throws up the tennis ball or foxtail and hits it him or herself. After the player hits the ball, he or she is to run the bases as far as possible before the ball gets back to the pitcher's hand. If a runner is between bases when the ball reaches the pitcher's hand, that player must return to first base. There are no outs. If a runner doesn't think he or she can make it to the next base, they can stay where they are. There can be many runners on one base at a time. A team is at bat until all players on that team have batted. They then take the field and the other team bats. The running team scores by running past home plate. Runners who have scored get a free trip back to first (they keep going around the bases). The team in the field can score too. They are awarded a point when they catch a batted ball on the fly and when they catch a runner or runners between bases by getting the ball back to the pitcher's hand. Runners on the team at bat run the bases until their team takes the field. There's no particular reason why this game is called "Swedish Softball." One thing is for sure, everyone is active and it is fun!

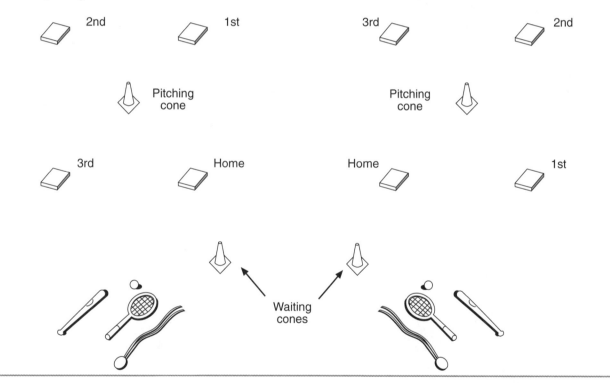

••••••• Three-Legged •••••• Races

Equipment: Gunny Sacks or Safety Ties

Your basic three-legged race. Kids love this, and it definitely works on cooperation.

••••• Across the River •••••

Equipment: Various

A relay race where objects are placed along the path so that students pretend they are going around trees, jumping over rivers, leap-frogging over stumps, and so on. This relay becomes so much fun that the kids forget about what their time might be.

Power Walk

Equipment: Stopwatch

Power-walking or race-walking is a great way to increase the heart rate for a longer period of time. Challenge your students to see if they can walk as fast as you can! This is a very fun activity with heart rate monitors. The kids are very surprised that their heart rate increases so much just from walking! You can also try partner power-walking.

Prediction Run

Equipment: Stopwatch

This is a motivational strategy that takes the emphasis out of winning when running. Set up a running route. The distance can be from 400 yards to 2 miles. Students will write down in the Activity Logs of their Radical Wellness Books the predicted time (PT) they think it will take them to run the course. When the kids return from the run, have them log in their Activity Logs the actual time (AT). Subtract one from the other. How close are the scores?

Bocce Ball

Equipment: Bocce Balls and Cones

This game is excellent for windy days, and is also a great game that students can play with their grandparents. Students will come back to school and share how they introduced this to their families and how much fun they had. Bocce is played with eight large balls and one smaller target ball called the jack. The cones are used to set up the courts, two cones on each end approximately 25 feet apart. There are four balls to a side, or team, and they are made in two colors to distinguish the balls of one team from the four balls of the opposing team. The object of the game is to get your team's balls closest to the jack. The closest ball gets three points; the second closest ball, two points; and the third closest ball, one point. Students take turns rolling (*not* overhand throwing) the bocce ball. Players can knock other players' balls out of the way if they choose. Add up points each round, and repeat.

25 feet

Hot Swatter

Equipment: 8 Frisbees, 8 Foam Sticks

Assign a maximum of six students per group. One student is "it" and has the stick. All others form a circle three yards from a Frisbee, which is now in the center. The student who is "it" now strikes a participant on the leg and lays the stick on the Frisbee. (Players can't throw the stick, and they must touch the Frisbee before letting go of the stick.) The student that was struck races in, grabs the stick, and tries to hit the person who's "it" before he or she can get to the vacated spot. If they miss, then they are the new "it" and strike another. If they hit them, then they have to lay the stick down, and get back to the spot before they get hit again.

Skin the Snake

Equipment: Boom Box

Divide the class into teams of six. Have each team find a space and get into file formation behind a leader. Be sure the kids have enough space. Have students spread their legs apart; lean over, putting their right hands forward to grasp the hand of the player in front of them; then they put their left hands back between their legs, to grasp the extended hand of the player behind. They should hold the hands of both players throughout the game. On the signal "Go," the last player lies down as the rest of the team backs up over him or her, straddling the player with their legs apart. Then each player, in turn, lies down for the team to shuffle backward over them until everyone is lying down, still holding hands. The last player (first to lie down) gets to his or her feet; then straddle-walks forward over the rest of the team, pulling each one in turn to the standing position until all are back in original position. Emphasize that players keep their legs in close while lying down. Remind players to keep the hand-hold at all times. Warn players to walk with legs wide apart, to avoid treading on their teammates. This activity really works on flexibility, but definitely is best when the boys and girls are separated.

Scooter Boards

Equipment: Scooter Boards, Balls, and Goals

This activity is played on an indoor or outdoor basketball court with a smooth surface using a playground ball. The object of the game is to throw the ball through the opponent's goal. The rules are the same as soccer except that the players must stay seated on the scooter boards. There are six or fewer players on a team. After a goal is scored, the opposing team brings the ball up the court as in basketball. The game may be played with more than one ball. The goalie is the only player permitted in the goal area. The game starts with the ball in the center of the court.

Bonus Ball

Equipment: 55 Tennis Balls

This is a high-energy relay. Divide the class into six teams, numbered one through six, with no more than eight players per team. You'll need 55 tennis balls for this activity. In advance of the class, divide the tennis balls into six groups of eight balls, numbered one through six, and one group of seven. Mark each of the balls in the groups with the appropriate number (for example, "1" for the balls in the first group, "2" in the second group, etc.). Mark the balls in the group of seven balls with "BB" for bonus ball. Each team has a #10 can (the container tennis balls come in) or an old coffee can at the front of their line. The teams line up parallel to one another at one end of the playing area. All the tennis balls are at the other end, just mixed up on the ground. On the starting signal, the first four players run forward to find a tennis ball with their team's number on it. Once the player has found a numbered ball belonging to his or her team, he or she returns and places it in the team's #10 can. That player goes to the end of the line as the next player runs and tries to find a ball with the team's number. Bonus balls are "wild" and can be picked up by any team player once the team has found five or more of its numbered balls. Score one point for the numbered team balls and two points for a bonus ball. Tell the students to keep it a secret if they find a bonus ball. This makes it more exciting when totaling up scores.

·····Inner Tube Relay·····

Equipment: Bicycle Inner Tubes

Divide the class into teams of four students. Divide each four-person team into pairs. Send one pair to the start/finish line and the other pair 40 to 60 feet away. The first person at the start line runs to the teammates at the opposite end, holding on to the inner tube. One teammate joins with the first person, holding on to the tube. The two of them run back toward the start/finish line to pick up the third teammate. The three teammates, all holding on to the inner tube, run back to pick up the fourth teammate. All four return to the start/finish line, running together, and all holding on to the inner tube. Try groups of 8, or 16, or even the whole class!

········Jump Rope········ Challenges

Equipment: One Giant Rope, Lots of Single Ropes, Station Cards, and Boom Box

Giant Rope. Two students take the rope by its ends and begin turning. The rest of the students will be jumpers, lining up single file. The students proceed to pass through the turning rope. Explain to the students how to judge their timing, so that they jump in when the rope is at its highest point, and how to jump out. Change the rope turners when needed. Challenge students to go through the turning rope singly, then two by two, four by four, eight by eight, and so on, until the entire class goes through the rope at once.

Station Cards. Use Jump Rope Station cards to teach different jumping skills to music. For example, one station might instruct students to jump on their right foot. Other stations would have them jump on the left foot, jump rope backwards, crisscross their arms as they jump, and so forth. I always introduce rope skills as the best conditioner for athletics to preempt any student who might think of jumping rope as a "sissy" thing to do.

·········Juggling·········

Equipment: Juggling Scarves and Boom Box

Each student gets three scarves: two scarves are put in the waistband and one scarf is in a hand. Have the students toss the scarf up to the music and catch it overhand (so the knuckles are facing up). Next, have the students do two-scarf juggling with both hands: cross the two scarves overhead, drop them, and catch them on top of the scarves. When this is mastered, cross one scarf across the body overhead, then the other (crisscross, applesauce). Students should say "crisscross" and "applesauce" outloud while they are juggling the scarves.

Next is two-scarf juggling with one hand. First demonstrate the proper holding technique. Hold one scarf against the palm with the middle finger, ring finger, and index finger. The other scarf goes between the thumb and index finger of the same hand. Put the hand you are not using behind your back. Practice with one hand, then the other.

Finally, have the students do three-scarf juggling with both hands. Again, demonstrate the proper holding technique for the students. Put two scarves in one hand (as previously explained) and one scarf in the other. The first scarf to be thrown is the scarf held with the thumb and the index finger in the hand that is holding two scarves. Before it begins to fall, toss the scarf in the other hand (that's holding only one scarf) in the opposite direction, so you are making an *X* across your body with the two scarves. After you throw the second scarf, your hand comes down to catch the first scarf on top. Then you toss the third scarf (the one held against your palm with three fingers) across your body, and then that hand comes down to catch the second scarf on top, continuing this process of juggling scarves one right after the other. Yippee!!

Four-Square

Equipment: Playground Balls and Squares on Floor

Introduce this game as "Middle School Four-Square"—which is nothing like the game they played in elementary school. This is very fast paced, which requires a lot of agility and quick reaction time. The students must keep their fingers pointed down. If the ball bounces on the line, the student is out. The server must say service. Students really enjoy this game. The differences from elementary school four-square are the fingers pointing down and the fast-paced action.

Spinjammers and Frisbees

Equipment: Spinjammers and Frisbees

Kids love Frisbees. The Spinjammer is a type of Frisbee that has a special center device that enables the students to spin the Frisbee on their finger. Spinjammers and Frisbees can be used for great catch games. Take the students through the progression of throwing and catching a Frisbee. (1) Grip: Grasp the disc as if you were going to fan yourself. (2) Step-throw: Place your feet along the line of intended flight with your throwing-arm side toward the target, and step toward the target as you throw. The backswing should involve a turn of the upper body. Have fun!

Foxtail Golf

Equipment: Foxtails, Hoops, and Cones

Set up a golf course as you would Frisbee golf, except use foxtails. For example, a cone can be where you tee off, and the hula-hoop is the hole. If you have visible flags you can stick in the center of the hoop for a visual cue, go for it. The object of the game is to get the foxtails into the hoops.

Freaking Frisbees

Equipment: Frisbees and Two Large Tubs

The object of the game is to throw the Frisbee into the tub. The field is about 50 yards with two large tubs at either end. Each tub is in the center of an inner circle (5 yards in diameter) and an outer circle (9 yards in diameter). Each team has two goalies who each hold a Frisbee to knock Frisbees away from the tub. Goalies have to stay between the inside circle and the outside circle. No other player can be inside that area. Goalies cannot touch anything inside the inner circle where the barrel is located. All students have a Frisbee. Both teams line up 20 yards apart, and, on the command "Go," all students throw their Frisbees toward their goal.

Here are additional rules of the game: (1) No student can have more than one Frisbee. (2) All Frisbees that touch the ground and are picked up by anyone must be tossed back one throw to someone on their team before being tossed forward toward their goal; in other words, just find a Frisbee and throw it back to a teammate. (3) All Frisbees inside the goalie circle must be thrown out by the goalies only. (4) A Frisbee inside the tub equals five points; a Frisbee inside the inner circle equals one point. (5) The game continues until all Frisbees are inside the inner circle. (Don't worry, the goalies don't get thrashed by Frisbees.) When there are only a few Frisbees left, the action continues. Remember, if a Frisbee touches the ground, anyone can grab it, so the direction the Frisbees are going constantly changes.

Zwirl Footballs and More

Equipment: Zwirl Footballs, or Any Type of Throwing Object

A variety of neat things to throw excites most kids. There are many products out there that make cool noises, fly, or glide. Try to expose your students to throwing different objects and experiencing the different flights they may take. Students partner up or form groups and practice throwing and catching.

Star Wars

Equipment: 4 Folding Mats, 50 Yarn Balls, 2 Trash Can Lids, 2 Jump Ropes to Cover Goal Opening, Boom Box, and *Star Wars* Music

The object of the game is to keep balls out of your space station by deflecting them while getting as many as possible into your opponent's station. Place at both ends of the playing area approximately 50 feet apart two folding mats, standing on their ends and locked together to make a semicircular "fort." Place a jump rope in front of the "fort" to indicate a goal box. These are the "Starship Space Stations." Scatter yarn balls in the play area.

How to play: (1) Two galaxies are at war and are firing "death stars" at each other's "Space Stations." Neither army can cross the battle line (the midline). (2) Each army has a special guard who stands in front of the "Space Station" and possesses a "star shield" (trash can lid) that repels "death stars" (yarn balls). All warriors may block incoming "death stars" with their bodies. (3) Warriors may only possess one "death star" at a time and may throw from anywhere on their side of the battlefield. (4) "Death stars" may not be removed from the "Space Station" until the end of the battle, after they have been counted. (5) For special effect, the activity is enhanced by playing the *Star Wars* theme music. When the music stops or when the whistle is blown, both armies must cease fire. Each star shield guard counts all the "death stars" in his or her "Space Station." The team that has more "death stars" in its "Space Station" loses the war. (6) Change star shield holders and start a new battle.

Partner Sit-Ups

Equipment: Boom Box and Yarn Balls

Partners sit facing one another, with knees bent, feet flat on the ground. One student holds a yarn ball. Pass the ball back and forth while performing sit-ups. Next, give all students a ball and sit in a big circle. When the music starts, on count one, the students tap the ball to the outside edge of their right feet. On count two, they lie back with arms overhead and tap the ball on the ground. On count three, they sit up and tap the ball to the side of their bent knees On count four, they pass the ball under their bent knees, transferring it to their left hands. The ball is now ready to be picked up by the person on the left. The person on the left grasps it in their right hand and all repeat the same pattern.

Fling-Its

Equipment: Fling-It Nets and Balls

Fling-It is a net and ball game that has been specially designed to encourage and challenge players to communicate, cooperate, and coordinate their efforts in tossing a ball. You can use old pillowcases, towels, or sheets if you don't have fling-it nets. Divide the class into groups of four. Each group has a fling-it net. Inside the net is one ball. At a count of three, fling the net up to shoot the ball into the air and catch it in the net. How high can you fling-it? There are many games you can create with these nets: throw the ball up in the air and catch it; throw it to another group; create a fling-it for the entire class; and so forth. How about flinging chickens? Or fish? Or a variety of equipment at one time? Does the different equipment travel and fall at different speeds?

Surf City

Equipment: Boom Box and Surf Music (King of the Surf Guitar)

Part 1: Grapevine right (counts 1-4); grapevine left (counts 5-8); grapevine right (counts 9-12); and grapevine left (counts 13-16).

Part 2: Step forward with right foot; touch left foot next to right (counts 1-2). Step backward with left foot; touch right foot next to left (counts 3-4). Repeat (counts 5-8). During these steps the arms move like the "wave": up high when you step forward and down low when you step backwards.

Part 3: Walk backwards right, left, right, together (counts 1-4). Jump to straddle position (counts 5-6). Jump one half turn with the feet landing together (counts 7-8; you are now facing backwards). Repeat parts 1-3 facing this new direction.

Part 4: Chassé with right foot in front (step, together, step) (counts 1-2). Step on left foot in front (count 3). Step back on right foot behind (count 4). Chassé backwards with left foot (counts 5-6). Step behind with right foot (count 7). Step forward on left foot (count 8). Repeat entire dance.

Part 5: Chassé sideways two times leading with the right foot: step right foot to side, left foot goes behind right, arms "swoosh" up high and to the right, and the head looks up (counts 1-4). Chassé sideways to the left two times leading with the left foot: step left foot to side, right foot goes behind left, arms "swoosh" low and to the left, head looks down (counts 5-8). Repeat part 5 (counts 9-16). Lift head and hold final position for a few seconds while taking a musical break. Improvise "surf" moves for 16 counts—anything goes!

Part 6: Step right to side, touch left toes next to right. Fingers "snap" when you touch left toe next to right foot (counts 1-2). Step left to side, touch right toe next to left. Fingers "snap" when you touch right toe next to left foot (counts 3-4). Repeat (counts 5-8). Walk backwards right, left, right, together (counts 1-4). Jump to straddle position (counts 5-6). Jump a straddle half turn with feet landing together (counts 7-8). Repeat part 6 facing the new direction.

The dance now begins all over again from part 1. Do whatever you feel like at the end if the dance does not fit the entire song. Be creative and have fun!

Choreography by Vicki Sullivan, 1998. Used by permission.

Goal Ball

Equipment: Basketballs and Jerseys

This lead-up game involves dribbling and passing. Tape four-by-six-foot goal boxes into the four corners of the basketball court. Each team has two of the goal areas. The object is to score by passing the basketball to a teammate inside one of the team's goal areas. The game begins with either a center jump or by one team inbounding the ball at the *x* (see diagram). The players move the ball down the court to score by combining dribbling and passing. A goal is scored when a teammate in the goal box catches a passed ball in flight. Opponents attempt to prevent a score by guarding players, but cannot enter the goal box. A ball going out of bounds is awarded to the opponents for a throw-in at that spot. After a goal, the opposing team puts the ball in play at the *x*. If a violation occurs, the ball is awarded to the offended team for a throw-in. The following constitute violations: traveling; contacting an opponent (foul); bouncing the ball to the teammate in the goal; stepping into the opponent's goal. The game is designed for 10 players. The players can be allowed to play full court, or they can be separated into offensive and defensive teams that must remain on their halves of the court. One modification of the game is to have no one assigned to the goal areas. Therefore, any player may enter the box at any time to receive a scoring pass.

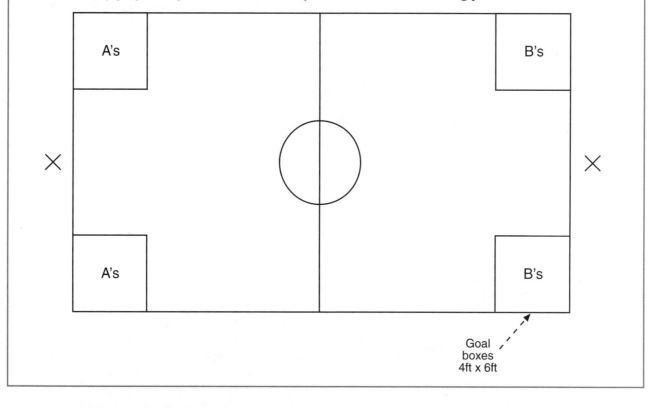

Goal boxes 4ft x 6ft

Mini-Basketball Games

Equipment: Basketballs and Jerseys

Because the kids are dying to play a game, I make mini-games (three on three). With one day of this, the kids have had the feel of a big game, yet all the kids have been involved.

Toe Tag

Equipment: Boom Box

Partner up back to back in general space. Partners face each other with arms on shoulders. The object of the activity is to tap the other person's toes. Switch partners a few times. This is lots of fun!

Putt-and-Strut Golf

Equipment: Golf Clubs and Whiffle Balls

After you briefly go over the proper grip of a club, the students will be ready to challenge themselves in making a putt. To make golf holes, flatten one side of a No. 10 can (a tennis ball can) and lay it on its flat side so that it does not roll. Students should start one foot from the hole, then slowly back up each time. This might be all it takes to get a kid "hooked on golf."

Soccer Croquet

Equipment: Soccer Balls, Coat Hangers for Wickets, and Goals

Using the coat hangers for wickets, design a gate for the soccer ball to pass through. Number the gates and follow in order the numbers one to nine. Have about 30 feet between numbered wickets to help give players enough room to play unhindered. After completing all wickets, the player gets to dribble for a goal shot. Arrange players at different wickets to start the activity.

Sideline Basketball

Equipment: Basketballs and Jerseys

This is another great lead-up game that involves passing and shooting. It is a participation activity that can be played with 16 students per court (8 players per team). The teams are positioned so that half of each team is on the court at one time, and the other half is positioned along the sidelines, leaving 4 players per team on the playing court. These players can move from end to end or be restricted to half-court play. The game begins with a center jump. Scoring and fouls are the same as in basketball. When the defensive team obtains possession of the ball, they must pass it to at least one sideline player before it can be shot. The sideline player cannot shoot the ball, but only pass it to an on-court teammate. After a basket or three to four minutes of play, the on-court and sideline players exchange places. The game can be modified by allowing on-court players to dribble; by requiring more than one sideline pass before a shot is taken; and so on.

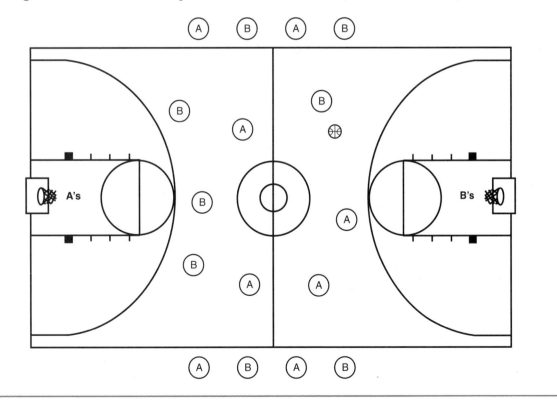

Partner Balances

Equipment: Boom Box

Have the students sit back to back on the floor with knees bent. Then have them push into each other's backs at the same time to try to stand up. Have them try it a few times. Next, try groups of four, five, six, and so on. Kids enjoy this activity. Then debrief, talking about how both or all people need to cooperate.

Yo-Yos

Equipment: Yo-yos and Boom Box

You can't go wrong with yo-yos. Turn on the music and let them play. My students automatically form groups to teach each other different tricks. This is lots of fun. To add aerobic moves to playing with yo-yos, have the kids challenge themselves to race-walk and yo-yo at the same time.

Basket Bowl

Equipment: Nerf Balls and Tubs

This game is a cross between basketball and hockey with a hockey goal (tub) at each end of the court and small utility balls for equipment. The players dribble the Nerf balls and pass them as is done in basketball, except for one major difference: more than one ball, and as many as five, may be in play simultaneously. This tactic really speeds up the game and spreads the players out across the court rather than being crowded around one player with the ball. In this game, as in basketball, no contact is allowed. The object of the game is to score as many points as possible by throwing the balls into the goal, which is protected by a goalie who considers the area his or her private domain. The goalie's job is much more challenging because his or her attention is divided among the many in-coming balls. This game can be played on a basketball court with the free throw lane as the goal area, or on an open field, which encourages passing the ball rather than dribbling. I highly recommend that the goalie wear eye protection because of the many balls in play coming from all directions.

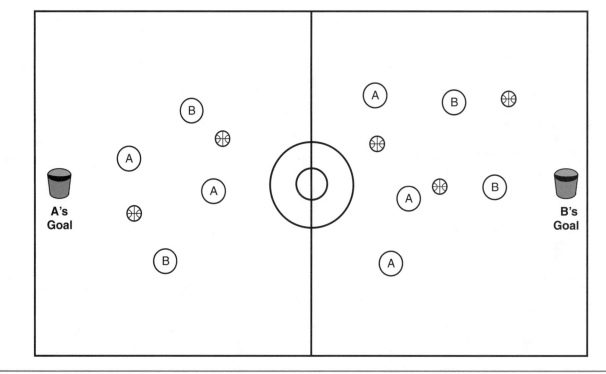

Ribbon Balls

Equipment: Ribbon Balls and Boom Box

My students love these balls! They are rubber balls with a long ribbon streaming out. Put on the music and the kids will create cool movements. You can purchase them in a sports supply catalog. The following are suggested movements: circles, side circles, above the head circles, figure eights, swings, using two ribbon balls at one time. Note that it's not a good idea to let go of the ribbon balls as they can become tangled and knotted up.

Electric Slide

Equipment: Boom Box and Country Music

Line dances are a great way to teach kids rhythm and dance without having to find a partner. Any fun upbeat music is recommended.

Counts 1, 2, 3, and 4: Grapevine step to the right (step right; cross left foot behind; step right; touch left foot beside the right). Say, "Right behind right touch."

Counts 5, 6, 7, and 8: Grapevine to the left (step left; cross right foot behind; step left; touch right foot beside the left). Say, "Left behind left touch."

Counts 9, 10, 11, and 12: Step back on the right foot, step back on the left foot, step back on the right foot, and touch the left foot beside. Say, "Back, two, three, touch."

Counts 13 and 14: Step forward on the left foot and touch the right foot beside it. Say, "Left touch."

Counts 15 and 16: Step back on the right foot and touch the left foot beside it. Say, "Back touch."

Counts 17 and 18: Step forward with the left foot, make a quarter turn to the left while brushing the right foot past the left, and repeat counts 1 to 18 until the end of the song. Yahoo!

Centerfield

Equipment: Boom Box and Music (by John Fogerty)

Introduction: Claps (counts 1, 2, 3-and 4, 5, 6, hold, and 8). Repeat claps five times. Next, do bicep-builders (make a fist, bend arm at elbow, then straighten) four times, and trunk-twisters (put hands on hips and twist) four times.

Part 1: Slap knees, and clap hands four times. Reach up with both arms and clap hands four times. Repeat part 1.

Part 2: Reach to right side, touch ground (counts 1-2), return to starting position and clap (2 counts). Repeat on the left side. Do this for a total of 2 sets of 8. While standing, right foot over knee, left elbow on right knee (counts 1-4), tap left toe (4 counts). Repeat with the opposite side.

Part 3: Chorus. Alternately reach above head four times, clap hands 1, 2, 3, and 4, snap fingers two times on the word "today." Stand up and alternately reach overhead (may add aerobic bounce) four times. Hustle-jog forward (8 counts), point to self with right arm, elbow high (4 counts). Add left arm (4 counts). Return to imaginary seat, dust off gluteus maximus, dust off bench, sit down.

Repeat part 1. Repeat part 2. Repeat part 3, Chorus. Repeat Introduction. Repeat part 1. Repeat part 2. Repeat part 3, Chorus, until end of song. End sitting on bench, foot crossed over knee, elbow on knee, chin in hand, and smile!

Hand Jive

Equipment: Boom Box and Jive Music

While seated, slap thighs two times, clap two times, cross right over left hand twice, and cross left over right hand twice (counts 1-8). Next, with hands fisted, hit right on top of left two times, and hit left on top of right two times (counts 9-12). Then, "hitchhike" twice with right hand and twice with left (counts 13-16). This is an excellent activity to get quick brain activation, and it's a whole lot of fun!

·····Throw and Run·····

Equipment: 32 Cones and Eight Soft Balls

This is a very modified softball-type game without bats or bases. Set up a hitting cone, running cone, and side boundary cones for a skinny field with no end boundaries. There should be at least 6 players per playing area. If you have 48 students in your class, set up eight fields of 6 players. Positions are catcher, thrower, and pitcher, and 3 fielders. The pitcher tosses the ball underhand to the batter, who catches it. The batter then can throw the ball anywhere in fair territory, which is inside the boundary cones. The batter's goal is to run around the boundary cones and get back to home base before the ball does. The ball must be thrown to all of the fielders before throwing it home. The fielders need to set up a relay system to get the ball to all the players quickly. Players then rotate one position clockwise so that everyone gets an equal chance to play all positions.

·····Slap Leather·····

Equipment: Boom Box and Music

Feet start together with the weight on the balls of the feet. On the first 2 counts the heels fan out, on the next 2 counts the heels come back together (counts 1-4). Repeat (counts 5-8). Then, touch the right heel in front, then back together; touch the left heel in front, then back together (counts 9-12). Repeat (counts 13-16).

Next, tap right heel in front twice, then tap right toe behind twice (counts 17-20). Tap right heel in front, tap right heel out to the side, tap right toe behind the left foot, and tap right heel out to the side again (counts 21-24). Lift the right foot off of the ground and slap the inside of the shoe with the left hand; swing the foot out and slap with the right hand while doing a quarter turn counterclockwise (counts 25-26). Grapevine to the right; on the fourth step do a chug (lift left knee up and clap) (counts 27-30). Grapevine to the left; on the fourth step do a chug (counts 31-34). Step back on the right foot, left foot, right foot, chug (counts 35-38). Stomp the left foot and stomp the right foot beside (counts 39-40). Repeat. Hee Haw!

·········Pyramid Building·········

Equipment: Boom Box

Start with two students per pyramid. Safety is critical in these activities. Remember to (1) spread students out in personal space; (2) provide mats for cushion; (3) make sure that warmups have been thorough. Here is an example of a two-student pyramid: swan balance, back and knee, Y-balance, thigh balance, back-down-and-through. This may be as far as you want to take the pyramid lesson. At this point, the students have had a taste of it, and the interested ones will be motivated to find out more about gymnastic activities in their community. If comfortable, graduate to three students per pyramid. The following is an example of a three-student pyramid: T-balance, knee stand, thigh stand, and supported thigh stand. Pyramid building is all about balance, so be sure you have the kids talk about the process.

Hawaiian Banana Ball Mini-Games

Equipment: 20 Cones, 5 Bright Yellow Balls, and Football Flags

Set up five mini-fields (depending on your class size) with two cones at each end for the goals. The game begins with both teams (maximum of five on each team) lined up in the middle of the field, approximately ten yards apart. The game starts with anyone throwing to a teammate. The ball can be passed forward or backwards. To score a touchdown (three points), cross the end zone with ball and flags on, but you can only take three steps in a row. No running for more than three steps! Thus the ball will need to be thrown to someone. The defensive team tries to de-flag the offense. All offensive players are available catchers. The passing team must make at least three completed passes to three different teammates before scoring; you can have more passes, but not fewer. No blocking is allowed. It is the other team's ball if a ball touches the ground, the ball is intercepted, or a flag is pulled with the ball in the player's hand. There are no boundaries, in order to promote more movement and less down time. Penalties result if guarding the flag or blocking occurs. The defense must be three feet back from the offensive player, except when attempting to pull a flag. The defensive player has three seconds to get three feet away again. I write the following on a dry-erase board for the kids: Just think of threes.

Triangle Soccer

Equipment: Soccer Balls and Cones

Assign one soccer ball and three cone markers per group. Use groups of four players. Three players form a triangle and pass the ball around from player to player. Use cones to mark the triangle formation. As the ball is passed to another player, all of the three players move one space clockwise. The fourth player will try to intercept the ball. The players should try and move to an open place to receive the passed ball. Rotate players throughout the drill so that everyone gets to play defense.

Mini-Football Games

Equipment: 20 Cones, 5 Footballs, and Jerseys

Incorporate mini-games throughout the year. The kids really enjoy them, and it satisfies their need to play traditional games. Everything is in threes: for example, at least three people on a team, three seconds and get rid of the ball, and three points per goal. Other rules could include requiring everyone on a team to touch the ball before a goal is made, and removing the boundaries. Set up five mini-fields; this creates much action. Emphasize safety. At this point, don't mention the technical rules of football, but emphasize that the object of the game is to get personal space so the ball can be passed to you and to keep moving!

Zone-Passing Basketball

Equipment: Basketballs, Jerseys, and Cones

This is a great way to teach passing. Separate the court into four zones. Number the zones one, two, three, and four, and mark off with cones. Divide class into groups of 9, 18 per court. Three students are in each zone, alternating zones, and 3 students are at an end zone. For example, team A will start with 3 people in zone one, 3 people in zone three, and leave 3 people behind an end line that's not adjacent to their team. Team B will start 3 people in zone two, 3 people in zone four, and leave 3 behind an end line that's not adjacent to their team. The game begins with a center jump. The ball then must be played by passing (chest, bounce, or overhead) from one zone to the next. Players cannot leave their zone. A score is made when an end-zone player catches a pass beyond the end line. After a score, or following a dropped end-line pass, the opposing team gains possession in its nearest zone. The ball cannot be dribbled, held for more than five seconds, or passed over two zones. Passing within the same zone is allowed. Players should be rotated from zone to zone every four to five minutes.

Basketball Fun

Equipment: Basketballs and Boom Box

I try to make the passing, dribbling, and shooting drills fun for the kids. With music playing, work on the different skills.

Dribbling drills: (1) Stand stationary in personal space while dribbling; switch hands; kneel down; kneel on other knee; sit down with legs straight out while dribbling; and dribble in and out of legs in a figure-eight fashion. (2) Dribble across the court, then up and back, using right hand, left hand, and both hands.

Passing drills: (1) Pass to a spot on a wall and rebound; pass to a partner; pass to a group in a circle. (2) Combine dribbling across the court and passing to the first person in line.

Shooting drills: (1) Students form two single-file lines facing the basket. One line shoots lay-ups while the other line rebounds the shots, one person at a time. After rebounding, the student is to complete a chest or bounce pass to the next shooter as that person moves toward the basket. (2) Five students spread around the key marked by five cones, shooting from each spot and switching places.

Aerobic Card Fun

Equipment: Tons of Playing Cards

Have the students run or race-walk, and give them a playing card every time they pass a designated spot. Have different challenges: collect cards all the same suit, collect numbers in a row, and so on. Be sure to remind students that trading cards with fellow classmates is not allowed. Don't call this a "poker run" to prevent any misunderstanding of an inappropriate activity at school. Remind the students that they can't swap cards.

Four-Square Paddle Tennis

Equipment: Playground Balls and Squares on Floor

This game is played exactly the same as four-square, except with paddles and a small ball. If the ball bounces on the line, the student is out. The server must say "Service." This is a great variation to a simple game.

Tunnels

Equipment: Soccer Balls and Stopwatch

Have students partner up. One partner is a one; the other partner is a two. Instruct all ones to find personal space and straddle stand. The twos will dribble through the legs of the other half of the class (the ones). Dribblers try to dribble through as many tunnels as possible during a time limit. Roles rotate.

Takraw

Equipment: Buka Balls, Volleyball Net

Takraw is a net game that is fast paced and action packed. It is played by two opposing teams of three players each. Each team is permitted to strike the Buka ball three times before it must cross the net, much like volleyball. The only difference is that the ball can be hit all three times by the same player. The game is initiated when one of the forward players tosses the buka ball to the back. The back must then kick the ball with the foot that is outside the serving circle into the opponent's court in one try. A game is won by the first team scoring 15 points. Like volleyball, a team may only score a point while serving. A set is won by winning two out of three games.

Badminton Fun

Equipment: Badminton Rackets, Birdies, Yarn Balls, and Balloons

This is a great way to work on team cooperation. Divide the class into groups of eight players. Each group forms a circle, with players about two feet apart. On your signal, one player from each group hits a balloon into the air. The players in each group will try to keep the balloon in play for as long as possible. Start with a 20-second time limit, and then work up to see who can keep the balloon in play for more than a minute. Add balloons, and see which group can keep the most balloons up. Next, try yarn balls, and then move on to birdies.

Volleying Drills

Equipment: Nerf Balls and Softie Volleyballs

Bumping, setting, and serving—all three skills are learned first by oneself, then with a partner, then as a group.

Bumping

(To self):
1. toss to self, catch on forearms
2. toss, bump, catch
3. bump repeatedly to keep ball up in air
4. bump repeatedly to wall

(To partner):
1. toss to partner to bump back to you and catch, and switch
2. toss so partner has to move to bump back to you and catch, and switch
3. toss to partner to keep it up as long as you can, and switch
4. bump to wall, both partners taking turns simultaneously
5. bump to each other, back and forth

(As a group of four to six people in a circular formation): keep it up as long as your group can, repeat

Setting

(To self):
1. toss and catch in fingers
2. toss, set, catch
3. keep ball up by setting repeatedly
4. set to wall

(To partner):
1. toss to partner to set back to you and catch, and switch
2. toss so partner has to move to set back to you and catch, and switch
3. toss to partner to keep it up as long as they can, and switch
4. set to wall, both partners taking turns simultaneously
5. set to each other, back and forth

(As a group of four to six people in a circular formation): keep it up as long as your group can, repeat

Serving

(To self): serve to wall, and catch
(With partner):
1. serve to partner, and switch
2. serve to hoop, and switch

(As a group of four to six people in a circular formation): serve to group, and switch

Push-Up Wave

Equipment: Boom Box

Have the entire class form a large circle by holding hands. When a circle has been created, drop hands. All students get in the push-up starting position while in the circular formation. Designate one student to be the starting person. On the signal to start, the students hold themselves about one inch off the ground in a push-up position. Then everyone goes down in a "wave" order. When the "wave" comes around again the students push themselves back up to the starting position. Challenge the class to see how many times they can do the "push-up wave"!

Elvis Dance

Equipment: Boom Box and "Heartbreak Hotel" Music

Before teaching this dance, get real silly by practicing Elvis poses.

    First line: right hand flares out
    Second line: left hand flares out
    Third line: twitch your shoulders
    Heartbreak Hotel: shake hips
    Chorus first line: walk up 1, 2, 3
    Chorus second line: walk back 1, 2, 3
    Chorus third line: walk up 1, 2, 3
    On the instrumental section we do our "Elvis Walk" around the room. Sunglasses are great props to have the kids wear—they love it!

Human Ladders

Equipment: 10 Baseball Bats

This activity is all based on trust. Much discussion about counting on each other needs to be involved before attempting this. Students are paired and given one baseball bat, which will form a "rung" of the ladder. Several pairs, holding onto a bat/rung at waist height and standing very close together, form the horizontal ladder. A climber starts at one end of the ladder and proceeds to move from one rung to another. As the climber passes by, the pair holding that ladder rung may leave their position and proceed to the other end of the ladder, extending the ladder length indefinitely!

Jump Bands

Equipment: Jump Bands and Boom Box

Students are organized into groups of six. Two students are the "enders" and loop the bands around their ankles while standing approximately six feet apart or until the bands are taut. Enders jump to the count of one, two, three, four. On counts one and two, the enders jump with feet apart about one foot. On counts three and four, the enders jump twice with feet together. The other students are the jumpers and maneuver through the bands by hopping or jumping: for counts one and two they hop in between the bands, and for counts three and four they jump outside the bands. Use Station cards once the students get the general hang of these. Stations might be inside, outside, jump in, jump out, create a plus, rotate around, and so on.

Aquatic Activities

Equipment: Swimming Pool

As always, whenever you are around a pool, the extra safety sensor in your mind and body needs to go off. When teaching aquatic activities, you're caught between a rock and a hard spot. You either have kids wait on a pool deck or pool wall for instructions, or you let them continually move in the water the entire class (and they will) for free activity time. Of course, only allow free play if all students can touch the bottom at all times if needed. The weaker swimmers are at one end or side of the pool. This does not mean that the free time is unstructured. Set some ground rules, such as three safety whistles and all kids need to be at the pool wall, pull themselves out, and sit on the edge of the pool deck within 10 seconds. That's a great upper body workout in itself. Aquatic activities provide awesome water resistance to tone up the body and keep the heart pumping. When class sizes are large, it is best to team-teach with another teacher in order to provide more supervision. Keep students moving constantly during the entire class, with spinning, exploring, kicking, somersaults, gliding, and more. These are all superior movements for brain and vestibular development.

Tetherball

Equipment: Tetherballs

This is always a favorite with the kids. Many middle schools don't have tetherballs set up anymore, which is a real shame. This activity can be challenging, nonstop, and fun. A tetherball hangs from a rope connected to a pole. The object of the game is to strike the tetherball so the ball and the rope wrap around the pole. However, there is an opponent who is trying to strike the ball and have it wrap on the pole going in the opposite direction.

Trust Falls

Equipment: Boom Box

Trust Falls really test how far you can sway until you lose your balance—and how much you can trust your buddies to take care of you. Form groups of three players. All players in each group stand facing the same direction, with one player about 18 inches in front of the two. The two back players—the "catchers"—reach forward to almost touch the front player with their hands. The front player stiffens all the muscles in his or her body and slowly leans backward until he or she falls into the arms of the two catchers. The falling player should try to keep the arms at the side as he or she falls. The catchers should almost touch the falling player with their hands before he or she falls. When they catch the front player, they should push him or her gently to a standing position. Have the front player repeat the fall, but this time allow him or her to fall a little farther backward before they catch him or her. Have the catchers let the player know that he or she can trust them. Change roles until all players in the group have experienced the Trust Fall. Next, with eight students, form tight circles with a student in the middle. The middle student stiffens up and the outer circle gently pushes the student in different directions. Change roles. Some students might be uncomfortable at the prospect of unwelcome touching. The falling person could cross his or her arms over the chest for a more self-protective posture.

Big Ball Throw

Equipment: Giant Ball, 50 Yarn Balls

Put a giant ball in the center of the playing area. There are two teams on each side of the area; they must stay on their own side. You may have four teams, in which case you should put the ball at the intersection of four squares. Each team has two retrievers that may go anywhere in the playing area. The retrievers return the balls to the players. The object of the game is for the teams behind the lines to throw yarn balls at the giant ball and have it pass over the other team's playing area. If the retriever gets hit with the large ball, that team gets one point; the goal is not to have any points. Repeat. This is super fun stuff!

Rounders

Equipment: 2 Soccer Balls, Cones, and Bases

Set up two softball playing areas so two games can be going on at once. Divide your class into four teams. Teams or players do not pitch to each other. Each batter kicks the soccer ball him- or herself. After the player kicks the ball, he or she is to run the bases as far as possible before the ball reaches the pitcher's hand. If a runner is between bases when the ball reaches the pitcher's hand, that player must return to first base. There are no outs. If runners don't think they can make it to the next base, they can stay where they are. There can be many runners on one base at a time. A team is "up" until all players on that team have kicked. They then take the field and the other team kicks. The running team scores by running past home plate. Runners who have scored get a free trip back to first (they keep going around the bases). The team in the field can score too. They are awarded a point when they catch a kicked ball on the fly and when they catch a runner or runners between bases by getting the ball back to the pitcher's hand. Runners on the team at bat run the bases until their team takes the field. It's okay if it gets a little crowded on a base. At least you can have more students at one time experiencing running bases, instead of the usual, three strikes and you're out. In that scenario, many times a student won't get to run a base at all!

Squat Thrusts

Equipment: Boom Box

This is an activity for experiencing variations in a low center of gravity. Two people face one another and try to nudge each other off balance by pushing their palms against one another. The players are positioned so that the balance points are on the balls of the feet. The object is not to move more than a foot. An effective strategy is not to always try to make contact with the other player's palms, but to occasionally make a move in one direction or another in order to get the opponent to lose his or her balance. This is very entertaining.

2x4 Quicksand Save

Equipment: 2x4s or Polyspots

The object of the game is to cross the Quicksand River without falling in and saying, "Bye-bye." The class forms groups of 10 people. The groups line up single file at one side of the Quicksand River. The first person in each line has enough 2x4s or polyspots for each student in the line. The first person drops a spot and steps on it, then passes the spots back to the next person to do the same, and so on, until everyone in the group is standing on one board or polyspot. This is when the challenge comes. The last person has to pick up his or her board or polyspot and pass it down the line. In order for this to happen everyone in the line has to cooperate and lift one leg so that the person next to them can step on it (every board or spot must be in contact). If someone on a team is not in contact with a board or spot, that stepping stone has gone into the quicksand, and the teacher gets it. The next to the last person will have to hold on to the last person so that he or she can reach down and pick up the board or spot and pass it to the front. When the first person receives the spot, he or she tosses it down and the process begins again. The distance of the Quicksand River is about 20 feet, but you can vary that length as students become proficient at the game. If someone falls into the Quicksand River, the team needs to start over. Good luck!

Kickball Basketball

Equipment: Rubber Playground Ball and Jerseys

There are six students on each team. One team is up to kick. One corner of the basketball half-court is home, one corner is first, one corner is second, and one corner is third. Out "court" team has a pitcher who rolls the ball to the first player up; that player kicks the ball and runs the bases (or corners). The out "court" team passes to everyone on the team and has to make a basket before the runner gets home. The running team gets one point every time they pass home, and they keep running the bases. The out "court" team gets five points if they make a basket before the running team player who kicked the ball makes a home run. All the running team players kick, and then go out "court," and vice versa.

Strikeball Basketball

Equipment: 3 Playground Balls

There are six students on each team. One team is up to strike the ball. One corner of the half court is home, one corner is first, one corner is second, and one corner is third. Out "court" team has a pitcher who bounces the ball to the first player up; that player strikes the ball with their hand and runs the bases (or corners). The out "court" players have to be over ten feet from each other. The out "court" team passes to everyone on the team and has to make a basket before the runner gets home. The running team gets one point every time they pass home, and they keep running the bases. The out "court" team gets five points if they make a basket before the running team player who strikes the ball makes a home run. All running team players strike and then go out "court," and vice versa.

Group Tugs

Equipment: Tug Ropes

Circle Tug-of-Peace: tie a tug rope securely in a circle formation. Have students hold on to the rope, with a cone centered in the middle. When signaled, the students should all pull at the same time, trying to pull the other side of the circle over the cone.

Line Tug-of-Peace: pull until a group is across a line.

Team Tug-of-Peace: get a rope that can be pulled four ways (the shape of a plus sign). With the cone in the middle, tug away. Kids love tug games. Debrief them about how this relates to balance, muscular strength, and endurance.

One-on-Five Volley

Equipment: Nerf Balls and Soft Volleyballs

This is a fun activity. Use one ball and one court per six players. One player (the tosser) has one side of the net all by him or herself. The other five are on the opposite side of the net in scattered formation. The single player gets to toss, not serve, the ball over the net five times. Everyone plays his or her own area, calls the ball, and bumps the ball on the first pass. Keep the ball going as many times as desired until it crosses the net. In this game, you can work on helping your students to bump the ball to the middle front position. That person sets the ball to the outside front person, who can hit the ball over the net. When the tosser has tossed the ball five times, all players rotate, with a new tosser. Repeat.

Thunder Bumper

Equipment: Soft Volleyballs

There is one ball and court for every five students. One player (the tosser) has one side of the net all by him or herself. The other four are on the opposite side of the net: one in the front row, the other three in the back. The single player tosses the ball over the net. One person calls the ball and bumps it up to the middle front position. That person sets it. Rotate. Keep varying the spot to which the ball is tossed over the net.

Hacky Sacks

Equipment: Foot Bags

First, have the kids practice tracking the foot bags by throwing them. These are the instructions to use: Throw the bag up, and catch it. Throw the bag up, and catch it behind your back. Practice dropping the hacky sack on your thigh, and catching it. The leg should be lifted so that the sack can contact the thigh; switch legs. Next, try the kicks. Kick with the inside of the foot, keeping the foot in front of you. Drop, kick with the inside of the foot, and catch. Switch legs. How about the outside of the foot? Drop the bag off the outside of the foot, and catch. Switch legs. After mastering single drops and catches, try two kicks in a row, then three, and so on. After that, partner up, or practice in groups. Do the same progressions with buka balls. Go for it!

Kick and Run

Equipment: 32 Cones and Soccer Balls

This is a very modified soccer game. Set up a kicking cone, running cone, and side boundary cones for a skinny field with no end boundaries; have approximately six students per team. Positions are catcher, kicker, and pitcher, and the rest are fielders. There is an underhand toss by the pitcher to the kicker who catches the ball. The kicker then can kick the ball anywhere in fair territory. The goal of the kicker is to dribble another soccer ball around the running cone and back to home base before the ball makes it back. The ball must be kicked to all of the fielders before kicking it home. The fielders need to set up a relay system to get the ball to all players quickly. Players then rotate one position clockwise so that all players get equal chances to play all positions.

Volleyball

Equipment: Soft Volleyballs

Play the real thing! Six players per team.

Soccer Drills

Equipment: Soccer Balls

Soccer drills are always great for teaching the concept of striking with the lower body. Students should work on the skills of dribbling, trapping, and passing. All three skills are taught self, partner, then group.

Dribbling

Dribbling involves tapping the ball under control to move it down the field.

(To self): Have students use instep to tap the ball. Remind them to concentrate on keeping their balance and looking ahead while they dribble.

(To partner): Have students use instep to tap the ball to a partner alongside of them approximately ten feet away. Again, remind them to concentrate on keeping their balance and looking ahead while they dribble.

(With group): Have students create groups of three. Groups line up in an approximate row about 10 feet from each other. One group member uses instep to tap the ball to another group member down the line. The center person will have the ball dribbled to them from the right and left. After a couple of minutes, rotate who is in the center.

Trapping

Trapping the ball is stopping it with different parts of your body.

(To self): Tell students to raise one foot up as the ball approaches and wedge the ball between the sole of the foot and the ground. Next, students meet the ball with the inside or outside of one foot and pull the foot to the side to stop the ball, first inside then outside. The "thigh trap" is performed by meeting the ball in the air with the thigh. As the ball hits the thigh just above the knee, students should drop their leg back so that the ball will fall to the ground.

(To partner): Have students practice the trapping skills with a partner with the same set-up as the dribbling skills.

(To group): Have students practice trapping in the same group formation as the dribbling skills.

Passing

Passing is kicking the ball to an open player.

(To self): The push pass is performed by placing the nonkicking foot close to the ball and using the kicking foot with a pushing motion. The lob pass is made if the ball is up in the air. The kicking leg is lifted and swings upward facing the ball. The player puts the bottom of the foot on the ball and pulls the ball backwards when using the draw pass. The flick pass uses the outside of the foot. The ball is contacted in the little toe area and the leg swings out to the side from the hip.

(To partner): Have students perform the passing drills to a partner, using the same format as previous skills.

(To group): Have students perform the passing drills in three-member group line format used in previous skills.

Racket/Paddle Bucket Stations

Equipment: 8 Giant Buckets, Racket/Paddle Equipment, and Boom Box

Put at least 6 of one kind of racket equipment in each bucket, using eight buckets, totaling 48 racquets plus the object you are hitting. If you have more students, add more equipment. The buckets are set up similarly to Station cards in that they are around a boom box in circular fashion. To begin, students are to sit in the center of the buckets without touching the boom box while the teacher demonstrates what is at each bucket station. Next, students are to report to a bucket without touching anything. The teacher needs to make sure that there are not more than six people at each bucket so that each student has a piece of equipment. Examples of rackets could be badminton, tennis, paddles, racquetball, and smash ball. Of course, each bucket will need balls or shuttlecocks or whatever object you decide to have the students practice with. Then, when the whistle blows, the students participate at that station, practicing handling the equipment. In a few minutes, the students rotate clockwise from one bucket to the next, remembering to put their equipment in the bucket before doing so. They truly love this because they always have a piece of equipment, and they can practice in a fun format. This is a great way to utilize equipment that you may only have a few of, but enough to fill up one bucket.

Triangle Hockey

Equipment: Hockey Sticks, Balls, and Cones

Assign one hockey ball and three cone markers per group. Use groups of four players. Three players form a triangle and pass the ball around from player to player. Use cones to mark the triangle formation. As the ball is passed to another player, all of the three players move one space clockwise. The fourth player will try to intercept the ball. The players should try to move to an open place to receive the passed ball. Rotate players throughout the drill so that everyone gets to play defense.

Mini-Hockey Games

Equipment: 20 Cones, 5 Hockey Nerf Balls, Lots of Sticks, and Jerseys

In mini-hockey, the game starts in the center of the field with teams of six or less squaring off. To square off, two students (one from each team) face each other with their hockey sticks on the sides of the ball. Count one, tap ground with stick; count two, tap shaft of stick; and count three, tap ground again, then hit the ball. It is very crucial that the kids do not high stick, that is, that they keep the hockey sticks waist level or lower. As in the other mini-games, everything is in threes. For example, at least three people on a team; three seconds to get rid of the ball; three points per goal. Everyone on the team has to touch the ball before a goal is made and there are no boundaries. There are five minifields set up, which creates much action. I emphasize safety regarding keeping the ball on the ground and the sticks waist high, and so on. I emphasize that the object of the game is to get personal space so the ball can be passed to you.

Hit and Run

Equipment: 32 Cones, 8 Tennis Rackets, and 8 Tennis Balls

This is a very modified hitting game. Set up a hitting cone, running cone, and side boundary cones for a skinny field with no end boundaries. There should be six or fewer players on a team; positions are catcher, kicker, and pitcher, and the rest are fielders. Begin with an underhand toss by the pitcher to the hitter who catches the ball. The hitter then can hit the ball anywhere in fair territory—anywhere between the side boundary cones. The goal of the hitter is to run around the boundary cones and back to home base before the ball makes it back. The ball must be thrown to all of the fielders and the pitcher before throwing it to the catcher. The fielders need to set up a relay system to get the ball to all players quickly. Players then rotate one position clockwise so that all players get equal chances to play all positions.

·····PVC Water Relay·····

Equipment: 6 PVC Pipes, 6 Giant Tubs, 6 Cans, at Least 24 Paper Cups, and Water

This is a great way to incorporate teamwork. The relay is set up with six giant tubs full of water in a row, about 10 feet apart. Opposite each tub is a can, as far away from the tub as you like. Each tub has a 1½-inch diameter PVC pipe cut about 4 feet long. The pipes have a bunch of holes drilled in them. A paper cup should be beside each tub. The object of the game is to transport water from the tub to the can via the PVC pipe. And yes, because of the holes in the pipe, water will squirt out at the kids. The students need to work together and plug them up so they can fill the pipe up with water. Total cooperation is needed. The cup is used to pour the water; it can't be used for the bottom of the pipe. Extra cups are for the replacement of broken ones. This game is a blast.

·······Sheet Races·······

Equipment: 6 Bed Sheets, 6 Giant Tubs, 6 Cans, at Least 24 Paper Cups, and Water

This is another great water game. The relay is set up with six giant tubs full of water in a row about 10 feet from each other. Opposite each tub is a can, as far away from the tub as you like. Each tub has next to it one paper cup and a bed sheet. The object of the game is to transport water from tub to can via a student sitting on the sheet holding the paper cup of water. The other students grab the corners of the sheet and drag the one student sitting with the water. They run down to the can. The student on the sheet pours the water into the can, gets out of the sheet, and all the team members run back to the tub. Another student gets the cup full of water and sits on the sheet. Repeat until all team players have gone. Extra cups are for the replacement of broken ones. This will be, by far, one of your students' favorite activities. And what a workout it is! The kids are exhausted by the end of the class.

·····"Wet 'n' Wild"·····
Water Transport

Equipment: 4 Buckets, at Least 36 Paper Cups, and Water

This is a fun water game. Students are divided into two groups. Both groups sit shoulder to shoulder on the grass in two lines, facing each other. The lines should be about 10 feet apart from each other. Put a bucket at the ends of both lines; each line should have a full bucket of water and an empty bucket. The full bucket has 12 cups setting next to it. The object of the game is to transport water from the full bucket via the cups to the empty bucket from one student to the other. When water is poured into the empty bucket, the empty cups are sent back to the full bucket by the students, passing them one to the other. This is like an assembly line. Each student can only have one full cup in hand at one time, or one empty one. There will be two things going on at once. Full cups are traveling towards the empty bucket, while the empty ones are going back. Extra cups are for the replacement of broken ones. This is fun, fun, fun.

·····Water Watchout·····

Equipment: 6 Tubs, 6 Cans, at Least 24 Paper Cups, and Water

Divide students into six groups. The relay is set up with six giant tubs full of water in a row about 10 feet from each other. Opposite each tub is a can as far away from the tub as you like. Each tub has next to it one paper cup. The object of the game is to transport water from tub to can via a cup balanced on the head of the first student in line. Repeat until all team players have gone. Extra cups are for the replacement of broken ones. Don't worry, the students are not standing around in line, as this game moves faster than you think. This is another fun activity.

PART III

The Kids' Radical Wellness Book

PE-4-ME:
Radical Wellness Program

Rules

1. **Be kind**

2. **Be courteous**

3. **Give your best effort**

4. **Bring Radical Wellness Book to class daily**

From *PE-4-ME* by Cathie Summerford, 2000, Champaign, IL: Human Kinetics.

PE-4-ME Radical Wellness Program

Activity Log

Date	Fitness Activity	Minutes	Heart Rate	Comments

From *PE-4-ME* by Cathie Summerford, 2000, Champaign, IL: Human Kinetics.

PE-4-ME Radical Wellness Program

Be Fit at Home Checklist

Directions: This checklist is designed to give you credit for being active outside of class. Select one of the activities listed below, or any other activity where you are moving. The selected activity should be performed continuously for 30 minutes. You earn three points for every 30 minutes of exercise. At the bottom of this page, continually add up points by circling the numbers. Can you make it to 100?

Be a PE-4-ME Mover and Shaker!

Activities

- ☐ Fast walking
- ☐ Jogging
- ☐ Rope jumping
- ☐ Soccer
- ☐ Basketball

- ☐ Swimming
- ☐ Aerobics
- ☐ Weight lifting
- ☐ Volleyball
- ☐ Bike riding

- ☐ Rollerblading
- ☐ Skateboarding
- ☐ Skiing
- ☐ Other

Home Activity Point Chart

1	2	3	4	5	6	7	8	9	10
11	12	13	14	15	16	17	18	19	20
21	22	23	24	25	26	27	28	29	30
31	32	33	34	35	36	37	38	39	40
41	42	43	44	45	46	47	48	49	50
51	52	53	54	55	56	57	58	59	60
61	62	63	64	65	66	67	68	69	70
71	72	73	74	75	76	77	78	79	80
81	82	83	84	85	86	87	88	89	90
91	92	93	94	95	96	97	98	99	100

Student name _____

Parent's signature _____

Physical Education teacher _____

Date completed _____

From *PE-4-ME* by Cathie Summerford, 2000, Champaign, IL: Human Kinetics.

Name _____ Date _____ Period _____

PE Teacher's Name _____

What Is Physical Education?

Please circle *T* for true or *F* for false.

• •

T	F	1.	Physical Education and PE are different names for the same class.
T	F	2.	PE is glorified recess.
T	F	3.	Physical Education provides all students the opportunity to gain an appreciation for obtaining and maintaining an active, healthy lifestyle.
T	F	4.	Research shows that if you feel good about yourself, you will probably do better academically.
T	F	5.	It's okay to "blow off" PE because you do not get a grade.
T	F	6.	Citizenship is not important in Physical Education.
T	F	7.	PE is coeducational.
T	F	8.	Health concepts are an important part of Physical Education.
T	F	9.	PE is the same as athletics.
T	F	10.	The locker rooms are just fun places to "hang out."
T	F	11.	It is very important to follow the rules in Physical Education.
T	F	12.	PE involves the study of movement.
T	F	13.	In PE, there aren't any homework assignments or projects.
T	F	14.	It's okay not to dress out for PE if you don't feel like it.
T	F	15.	If you are absent, you should make an effort to make up work. It is your responsibility, not the teacher's.
T	F	16.	In Physical Education, "put-downs" are acceptable.
T	F	17.	Being disrespectful toward yourself, fellow classmates, and the teachers are appropriate behaviors.
T	F	18.	Safety is critical in Physical Education, including your time in the locker rooms.
T	F	19.	If all students and teachers worked together to make this the best year, everyone would be better off.
T	F	20.	Jewelry, including watches, chains, rings, earrings and bracelets, is safe to wear in your PE class.

In the space below, please write down questions you may have regarding Physical Education:

From *PE-4-ME* by Cathie Summerford, 2000, Champaign, IL: Human Kinetics.

Physical Education Handbook Review

Please circle *T* for true or *F* for false.

• •

T   F   1. The purpose of the handbook is to acquaint you with the procedures and policies that will help you to do a better job during your enrollment in Physical Education.

T   F   2. Dressing out for PE shows responsibility on the student's behalf.

T   F   3. If everyone keeps his or her eyes to him or herself when dressing out in the locker room, then no one will be looking at anyone else.

T   F   4. When swimming, it is okay to bring your bathing suit only, not your regular PE clothes.

T   F   5. It's okay to flush whatever you want down the toilets.

T   F   6. Sodas are to be purchased after you have dressed for your next class.

T   F   7. It's okay to dress in the bathrooms.

T   F   8. It would be a great idea to read the Information Board located in the locker rooms everyday.

T   F   9. In Physical Education, it's okay to share your PE clothes with your friends.

T   F   10. During announcements, students should sit down and listen. After announcements, students then are allowed to get dressed in their PE clothes.

T   F   11. It doesn't matter if you leave your PE clothes lying around the locker rooms. The PE teachers will pick up after you.

T   F   12. Chewing gum is allowed in the locker room, as long as you don't blow bubbles.

T   F   13. Sugar (candy, cookies, gum, and soda) attracts ants.

T   F   14. Dressing out for PE is optional.

T   F   15. If you decide to behave inappropriately, you will face unpleasant consequences, such as a referral.

T   F   16. It would be a smart move to wait until it is freezing cold before you think about bringing sweats for PE.

T   F   17. It's okay to wear street clothes under your PE clothes.

T   F   18. Your name should be on your PE clothes.

T   F   19. It's fine to leave the locker rooms when dressed, even if it is before the passing bell rings.

T   F   20. Teamwork is very important in the locker rooms.

In the space below, please write down the PE clothing requirements:

From PE-4-ME by Cathie Summerford, 2000, Champaign, IL: Human Kinetics.

Name _____ Date _____ Period _____

PE Teacher's Name _____

PE-4-ME Radical Wellness Program

Locks and Locker Room Guidelines

Please circle *T* for true or *F* for false.

• •

T   F   1. It's okay to tell your best friends your lock combination.

T   F   2. We dress out for PE for safety in class, to protect our street clothes, and to show responsibility.

T   F   3. Sandals are appropriate PE shoes.

T   F   4. It is okay to leave wet swimsuits and towels in the lockers.

T   F   5. Your combination lock can go on anyone's locker.

T   F   6. If you can't be responsible for locking your locker, you will lose the privilege of having a locker.

T   F   7. If you leave clothes in the long lockers, no one will ever know.

T   F   8. You can wear your friend's PE clothes.

T   F   9. You are to stay in locker rooms at all times, unless instructed by the PE teachers to wait for the bell outside.

T   F   10. You are allowed to leave the locker room from any door you feel like using.

T   F   11. If you leave clothes lying around the locker rooms, your clothes will be taken to the lost and found. If your clothes are not claimed in one week, the clothes will be donated to charity. If you are irresponsible, your Mommy or Daddy will come to school to help you get dressed.

T   F   12. If you forget your sweats on a cold, windy day, it is okay to "borrow" a pair from the PE loaner clothes.

T   F   13. Loaner clothes are used on an emergency basis only. You will be monitored carefully if you are abusing this luxury.

T   F   14. It is your responsibility to memorize your lock combination.

T   F   15. If you decide to behave inappropriately, you will face unpleasant consequences, such as a referral.

T   F   16. You are allowed to use the long lockers during your PE class time only. It is your responsibility to put your lock and belongings back in your small locker.

T   F   17. PE clothes only need to be washed once a year.

T   F   18. If you put your clothes in another person's locker, both of you will receive a referral and lose all locker privileges.

T   F   19. If everyone works together, the year will be great.

T   F   20. Using *T* as yes, and *F* as no, are you ready to be issued a lock?

In the space below, please write down three reasons for losing locker privileges:

From *PE-4-ME* by Cathie Summerford, 2000, Champaign, IL: Human Kinetics.

Name _____ Date _____ Period _____

PE Teacher's Name _____

 **Radical Wellness Program**

Locker Room Boot Camp Final Assessment

On a piece of scratch paper provided by your teacher, write down your locker combination 25 times without anyone seeing it (**top secret!**). Please, write only the combination, not your lock number.

• •

Now that you have done that, please write in the space below what your locker number (not combination) is.

_____

What are the PE clothing requirements?

_____

_____

Whose responsibility is it to lock your locker? What happens when locks are not locked?

_____

_____

_____

What would you like to improve on in Physical Education this year?

_____

_____

_____

_____

_____

_____

I promise, as a student in Physical Education, I will abide by the policies and procedures set forth in Locker Room Boot Camp.

Name _____ Date _____

Parent Signature _____ Date _____

From *PE-4-ME* by Cathie Summerford, 2000, Champaign, IL: Human Kinetics.

Name _____ Date _____ Period _____

ACTIVITY #1

PE-4-ME Radical Wellness Program

Class Act

In physical education it is critical that each class member cooperates with the others in the class. If one student decides not to follow directions, the entire class is affected. If someone in your PE class were not being a team player, what would you say to that person? Please share on the following lines.

● ●

_____

_____

_____

_____

_____

_____

_____

_____

_____

_____

_____

_____

_____

_____

_____

_____

_____

_____

_____

_____

_____

_____

From *PE-4-ME* by Cathie Summerford, 2000, Champaign, IL: Human Kinetics.

Name _____ Date _____ Period _____

ACTIVITY #2

PE-4-ME Radical Wellness Program

Superstars

Everywhere you look these days, you can see famous athletes promoting products. But what about promoting athleticism? A lot of people admire athletes. Through TV and magazines, athletes are recognized around the world for their healthy bodies and minds. And sometimes they're recognized for their healthy attitudes, too.

• •

Can you think of someone—famous or not—who meets that description?

_____

_____

_____

_____

What do you admire about that person?

_____

_____

_____

How are you and that person alike?

_____

_____

_____

_____

What would you like to say to your role model?

_____

_____

_____

_____

From *PE-4-ME* by Cathie Summerford, 2000, Champaign, IL: Human Kinetics.

Name _____ Date _____ Period _____

ACTIVITY #3

 **Radical Wellness Program**

Symbolizing Movement in Pictures

Congratulations! The local after-school sports club has asked you to draw a mural for their playground wall. The mural can be anything you want, but it should encourage people to participate in physical activity. Draw your mural in the space below.

• •

From *PE-4-ME* by Cathie Summerford, 2000, Champaign, IL: Human Kinetics.

Name _____ Date _____ Period _____

ACTIVITY #4

 **PE-4-ME Radical Wellness Program**

Symbolizing Movement in Words

● ●

What does movement sound like? Feet slapping the ground, wind in your hair, heart pumping in your ears? List six verbs—moving words—describing your favorite sport (like kick, run, jump).

1. _____   4. _____

2. _____   5. _____

3. _____   6. _____

Now list six nouns—person, place, or thing words—of your sport (like net, bat, shoes).

1. _____   4. _____

2. _____   5. _____

3. _____   6. _____

Now use those words to create a word picture of your activity—a poem, a story, a haiku, or a song. Be creative and have fun!

_____

_____

_____

_____

_____

_____

_____

_____

_____

_____

_____

_____

From *PE-4-ME* by Cathie Summerford, 2000, Champaign, IL: Human Kinetics.

Name _____ Date _____ Period _____

ACTIVITY #5

PE-4-ME Radical Wellness Program

PE . . . Not a No-Brainer?

• •

1. Did you know that movement helps you to learn? When you move, neural (brain) pathways are formed that make way for more learning to occur. What activities are your favorite "ways to move"?

_____

_____

_____

_____

2. Why do you like these activities?

_____

_____

_____

_____

_____

_____

_____

_____

_____

_____

_____

_____

_____

_____

_____

_____

From *PE-4-ME* by Cathie Summerford, 2000, Champaign, IL: Human Kinetics.

ACTIVITY #6

 **Radical Wellness Program**

What's BDNF?

• •

1. Exercise triggers the release of BDNF (brain-derived neurotrophic factor), a chemical in your brain that enhances thinking and learning by boosting the ability of brain cells to communicate with each other. BDNF starts the chemical process. What exercises do you think would be good activities for becoming better thinkers?

_____

_____

_____

_____

2. Why do you think this exercise would be good for thinking?

_____

_____

_____

_____

_____

_____

_____

_____

_____

_____

_____

_____

_____

From *PE-4-ME* by Cathie Summerford, 2000, Champaign, IL: Human Kinetics.

ACTIVITY #7

 **Radical Wellness Program**

Heart-Brain Buddy System

Most people think the brain controls the heart. But new research is emerging that suggests that the heart may be more of a team player than previously thought. Wow! It's no wonder that people who participate in vigorous exercise have improved short-term memory, reaction time, and creativity.

● ●

The brain is enriched best by brain foods, nutrition, water, and exercise, as well as challenges and feedback. What foods would you consider to be brain foods?

_____

_____

_____

_____

_____

_____

_____

_____

_____

_____

_____

_____

_____

_____

_____

_____

_____

_____

_____

From *PE-4-ME* by Cathie Summerford, 2000, Champaign, IL: Human Kinetics.

Name _____ Date _____ Period _____

ACTIVITY #8

 Radical Wellness Program

Sound Body, Sound Mind

Exercise naturally relieves tension, helps the brain to find its natural stress level, and improves the functioning of our immune system (our body's protection) for up to three days. Exercise experiences feed directly into the pleasure centers in the emotional centers of the brain.

• •

My Favorite Sports or Activities

_____

_____

_____

_____

_____

_____

Ways to Improve

_____

_____

_____

_____

_____

_____

_____

_____

_____

_____

_____

_____

_____

_____

_____

From PE-4-ME by Cathie Summerford, 2000, Champaign, IL: Human Kinetics.

Name _____ Date _____ Period _____

ACTIVITY #9

Personal Excellence

• •

1. What is personal excellence?

_____

_____

_____

_____

2. How can I improve my personal excellence?

_____

_____

_____

_____

3. Is setting goals important?

_____

_____

_____

_____

4. In what physical education skills are you "most excellent"?

_____

_____

_____

_____

_____

_____

From *PE-4-ME* by Cathie Summerford, 2000, Champaign, IL: Human Kinetics.

ACTIVITY #10

 **Radical Wellness Program**

Do I Need an Attitude Adjustment?

Do you love to play soccer? Hate to swim? Everybody has different likes and dislikes, and that goes for physical activity, too. However, being mentally prepared to enjoy a new challenge can make it easier to like it. Are you ready to like PE?

• •

1. How do you usually feel about going to PE?

_____

_____

_____

_____

_____

2. Do you think there are differences between physical education and physical activity? What are they?

_____

_____

_____

_____

3. Who in your life has influenced how you feel about physical activity? How?

_____

_____

_____

_____

_____

From *PE-4-ME* by Cathie Summerford, 2000, Champaign, IL: Human Kinetics.

ACTIVITY #11

 **Radical Wellness Program**

How Competitive Am I?

Sometimes being competitive can be a great help to your personal excellence. When you compete with yourself, you can work toward improvement. But a competitive spirit can be overdone—if it makes you feel too frustrated to play, or if it leads to unsporting behavior.

• •

Think of a time you were competing against someone else. Did you enjoy the challenge? Or was it intimidating? Write a paragraph about how you felt.

_____

_____

_____

_____

_____

_____

Now think of a time you were competing against yourself—to get a better grade, or to improve your time at a puzzle, for example. How did that make you feel? Write a paragraph.

_____

_____

_____

_____

_____

How could you use competition to improve your personal excellence?

_____

_____

_____

From *PE-4-ME* by Cathie Summerford, 2000, Champaign, IL: Human Kinetics.

ACTIVITY #12

Thinking About Personal Excellence in Cooperative Activities

Cooperative activities are challenges where the object of the game is to work together.

● ●

Many games and sports require cooperation—and in many different ways. List as many ways to "work together" as you can think of.

_____

_____

_____

_____

_____

_____

_____

_____

What sports or games require cooperation?

_____

_____

_____

_____

_____

_____

_____

_____

_____

From *PE-4-ME* by Cathie Summerford, 2000, Champaign, IL: Human Kinetics.

Name _____ Date _____ Period _____

ACTIVITY #13

 Radical Wellness Program

Thinking About Personal Excellence in Competitive Activities

Competitive activities are contests where the object is winning.

• •

Have you ever played a game where someone was not playing fair? Were they cheating? Wanting to win at all costs? When you play games or participate in competitive activities, how do you try to achieve personal excellence?

_____

_____

_____

_____

_____

_____

_____

_____

_____

_____

Can you name six sports that are competitive? Circle your favorite.

1. _____

2. _____

3. _____

4. _____

5. _____

6. _____

From *PE-4-ME* by Cathie Summerford, 2000, Champaign, IL: Human Kinetics.

Name _____ Date _____ Period _____

ACTIVITY #14

Radical Wellness Program

Thinking About Personal Excellence in Social Activities

When we are not participating in a cooperative activity or a competitive activity, we may just be "hanging out" in a social activity. For example, eating lunch with our friends during the school day is a social activity.

• •

Do you try to include everyone in a conversation at lunchtime?

_____

_____

Do you give "put-ups" to people around you?

_____

_____

Are you fun to be with?

_____

_____

If you weren't listening, what do you think your friends would say about you? Do they think you try to achieve personal excellence in your social behavior?

_____

_____

_____

_____

_____

From *PE-4-ME* by Cathie Summerford, 2000, Champaign, IL: Human Kinetics.

ACTIVITY #15

Attitude Toward Fitness

Physical fitness doesn't just happen, one has to work at it. What is your fitness attitude?

· ·

When I think of my fitness attitude, I have to say I _____ to exercise. You see, since I was a little kid, I have _____ participating in sports. All of my life, I _____ when I do my best. I always give my best _____ when I participate. I really don't care if I _____ or lose, just as long as I _____ with my teammates. I don't "put-down" my _____. Even when I don't feel like it, I _____ to stay in shape. I like it when I do my _____.

I like to listen to music and _____. Moving to music or _____ is great _____. I like to dance with my _____.

Whether I am playing sports or dancing, I try to achieve personal _____. I _____ with my friends in various activities. I can settle a dispute with my _____. I think I am a good _____.

From *PE-4-ME* by Cathie Summerford, 2000, Champaign, IL: Human Kinetics.

PE-4-ME Radical Wellness Program

Target Heart Rate Sheet

	Example	For You
Boys start with 220 Girls start with 226 Subtract your age	220 –12	
Equals maximum times heart can beat/minute Subtract resting heart rate	208 –72	
Multiply by 60%	136 ×.60	
Add resting heart rate	81.60 +72.00	
Equals approximate target heart rate (THR)	154 Beats per minute	Beats per minute Your THR

From *PE-4-ME* by Cathie Summerford, 2000, Champaign, IL: Human Kinetics.

Name _____ Date _____ Perio

ACTIVITY #16

 Radical Wellness Program

The Parts of Physical Fitness

Health-related components of physical fitness:

Health-related components help you maintain good health. Your body systems, like the cardiovascular, respiratory, and muscular systems, all work together.

1. Cardiovascular endurance: Shows how efficiently your heart, circulatory system, and respiratory system work together over a long period of time.

   Examples to increase cardiovascular endurance: Running, cycling, swimming.

2. Flexibility: The ability of joints to move through their full range of motion.

   Examples to increase flexibility: Stretching, gymnastics.

3. Body composition: Shows the relative amounts of fat body mass to lean body mass.

   Examples to lower fat: All cardiovascular activities.

4. Muscular strength: The amount of power a muscle can produce.

   Examples to increase muscular strength: Weightlifting, gymnastics, using playground equipment.

5. Muscular endurance: A muscle's ability to produce power for a long duration.

   Examples to increase muscular enduarnce: Running, swimming, weightlifting.

Skill-related components of physical fitness:

Skill-related components help you perform the skills needed for sports and dance activities. They can help you find joy in active play.

1. Agility: The ability to change direction of movement quickly while staying in control of your body.

   Examples: Shuttle-run test, soccer, basketball, tag, dodge ball, football, dance.

2. Balance: The ability to maintain body equilibrium in different movements. The two types of balance are (1) static balance, which is maintaining your balance without moving, and (2) dynamic balance, which is balancing while you are moving.

   Examples: Sprinter in starting blocks, quarterback going out for a pass.

From *PE-4-ME* by Cathie Summerford, 2000, Champaign, IL: Human Kinetics.

3. Coordination: The ability to synchronize, or combine at the same time, movements of various body parts.

Examples: Hitting a golf ball, setting a volleyball, rallying a tennis ball, swimming.

4. Power: The ability to combine strength and speed. Here is a simple formula to remember: STRENGTH + SPEED = POWER.

Examples: Sprinting, high-jumping, discus throwing, swimming, figure skating.

5. Reaction time: The time between one of your senses recognizing a stimulus and your body moving in response.

Examples: Hitting a tennis ball with a racket, hitting a softball with a bat, and running out to catch a football.

6. Speed: The time it takes you to move a certain distance.

Examples: Track sprinters, football receivers.

From *PE-4-ME* by Cathie Summerford, 2000, Champaign, IL: Human Kinetics.

Name _____ Date _____ Period _____

ACTIVITY #17

 Radical Wellness Program

Components of Physical Fitness

Physical fitness is made up of health-related and skill-related components. There are five health-related parts of physical fitness: cardiovascular endurance, muscular strength, muscular endurance, flexibility, and body composition. There are six skill-related parts of physical fitness: reaction time, coordination, balance, speed, power, and agility.

• •

After each fitness term, write an *H* for health-related or an *S* for skill-related:

1. Muscular endurance _____
2. Power _____
3. Agility _____
4. Cardiovascular endurance _____
5. Reaction time _____
6. Speed _____
7. Flexibility _____
8. Muscular strength _____
9. Body composition _____
10. Balance _____
11. Coordination _____

You are a fitness expert or consultant in charge of planning a program for your customer. Your customer could be anyone who desires to be fit and healthy. What is an activity that your customer can do to improve on the health-related component of fitness?

Health-related component	Activity
Cardiovascular endurance	_____
Muscular strength	_____
Muscular endurance	_____
Flexibility	_____
Body composition	_____

From *PE-4-ME* by Cathie Summerford, 2000, Champaign, IL: Human Kinetics.

What is an activity that your customer can do to improve on the skill-related component of fitness?

Skill-related component	Activity
Agility	_____
Speed	_____
Balance	_____
Coordination	_____
Reaction time	_____
Power	_____

Invent a game or activity to improve performance in these components. Does your game include health-related or skill-related components of physical fitness?

_____

_____

_____

_____

_____

_____

_____

_____

_____

_____

_____

_____

From *PE-4-ME* by Cathie Summerford, 2000, Champaign, IL: Human Kinetics.

Name _____ Date _____ Period _____

ACTIVITY #18

 Radical Wellness Program

United in Fitness #1

Rate your fitness level in the health-related components of fitness.

On the following chart, perform the movement that is suggested. Check off the correct health-related part of fitness in the adjacent boxes.

● ●

Movement	Cardiovascular endurance	Flexibility	Body composition	Muscular strength	Muscular endurance
Jog for 3 minutes					
Do 50 bent-knee curl-ups					
Hang from a horizontal bar for 15 seconds					
Touch your toes					
Do 75 jumping jacks					
Do 10 push-ups					
Do 25 push-ups					
Jog in place for 3 more minutes in an effort to lower body fat					
Touch your hands behind your back					

From *PE-4-ME* by Cathie Summerford, 2000, Champaign, IL: Human Kinetics.

Name _____ Date _____ Period _____

ACTIVITY #19

PE-4-ME Radical Wellness Program

United in Fitness #2

Rate your fitness level in the skill-related components of fitness.

On the following chart, perform the movement that is suggested. Check off the correct skill-related part of fitness in the adjacent boxes.

● ●

Movement	Agility	Coordination	Reaction time	Balance	Speed	Power
Face forward, move side to side 15 times.						
Toss and catch a ball from one hand to the other 6 times in a row.						
Stand on one foot with eyes closed for 15 seconds.						
Run as fast as you can from one spot to another.						
Put a penny on the back of your hand. Toss it up; try to catch it with palm of hand facing ground.						
Walk on a curb or board for 1 minute without falling off.						
Carefully move a heavy weight.						
While skipping, toss a ball back and forth between left and right hands.						
Kneel down; jump up to feet without touching your hands to the floor.						
Spin around with eyes closed 10 times. Open eyes without moving.						
Jump rope super-fast 20 times in a row.						

From *PE-4-ME* by Cathie Summerford, 2000, Champaign, IL: Human Kinetics.

Name _____ Date _____ Period _____

ACTIVITY #20

United in Fitness Challenge Review

Analyze your individual fitness level based upon what you did in United in Fitness #1 and #2. Check off on the chart how you think you are doing in your health- and skill-related components of fitness.

● ●

Component of fitness	Need to improve	Good	Excellent
Cardiovascular endurance			
Flexibility			
Muscular strength			
Muscular endurance			
Body Composition			
Coordination			
Agility			
Reaction time			
Balance			
Speed			
Power			

From *PE-4-ME* by Cathie Summerford, 2000, Champaign, IL: Human Kinetics.

What component of fitness did you enjoy the most?

_____
_____
_____
_____
_____

In what component of fitness do you need the most improvement?

_____
_____
_____
_____
_____

From *PE-4-ME* by Cathie Summerford, 2000, Champaign, IL: Human Kinetics.

Name _____ Date _____ Period ____

ACTIVITY #21

 **Radical Wellness Program**

Muscles, Muscles, and More Muscles!

Have you ever lifted a really heavy box? Or opened a really tight jar lid? Sure you have. You can do that because you have muscular strength. You used your muscles to produce a force (lifting or turning) against resistance (the box or lid).

Have you ever been on a very long bike ride? Or felt like you could run forever? Those activities use your muscles too, but in a different way. They are examples of muscular endurance—using your muscles for a long time without making them overly tired.

Read the following examples. After each, write *MS* for muscular strength or *ME* for muscular endurance.

• •

Running a marathon   _____

Arm wrestling   _____

Hiking a three-mile trail   _____

Canoeing across a lake   _____

Lifting a heavy book   _____

Pushing a heavy cart   _____

Swimming laps   _____

Lifting heavy weights   _____

Lifting lighter weights for a longer time   _____

Wrestling   _____

From *PE-4-ME* by Cathie Summerford, 2000, Champaign, IL: Human Kinetics.

Complete the following definitions:

Muscular strength is

_____

_____

_____

Muscular endurance is

_____

_____

_____

In what games, sports, or activities do you use muscular strength?

_____

_____

_____

In what games, sports, or activities do you use muscular endurance?

_____

_____

_____

What can you do to improve your muscular strength and endurance?

_____

_____

_____

From *PE-4-ME* by Cathie Summerford, 2000, Champaign, IL: Human Kinetics.

Name _____ Date _____ Period _____

ACTIVITY #22

 **Radical Wellness Program**

Range of Motion

Flexibility is the range of motion around a joint or group of joints

• •

List five safe, appropriate stretching exercises for improving flexibility:

1. _____
2. _____
3. _____
4. _____
5. _____

Do professional football players need to work on flexibility? Why?

_____

_____

_____

What are some other fitness activities that require flexibility?

_____

_____

_____

Can you think of some household chores that may require flexibility, such as pulling weeds?

_____

As review, write down the five health-related components of fitness.

1. _____
2. _____
3. _____
4. _____
5. _____

From *PE-4-ME* by Cathie Summerford, 2000, Champaign, IL: Human Kinetics.

As review, write down the six skill-related components of fitness.

1. _____

2. _____

3. _____

4. _____

5. _____

6. _____

You have been hired by Physical Activity, Inc. to create an ad promoting health- and skill-related components of fitness for kids. What would your ad look like? Draw it below.

From *PE-4-ME* by Cathie Summerford, 2000, Champaign, IL: Human Kinetics.

Name _____ Date _____ Period _____

ACTIVITY #23

 Radical Wellness Program

Analyzing Movement

A locomotor skill can be described as how we move from one place to another. Examples of locomotor skills are running, walking, hopping, galloping, sliding, jumping, leaping, and skipping.

• •

List three types of locomotion:

1. _____

2. _____

3. _____

An animal:

4. _____

A place:

5. _____

Two adjectives:

6. _____

7. _____

A famous athlete:

8. _____

The Big Race

A hush fell over the crowd as the beginning of the race drew near. One by one, the athletes took their places. Suddenly, a gunshot started the race. They were off! The tortoise headed out of the gate, (1)_____ quickly. But immediately the rabbit came (2)_____ up behind. "Look at him go," you shout. "He's moving like a (6)_____ (4)_____!" And sure enough, the rabbit looks like he could keep (3)_____ all the way to (5)_____. "He's as (7)_____ as (8)_____," you think.

From *PE-4-ME* by Cathie Summerford, 2000, Champaign, IL: Human Kinetics.

ACTIVITY #24

 **Radical Wellness Program**

"Checking Out" Locomotor Skills

How would you move if you were . . .

• •

A football player trying to get to the end zone?

_____

_____

_____

_____

A baseball batter trying to lead off the base?

_____

_____

_____

_____

A ballet dancer trying to cross the stage?

_____

_____

_____

_____

A soccer player heading a ball?

_____

_____

_____

_____

From *PE-4-ME* by Cathie Summerford, 2000, Champaign, IL: Human Kinetics.

PE 14

ACTIVITY #25

 **Radical Wellness Program**

Agility and Reaction Time

Agility and reaction time are components of skill-related fitness. Define the following terms. (You may need to refer to activity 16.)

• •

What is agility?

_____

_____

_____

What is reaction time?

_____

_____

_____

Why are agility and reaction time important in many sports, games, and activities?

_____

_____

_____

_____

Create an activity that uses agility and reaction time. Once you have mastered this activity, try it out in your PE-4-ME class.

_____

_____

_____

_____

_____

_____

_____

From *PE-4-ME* by Cathie Summerford, 2000, Champaign, IL: Human Kinetics.

ACTIVITY #26

 **PE-4-ME** Radical Wellness Program

What Games, Sports, or Activities Use Throwing?

Do you throw overhand? Do you throw underhand? How about a sidearm motion? Do you throw with one hand or two hands? There are many ways to throw objects, including passes, flips, flings, and pushes.

• •

How many activities can you list where some form of throwing is included?

_____

_____

_____

_____

_____

_____

_____

_____

_____

_____

_____

_____

_____

_____

_____

From *PE-4-ME* by Cathie Summerford, 2000, Champaign, IL: Human Kinetics.

Name _____ Date _____ Period _____

ACTIVITY #27

 Radical Wellness Program

Power Throwing

A body in motion wants to stay in motion—and if it starts out fast, it wants to stay fast. Think about how that affects your throwing. If you want to throw farther, how can you improve?

• •

1. _____

2. _____

3. _____

4. _____

Make a picture below of how your arm should move when you throw overhand:

From *PE-4-ME* by Cathie Summerford, 2000, Champaign, IL: Human Kinetics.

Name _____ Date _____ Period _____

ACTIVITY #28

PE-4-ME Radical Wellness Program

Basketball Fun

If you were the teacher, what warm-up exercises would you have your students participate in prior to playing in a basketball activity?

• •

1. _____
2. _____
3. _____
4. _____
5. _____

The chest pass requires a two-hand pass from the chest of one player to another. What is another kind of pass in basketball?

_____

_____

What is a jump ball?

_____

_____

Below, diagram what a basketball court looks like:

From *PE-4-ME* by Cathie Summerford, 2000, Champaign, IL: Human Kinetics.

ACTIVITY #29

 **Radical Wellness Program**

Happenin' Hoops

You have just been assigned as the Recreation Director for the "Happenin' Hoops" Summer Camp basketball program. Your job is to create a basketball activity that the participants will enjoy. The activity has to be some variation of basketball; it can't be the actual game. What is the name of your activity, the object of the game, and how do you play it? Hoop . . . there it is!

• •

Name of activity:

_____

Object of game:

_____

_____

Directions:

_____

_____

_____

_____

_____

_____

_____

_____

_____

_____

_____

_____

_____

From *PE-4-ME* by Cathie Summerford, 2000, Champaign, IL: Human Kinetics.

Name _____ Date _____ Period _____

ACTIVITY #30

 **Radical Wellness Program**

Stepping Into It

While your arms are busy catching, what are your feet doing? If they're just standing there, you could be hurting your personal excellence. Using your whole body will help you make the catch, and will keep you from dropping it once you've got it.

• •

What should your feet be doing when you catch? (If you don't know, watch someone who catches well.)

_____

_____

_____

What should your eyes be doing?

_____

_____

_____

What should the rest of your body be doing?

_____

_____

_____

Set a goal. How can you improve your personal excellence in catching?

_____

_____

_____

_____

_____

_____

_____

From *PE-4-ME* by Cathie Summerford, 2000, Champaign, IL: Human Kinetics.

Name _____ Date _____ Period _____

ACTIVITY #31

PE-4-ME Radical Wellness Program

Balance

Your center of gravity affects your ability to stay balanced while standing still or moving. Your center of gravity is an imaginary point where all of the weight of your body is centrally distributed.

When moving, the center of gravity will change towards where most of your body parts move. When still, your center of gravity is at a midpoint in your body, around your abdominal area.

Your base of support also affects balance. The base of support is the part or parts of the body you are balancing on, and the area between them.

You are balanced when your center of gravity is between your base of support.

• •

Check off on the following chart what each activity requires:

Activities	High-centered gravity	Low-centered gravity	Wide base of support	Narrow base of support
Tackling in a football game				
Walking across a balance beam				
Diving off a diving board				
Doing a handstand				
Hitting a tennis ball with a racket				
Slow dancing				
Kicking a soccer ball				

From *PE-4-ME* by Cathie Summerford, 2000, Champaign, IL: Human Kinetics.

Name _____ Date _____ Period _____

ACTIVITY #32

PE-4-ME Radical Wellness Program

Principles of Balance

Draw a picture demonstrating the principles of balance.

· ·

Is the center of gravity high or low?   _____

Is the base of support wide or narrow? _____

From *PE-4-ME* by Cathie Summerford, 2000, Champaign, IL: Human Kinetics.

156

Name _____ Date _____ Period _____

ACTIVITY #33

Learning About the Principles of Flight

Sometimes, while you are playing a game, you have to become airborn—that is, your whole body has to leave the ground. That's called "flight." To get off the ground, you use different parts of your body to generate force and push your center of gravity up.

• •

Let's take it one body part at a time. Jump using only your feet. Keep your arms straight at your sides and your legs as straight as possible. How high can you jump?

_____

_____

Now use your legs, keeping your arms at your sides. How can your legs help your flight?

_____

_____

Now add your arms. Can you jump higher? Farther?

_____

_____

Okay, you have just been selected for the All-School Slam Dunk Celebration to represent your school. Too cool! Describe below how you might "fly" to the hoop and slam in the basketball. What parts of your body gave you the flight?

_____

_____

_____

_____

_____

From *PE-4-ME* by Cathie Summerford, 2000, Champaign, IL: Human Kinetics.

ACTIVITY #34

Radical Wellness Program

Landing Safely Back to Earth

· ·

Shock absorption—how to land with the least impact on your body. What shock-absorbing tricks can you list?

_____

_____

_____

Why is it easier to jump and land with your feet apart than together?

_____

_____

_____

Think about science—every action has an equal and opposite reaction, which means that the harder the impact on an object, the more it will bounce. What happens if you drop a pen, compared to what happens when you drop an eraser? How about if you drop your pencil on its side, compared to on its eraser end?

_____

_____

_____

_____

_____

How can you make landing from flight easier on your body?

_____

_____

_____

_____

_____

From *PE-4-ME* by Cathie Summerford, 2000, Champaign, IL: Human Kinetics.

Name _____ Date _____ Period

ACTIVITY #35

Body Management

In your everyday life, the principles of balance, flight, and landing play an important role. List five typical situations in your day at school or home when these principles might affect you.

• •

1. _____

2. _____

3. _____

4. _____

5. _____

For the following professions, how would flight, balance, and landing come into play?

Professional basketball player _____

Police officer _____

Food server _____

Gardener _____

Firefighter _____

Window washer _____

Lifeguard _____

From *PE-4-ME* by Cathie Summerford, 2000, Champaign, IL: Human Kinetics.

Explosive Movement: Did You Know?

- Basketball is a game that uses explosive movement. Players stop and start, change directions quickly, take jump shots, and jump to defend shots.
- A basketball player may run five miles during four quarters of play.
- Worrying about the "other guy" distracts you from your game.
- Dancers also spend hours of training to develop explosive ability. They need to jump high and quickly change direction.
- The stronger your heart is, the more blood it pumps per beat.
- A stronger heart means you recover faster after exercise.
- A healthy heart and explosive movement go hand in hand. A healthy heart will return to its normal state in 2-3 minutes.
- A fit heart does enough work in one hour to lift 3,000 pounds—about the weight of a small car—with one foot off of the ground.
- Blood vessels in an average adult form a branching network of about 60,000 miles.
- If your heart beats 80 times per minute, that's 115,200 times a day and over 42 million times a year.
- What you eat can determine how you play.
- Your appetite actually decreases when you exercise.
- Buying a soda everyday can cost $150 to $300 per year.
- A candy bar a day can cost up to $180.
- You can improve your fitness with 20 minutes of exercise, three times a week.
- A pound of muscle is denser than a pound of fat.
- Rule #1 is to have fun!

From *PE-4-ME* by Cathie Summerford, 2000, Champaign, IL: Human Kinetics.

ACTIVITY #36

 **Radical Wellness Program**

Striking With Body Parts

• •

Your body is the greatest piece of sports equipment you'll ever have—it's free and it's always nearby! It's easy to see why striking with the body is an important part of many activities. What are different activities that require striking with a body part?

_____

_____

_____

_____

_____

What striking movements match the activity? (For example, kicking for soccer.)

Soccer   _____

Volleyball   _____

Basketball   _____

Takraw   _____

Handball   _____

Boxing   _____

Tetherball   _____

From *PE-4-ME* by Cathie Summerford, 2000, Champaign, IL: Human Kinetics.

Basic Rules of Volleyball

- There are six players per team: Three in the front row, three in the back row.

- At the time of the serve, all must be in their proper positions on the court.

- After the serve, all players may move to play the ball or cover the court area. However, a back-row player may not block at the net or play the ball over the net from above the height of the net if his or her body is in front of the 10-foot line.

- The server must serve the ball within the serve area, which is behind the end line. The server cannot step on the line or a foot fault occurs and a side-out results.

- On the serve, the ball must be hit or batted with the hand, fist, or forearm, and it must cross over the net without touching it. The ball must be playable within the lines of the receiving team's court.

- A ball landing on a line is considered in-bounds.

- After the serve, the receiving team must clearly hit the ball with any part of the body above (and including) the waist. Each team may hit the ball three times on its side of the net. No player can hit the ball two times in succession.

- A player may go outside the court's boundary lines to play a ball. A ball that is hit over the net from out-of-bounds must cross the net between or over the side-lines.

- Fouls occur when the ball is not played properly or rules are not followed. Fouls result in a point for the serving team or a side-out for the non-serving team.

- A replay can occur under certain circumstances.

- When a side-out occurs, the new serving team rotates clockwise: the right front player goes back to serve at the right back position.

- When a point is scored, the same server keeps serving. No rotation occurs.

- A game is played to 15 points. The winner must be ahead by 2 points.

From *PE-4-ME* by Cathie Summerford, 2000, Champaign, IL: Human Kinetics.

Name _____ Date _____ Period _____

ACTIVITY #37

PE-4-ME Radical Wellness Program

Fancy Feet

• •

Do you have fancy feet? How many ways can you kick a foot bag?

_____

Can you kick a soccer ball the same way? Why or why not?

_____

What skill or skills do you think you need to improve on?

_____

Okay, you are now in charge of the after-school soccer program. However, the principal doesn't want the activity to be soccer! It needs to be a soccer lead-up game or a soccer-type activity that is creative, challenging, and fun! Describe your activity below:

_____

_____

_____

_____

_____

_____

_____

_____

_____

_____

From *PE-4-ME* by Cathie Summerford, 2000, Champaign, IL: Human Kinetics.

A Short History of Soccer

The game of soccer has been thought to have originated from a Greek game called *Harpaston* or from an Italian game called *Calzio*. Both were forerunners of the game of soccer, which was played in England during the Middle Ages. During this time the game of soccer was very much a part of English life. The big game of the season was always played on Shrove Tuesday, the day before Ash Wednesday. This game was played by the peasants, but gradually grew in popularity over the years. In 1863, soccer became an official school game in England, complete with rules and regulations.

The first college game of soccer was played in the United States on November 6, 1869. Today soccer is played in most schools, colleges, and communities. The popularity of soccer is growing because of soccer's fast action and low investment costs. The United States Soccer Federation (USSF) governs play within the United States, while the United States Youth Soccer Association (USYSA) governs youth soccer for those 19 years of age and younger.

From *PE-4-ME* by Cathie Summerford, 2000, Champaign, IL: Human Kinetics.

Name _____ Date _____ Period _____

ACTIVITY #38

 **Radical Wellness Program**

Striking and Liking It

Striking with implements. What does this mean? In many activities, we use tools or instruments to hit an object, such as bats, rackets, hockey sticks, lacrosse sticks, golf clubs, and paddles.

• •

What are some activities that require you to strike with an implement?

_____

_____

_____

_____

What are some different implements used in activities?

_____

_____

_____

_____

Striking with equipment presents special challenges. Which would be easier, hitting a table tennis ball with a paddle or with a pencil? Why?

_____

_____

_____

Which would be easier, playing racquetball with a racquetball racket or a long-handled tennis racket? Why?

_____

_____

_____

_____

From *PE-4-ME* by Cathie Summerford, 2000, Champaign, IL: Human Kinetics.

ACTIVITY #39

PE-4-ME Radical Wellness Program

Match 'Em

Check the correct box that matches the sport with the accurate equipment.

● ●

	Cycling	Swimming	Skate-boarding	Croquet	Golf	Softball	Hockey
Puck							
Mallet							
Home plate							
Helmet							
Skating park							
Wood							
Iron							
Fins							
Wheel							
Stick							
Wicket							
Goggles							
Gears							
Mitt							
Spoke							
Lawn							
Base							
Club							
Snorkel							
Knee pads							
Handlebars							

From *PE-4-ME* by Cathie Summerford, 2000, Champaign, IL: Human Kinetics.

Name _____ Date _____ Period _____

ACTIVITY #40

PE-4-ME Radical Wellness Program

Fun Time

It's important to play. People do not get enough time to "just have fun."

• •

If you were given a free week to do whatever you wanted, what would you do? How would you spend your time? What are your favorite "free-time" activities?

Day 1 _____

_____

_____

_____

Day 2 _____

_____

_____

_____

Day 3 _____

_____

_____

_____

Day 4 _____

_____

_____

_____

Day 5 _____

_____

_____

_____

From *PE-4-ME* by Cathie Summerford, 2000, Champaign, IL: Human Kinetics.

Name _____ Date _____ Period _____

ACTIVITY #41

PE-4-ME Radical Wellness Program

Hurrah!

• •

What are three of your favorite activities in Physical Education that you participated in this year?

1. _____

2. _____

3. _____

Did anyone give you a "put-up" this year? Please explain.

_____

_____

_____

_____

_____

_____

Do you remember the coolest "put-up" you gave someone?

_____

_____

_____

_____

_____

_____

Did you give yourself a "put-up?"

_____

_____

_____

_____

From *PE-4-ME* by Cathie Summerford, 2000, Champaign, IL: Human Kinetics.

Name _____ Date _____ Period _____

ACTIVITY #42

PE-4-ME Radical Wellness Program

The Blame Game?

Whose fault is it when things go well in a game? Whose fault is it if they don't? Nobody wants to lose, but sooner or later it happens to everyone. How do you think you react to winning and losing? How do you think your classmates feel? Who has responsibility for your success or failure?

• •

Think of someone else in your class, but don't tell who it is. Fill in the following statements the way you think that person would.

1. I _____

   _____ physical education.

2. When we play a game, my team sometimes wins. That's because _____

   _____.

3. Sometimes, though, we lose. I think that's because _____

   _____.

4. The people on my team usually _____

   _____.

5. When I play well, it's because _____

   _____.

Is the person you chose fun to have in class? Does this person value the feelings of other classmates over winning, or is winning everything?

_____

_____

_____

From *PE-4-ME* by Cathie Summerford, 2000, Champaign, IL: Human Kinetics.

Name _____ Date _____ Period _____

ACTIVITY #43

 **Radical Wellness Program**

Stress-Busters

● ●

Stress can be brutal on the body. In this day and age, stress is more prevalent than ever. How do you manage stress? List your six top activities that make you "feel better."

1. _____

2. _____

3. _____

4. _____

5. _____

6. _____

Set a goal: what activity would you like to learn to reduce stress?

_____

_____

_____

_____

_____

_____

_____

_____

_____

From *PE-4-ME* by Cathie Summerford, 2000, Champaign, IL: Human Kinetics.

Name _____ Date _____ Period _____

Skills #1

 **Radical Wellness Program**

A Peer Evaluation Manners Checklist

· ·

Directions: Please evaluate your partner and yourself using the following scale:

Scoring #	What does it mean?
4	consistently / all of the time
3	usually / most of the time
2	occasionally / some of the time
1	rarely / seldom

Criteria	Self	Partner
Positive attitude during activities		
Hustles out from locker room		
Says thank you		
Welcomes new students to class		
Does PE-4-ME homework		
Helps the teacher		
Helps other students in class		
Is a team player		
Provides "put-ups" to peers		
Does not give up		
Provided input on this checklist		

Thanks for giving your best effort!

From *PE-4-ME* by Cathie Summerford, 2000, Champaign, IL: Human Kinetics.

Don't Call Me Retarded

Don't call me retarded
just because I'm slow
I crossed the line like all the rest
and finished fifth, you know.
Rafer Johnson shook my hand
and said I really tried.
And all the people cheered me
as I walked away with pride.
Then they pinned my ribbon on,
the one that said fifth place,
And it was just as pretty
as the one's who won the race.
When the others teased me
for coming next to last,
I told them, I'm not built for speed . . .
I can't run very fast.
But don't call me retarded,
if you want to be my friend.
I may not finish in the lead,
but I'll hang in 'till the end.
And when they put the medals on the others,
I'll take pride
that Rafer Johnson shook my hand and said,
"You really tried!"

Author Unknown

From *PE-4-ME* by Cathie Summerford, 2000, Champaign, IL: Human Kinetics. Reprinted by permission of Rudy Benton.

Name _____ Date _____ Period _____

Skills #2

 Radical Wellness Program

Goal Setting

Activity Goals for 1st Semester _____

• •

What my game plan is:

Month	Activity	How frequently?	Target month
September			
October			
November			
December			
What I actually did:			

Month	Did I do activity?	How frequently?	Where did I do my activity?
September			
October			
November			
December			

From *PE-4-ME* by Cathie Summerford, 2000, Champaign, IL: Human Kinetics.

Name _____ Date _____ Period _____

Skills #2

 **Radical Wellness Program**

Goal Setting

Activity Goals for 2nd Semester _____

• •

What my game plan is:

Month	Activity	How frequently?	Target month
January			
February			
March			
April			
What I actually did:			

Month	Did I do activity?	How frequently?	Where did I do my activity?
January			
February			
March			
April			

Wow! It's summer already.
What goal do I want to set for the summer break?

_____

_____

From *PE-4-ME* by Cathie Summerford, 2000, Champaign, IL: Human Kinetics.

Name _____ Date _____ Period _____

Skills #3

 **Radical Wellness Program**

A Group Evaluation Complimenting Checklist

Directions: Please evaluate yourself and your group using the following scale:

Scoring #	What does it mean?
4	consistently / all of the time
3	usually / most of the time
2	occasionally / some of the time
1	rarely / seldom

Criteria	Self	Group
Compliments a teammate		
Compliments everyone on the team		
Uses genuine appreciation		
Provides enthusiasm to group		
Does not give up		
Provided input on this checklist		

From *PE-4-ME* by Cathie Summerford, 2000, Champaign, IL: Human Kinetics.

Skills #4

**Radical Wellness Program**

A Group Evaluation High-Five Checklist

Directions: Please evaluate yourself and your group using the following scale:

Scoring #	What does it mean?
4	consistently / all of the time
3	usually / most of the time
2	occasionally / some of the time
1	rarely / seldom

Criteria	Self	Group
High-fives a teammate		
High-fives everyone on the team		
Sincere		
Provides enthusiasm		
Has a "can-do" attitude		
Provided input on this checklist		

From *PE-4-ME* by Cathie Summerford, 2000, Champaign, IL: Human Kinetics.

Name _____ Date _____ Period _____

Skills #5

A Peer and Self-Evaluation NO PUT-DOWNS Checklist

• •

Directions: Please evaluate your partner and yourself using the following scale:

Scoring #	What does it mean?
4	consistently / all of the time
3	usually / most of the time
2	occasionally / some of the time
1	rarely / seldom

Criteria	Self	Partner
Smiles		
Encourages		
Says nice things		
Gives best effort		
Helps out in class		
Is fun to be with		

Thanks for giving PUT-UPS!
NO Put-Downs.

From *PE-4-ME* by Cathie Summerford, 2000, Champaign, IL: Human Kinetics.

Skills #6

 **Radical Wellness Program**

A Peer Evaluation Speed and Power Checklist

I am the COACH. My partner is the PLAYER.

My name _____ Partner's name _____

● ●

Directions: Read each task to your partner. Start with the first task, mark OK if correct and give your partner a "put-up." If not correct, encourage your partner and try again. Mark OK and move on to the second task when correct, or, after five attempts, mark "almost" and go on.

Speed and power	Almost	OK
Head and eyes are focused in the direction of the movement		
Arms assist in providing force by swinging in the direction of the movement		
Quickly initiates movement		
With timing device, improves in three attempts		
Gives best effort		
Provided sincere input to this checklist		

From *PE-4-ME* by Cathie Summerford, 2000, Champaign, IL: Human Kinetics.

Name _____ Date _____ Period ____

Skills #7

 Radical Wellness Program

A Peer Evaluation Agility and Reaction Time Checklist

I am the COACH. My partner is the PLAYER.

My name _____ Partner's name _____

• •

Directions: Read each task to your partner. Start with the first task, mark OK if correct and give your partner a "put-up." If not correct, encourage your partner and try again. Mark OK and move on to the second task when correct, or, after five attempts, mark "almost" and go on.

Agility and reaction time	Almost	OK
Rotates the shoulders and/or hips in the desired direction		
Pushing with the outside foot		
Quickly initiates movement		
With timing device, improves in three attempts to respond to a stimulus		
Gives best effort		
Provided sincere input to this checklist		

From *PE-4-ME* by Cathie Summerford, 2000, Champaign, IL: Human Kinetics.

Name _____ Date _____ Period _____

Skills #8

 **Radical Wellness Program**

Moving a Body Through Space (Dance)

Partner Assessment

● ●

Directions: Please evaluate your partner and yourself using the following scale:

Scoring #	What does it mean?
4	consistently / all of the time
3	usually / most of the time
2	occasionally / some of the time
1	rarely / seldom

Criteria	Self	Partner
Knowledge of steps		
On count with music		
Enthusiastic while learning dance		
Provides "put-ups" to peers		
Does not give up		
Provided input on this checklist		

How did you do?

_____

_____

Are you ready to teach the class?

_____

_____

From *PE-4-ME* by Cathie Summerford, 2000, Champaign, IL: Human Kinetics.

Name _____ Date _____ Period _____

Skills #9

Frisbee Fun . . .
A Moving-An-Object-Through-Space
Self-Evaluation Checklist

• •

Moving an object through space	Check off here
Grasps the disc as if fanning self (thumb on topside)	
Throwing arm side toward target	
Steps forward with lead leg, then hip, then shoulder, and arm follows	
Turning with upper body	
Flicks wrist	
Follow through	

From *PE-4-ME* by Cathie Summerford, 2000, Champaign, IL: Human Kinetics.

Name _____ Date _____ Period _____

Skills #10

 Radical Wellness Program

A Self-Evaluation Throwing Checklist

Check it out! Let's check ourselves and see if we are throwing properly. Put a check next to each criterion if you have completed it successfully.

Criteria	Check off here
Limited body movement, arm dominated	
Shows opposition	
Follows through toward target	
Shows trunk rotation	
Can transfer throwing skills to a "game situation"	
Can throw with increased velocity and accuracy	

From *PE-4-ME* by Cathie Summerford, 2000, Champaign, IL: Human Kinetics.

Name _____ Date _____ Period _____

Skills #11

PE-4-ME Radical Wellness Program

A Self-Evaluation Catching Checklist

Check it out! Let's check ourselves and see if we are catching properly. Put a check next to each criterion if you have completed it successfully.

Criteria	Check off here
Arms extended toward thrower, shows avoidance reaction	
Can catch a bounced ball from a partner	
Can catch a variety of self-tossed objects	
Can catch a variety of objects at different levels with a partner	
Can transfer catching skills to a "game situation"	
Can catch an object thrown with increased velocity or catch an object while moving	

From *PE-4-ME* by Cathie Summerford, 2000, Champaign, IL: Human Kinetics.

Skills #12

PE-4-ME Radical Wellness Program

A Group Evaluation Balancing Act Checklist

Can your group do the following activities?

● ●

Balance	Check off here
Travel and stop in balance	
Balance on different body parts and bases of support	
Travel on low equipment	
Perform stationary balances on equipment	
Balance with a partner	
Balance on boards or medium beams	
Perform a balance sequence that combines stationary and traveling sequences	
All participants were team players	
All participants gave input to this list	

From *PE-4-ME* by Cathie Summerford, 2000, Champaign, IL: Human Kinetics.

Skills #13

A Group Evaluation Explosive Movement Checklist

Can your group do the following activities?

Explosive movement	Check off here
Perform a sudden burst of power	
Stay balanced	
Explain how explosive movement applies to a variety of activities/sports	
Practice five explosive movements in a row	
All participants were team players	
All participants gave input to this list	

From *PE-4-ME* by Cathie Summerford, 2000, Champaign, IL: Human Kinetics.

Name_____ Date _____ Period ____

Skills #14

PE-4-ME Radical Wellness Program

A Peer Evaluation: Striking With Upper Body (Arms)

I am the COACH. My partner is the PLAYER.

My name _____ Partner's name _____

• •

Directions: Read each task to your partner. Toss the ball to your partner. Start with the first task, mark OK if correct and give your partner a "put-up." If not correct, encourage your partner and try again. Mark OK and move on to the second task when correct, or, after five tosses, mark "almost" and go on.

Bumping task	Almost	OK
Athletic stance, knees bent		
Thumbs together, parallel, and pointed down		
Elbows straight, forearms even		
Ball contacts forearms		
Legs straighten and body moves forward on contact		
Hips face target		
Arms extend toward target		

Setting task	Almost	OK
Lines up ball with mid-line of body		
Knees bent, weight on both feet		
Thumbs together, fingers pointing diagonally upward		
Elbows rotated out		
Primary contact on thumbs, middle, and index fingers		
Gets under the ball		
Uses leg and arm extension on contact with ball		

From *PE-4-ME* by Cathie Summerford, 2000, Champaign, IL: Human Kinetics.

Name _____ Date _____ Period _____

Skills #15

 **Radical Wellness Program**

A Striking-With-Lower-Body
Self-Evaluation Checklist

Striking with lower body	Strongly agree	Slightly agree	Agree	Disagree
Limited body movement, leg dominated action				
Moves toward a stationary ball and makes contact with dominant foot				
Can kick a stationary or moving ball and follow through toward target				
Can demonstrate a variety of kicks (stationary, dropkick, moving ball) using various types of balls				
Can transfer kicking skills to a "game situation"				
Performs a variety of kicks, with defenders, showing increased velocity and accuracy				

From *PE-4-ME* by Cathie Summerford, 2000, Champaign, IL: Human Kinetics.

Name _____ Date _____ Period _____

Skills #16

PE-4-ME *Radical Wellness Program*

A Striking-With-Implements
Self-Evaluation Checklist

Striking with implements	Strongly agree	Slightly agree	Agree	Disagree
Limited body movement, arm dominated				
Shows side orientation and proper grip				
Steps forward and makes contact with a stationary object				
Steps forward and makes contact with a moving object				
Can transfer striking skills to a "game situation"				
Can strike a ball with increased velocity and accuracy				

From *PE-4-ME* by Cathie Summerford, 2000, Champaign, IL: Human Kinetics.

Fun Stuff #1

 Radical Wellness Program

Second Chances

I'll never forget today. Today was the day they posted the results of basketball try-outs. I woke up excited and nervous at the same time. Everybody wanted to be on the team, but we all knew that not everybody was going to make it.

The coach posted the names of the kids who made the team on the wall by the gym. After school, my best friend and I went down to check it out. A crowd of kids huddled around the list, reading anxiously. Some cheered and high-fived each other; others turned away silently, looking at the ground.

We moved in closer. The names were in alphabetical order. I scanned the list quickly. Chris's name was there near the top. Mine wasn't. I looked again, in case I missed it, but my name just wasn't on the list.

I had to swallow really hard and take a deep breath before I could look at Chris. "Congratulations," I said. "You were really good at tryouts. I'm sure you'll have a lot of fun on the team."

"Thanks," Chris said quietly. "So…you want to walk home together?"

"No, you go on ahead," I said. "I think I just want to be alone a little bit."

I walked away, focusing on the yellow tiles of the hallway, concentrating really hard on them so I wouldn't cry before I was away from everyone else. I concentrated so hard, in fact, that I didn't notice Coach Smith until we had nearly collided.

"Oh, sorry, Coach," I said. "I wasn't paying attention."

"No harm," Coach said. He paused. "I guess you've seen the list?"

"Yeah," I muttered, looking back at the ground.

"I'm really sorry we didn't have more spots open," he said. "You showed a lot of effort, and that counts for a lot. I hope you'll keep practicing."

"Thanks, Coach," I said. "But I guess maybe basketball just isn't my thing."

"I hope you're not saying that just because one tryout didn't work out for you. A real winner keeps on trying, you know. Just look at Michael Jordan."

I looked up at Coach. "What do you mean? Michael Jordan is the best player ever."

From *PE-4-ME* by Cathie Summerford, 2000, Champaign, IL: Human Kinetics.

"Sure, he is *now*. But he used to be a kid like you. And, believe it or not, he missed the cut on his school team. What if he had quit then? What if *he* had said 'basketball's not my thing'? Some people say he's the greatest basketball player who ever lived—and those people would never even have heard of him if he'd quit then. Now, you can do as you please, of course, but you seem to have a lot of fun while you're playing basketball. I hope you keep working at it, because I'd like to see you at tryouts again next year."

I thanked the coach and slowly walked home. Coach's words swirled in my head all the way. I tried to imagine Michael Jordan—the same Michael Jordan whose poster hung on my bedroom wall—feeling exactly the way I felt right then. Just a regular kid, walking home, wishing he could tell his parents he made the team.

"I'm home," I yelled when I walked in. "Hi sweetie," Mom said. "How was school today?" That's when I started crying. I ran to my own room, so I could be alone. After a while, when I was all cried out, someone knocked softly on the door. My mom came in and sat on my bed.

"I didn't make the team," I said.

Mom wiped my hair out of my eyes. "Do you want to talk about it?"

I shook my head no. We sat for a moment. "I'm sorry I disappointed you and Dad." Mom hugged me close. "You could never disappoint us by taking a chance. We're proud of you for trying."

I looked up at the poster over my bed. Michael Jordan hung in the air, suspended by the basket. "Mom, did you know Michael Jordan got cut from his school team? That's what Coach told me. I bet that's why he's so good. He had to get a second chance, so he had to work really hard. And, he knew how it felt to be disappointed, and he never wanted to feel that way again. But instead of playing safe, and not trying anymore, he worked really hard and took another risk, even though he might have been disappointed again."

"I didn't know that," Mom said. Then she ruffled up my hair. "Dinner's almost ready."

"I'll be there in a minute," I said. When she was gone, I looked up at my poster again. Jordan held the ball at the basket, jumping above the reach of the other players. It looked so easy—effortless, even. But was it really? Who knows how much effort it took to get back on that court after being told he wasn't good enough to play? It was a lot to think about. I shook my head to clear my thoughts, and jumped up to high-five the world's greatest basketball player before heading in to dinner.

From *PE-4-ME* by Cathie Summerford, 2000, Champaign, IL: Human Kinetics.

Name _____ Date _____ Period _____

Fun Stuff #2

 Radical Wellness Program

Swim With a Buddy

Find the words for water safety equipment hidden in the list of letters below. They describe equipment used by lifeguards. Remember that the words can run up, down, backward, forward, or diagonally.

• •

```
S D I V I N G B O A R D H S S S T E O P P
R I I K I S W I M S U I T P A E O O W E R
O U F L U T T E R I I H I D D A L G A E P
L Y V V S R A L U C O N I B U R Y T S J H
A K D H F H W W S A D C T X I E N H H B F
D H R X I D H A X H V K C O E S B R E W L
D T A C R Z J I R S H O I O R C U O P S B
E E O W S D P S M N J J F O E U Z W H I S
R L B P T N N M U V I E U D C E I R E K E
I E K Q A A R Y F N O N U L O T R O R C N
N P C B I T X E J W T R G D M U Z P D Y I
N H A Z D S S H A M H A U F I B X E S U L
R O B E K D A E E C E I N L L E H B C H E
X N H I I R F S M A H Z S L E A T A R E F
R E W V T A E J U H V I B T O S G G O A I
M M N T C U T Y H A T I N L L T P S O V L
S W P Z E G Y O J M W J N G J E I H K I W
S Q S O S E P U C F G W Y G P S M O O N D
Z K G R G F O B U Y W O J X L O F V N G F
T E W A V I S G M B N K M E F I L M L J X
C M S K I L T N W P P K K O A I N E O U R
E F H H K Y S I P S U N G L A S S E S G I
L K B T Y K N R X G P Z Q V T O U T O E R
P O F K I C K B O A R D X T S T E V O O Q
```

❑ Kickboard   ❑ Backboard   ❑ Lifeguard stand   ❑ Safety post   ❑ Suntan lotion
❑ Whistle   ❑ Warning flags   ❑ Shepherd's crook   ❑ Sunglasses   ❑ Rescue tube
❑ Reaching pole ❑ Binoculars   ❑ Throw rope bag   ❑ Telephone   ❑ Rules
❑ Heaving jug   ❑ Ring buoy   ❑ Swimsuit   ❑ Lifelines   ❑ Hat
❑ First aid kit ❑ Diving board   ❑ Ladder   ❑ Heaving line

From *PE-4-ME* by Cathie Summerford, 2000, Champaign, IL: Human Kinetics.

191

PE-4-ME Radical Wellness Program

Don't Be a Fool . . . Follow the Rules!

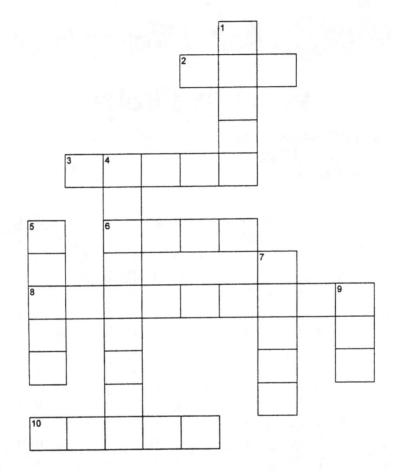

ACROSS

2 Only _____ person on the diving board at a time.
3 Always swim in _____ water, not murky water.
6 When using a slide, go down _____ first.
8 Don't swim when there is _____ and thunder.
10 Always swim with a _____.

DOWN

1 Never swim _____ the diving board.
4 The supervisor at the pool is the _____.
5 Be cool, follow the _____.
7 Never swim at _____ in unlighted areas.
9 Don't chew _____ while swimming.

From *PE-4-ME* by Cathie Summerford, 2000, Champaign, IL: Human Kinetics.

Name _____ Date _____ Period _

Fun Stuff #3

PE-4-ME Radical Wellness Program

Skeleton Crossword Puzzle

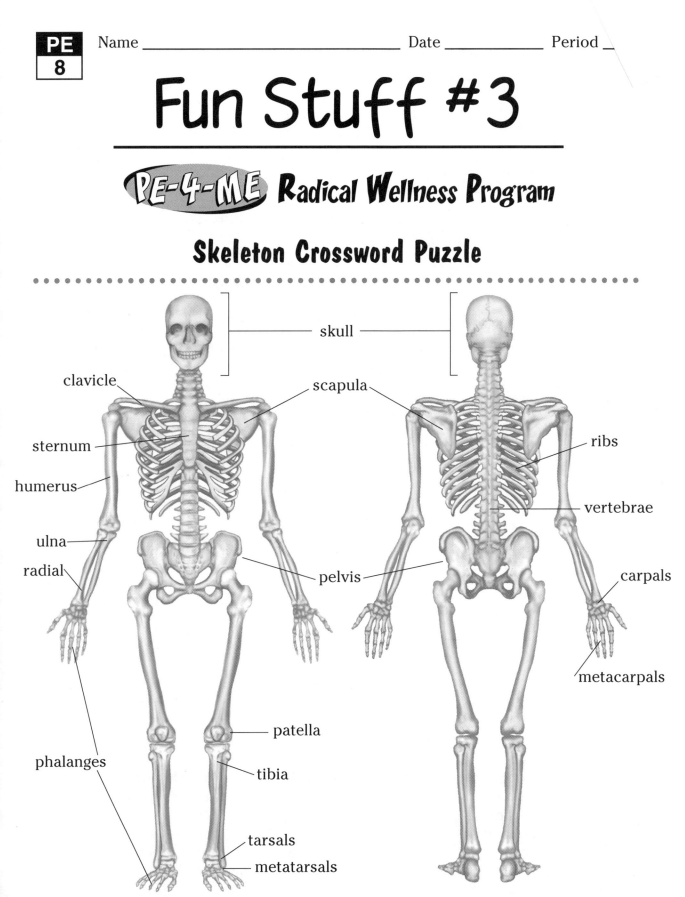

From *PE-4-ME* by Cathie Summerford, 2000, Champaign, IL: Human Kinetics. Originally published in *Essentials of Strength Training and Conditioning* by Thomas, Baechle, and Earl, 2000, Champaign, IL: Human Kinetics.

Skeleton Crossword Puzzle

ACROSS

1 shoulder blade
3 small bone in lower arm
4 chest bone
9 bones across top of hand
11 wrist bones
12 small bones in the spine
13 ankle bones
14 head

DOWN

1 chest bone
2 large bone in upper arm
5 bones across top of foot
6 tips of fingers and toes
7 collar bone
8 hip bone
10 knee cap

From *PE-4-ME* by Cathie Summerford, 2000, Champaign, IL: Human Kinetics.

Fun Stuff #4

PE-4-ME Radical Wellness Program

Pulse Rate

Do you ever feel like a couch potato? Your heart never does! It's constantly working—as you're about to discover.

• •

Your pulse rate is the number of times your heart beats in a minute. This rate changes with your level of activity. When you're calm and relaxed, you have a resting pulse rate. When you're running around or jogging in place, you have an active pulse rate.

To find your pulse rate:

Place your index and middle fingers on your wrist or neck. (Don't use your thumb; the pulse in your thumb may be strong enough to interfere with your count.)

Hold your fingers in place until you feel the steady beating of your pulse.

Count the beats for 6 seconds. Multiply this count by 10 to find the number of beats per minute.

My Resting Pulse Rate (when I'm calm and relaxed)

_____ beats in 6 seconds × 10 = _____ beats per minute

My Active Pulse Rate (after I've jogged in place for 1 minute)

_____ beats in 6 seconds × 10 = _____ beats per minute

Pulse Math

Calculate the number of times your heart beats each hour at its resting pulse rate. At this rate, how many times would your heart beat in a day? In a week? In a year? If you exercised for 20 minutes every day, how many times would your heart beat in a month?

From *PE-4-ME* by Cathie Summerford, 2000, Champaign, IL: Human Kinetics.

The American Sign Language Alphabet

Now it's time for finger exercises and communicating with your friends!

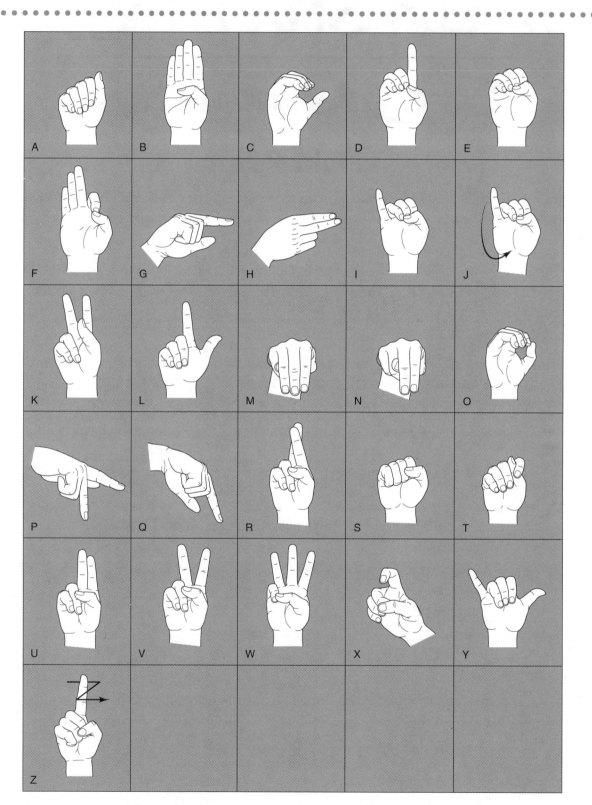

From *PE-4-ME* by Cathie Summerford, 2000, Champaign, IL: Human Kinetics. Originally published in *Motor Learning and Performance* by Richard Schmidt and Craig Wrisberg, 2000, Champaign, IL: Human Kinetics.

Name _____ Date _____ Period _____

Fun Stuff #5

PE-4-ME Radical Wellness Program

Swim Hidden Picture

Can you find the rabbit, snail, snake, key, bird, skate, and needle in this hidden picture? Good luck!

From *PE-4-ME* by Cathie Summerford, 2000, Champaign, IL: Human Kinetics. Copyright © 1995 by Highlights for Children, Inc., Columbus, OH. Reprinted by permission.

Math Fractions Boxing

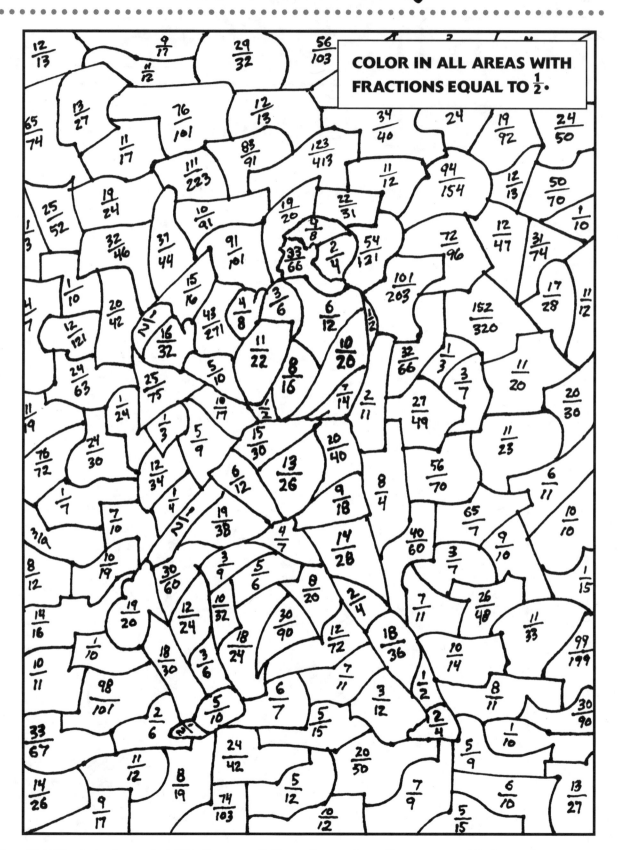

From *PE-4-ME* by Cathie Summerford, 2000, Champaign, IL: Human Kinetics. Printed by permission of Meghann Bell.

Name _____ Date _____ Period _____

Fun Stuff #6

 Radical Wellness Program

Sports Word-Search

Find and circle the words at the bottom of this puzzle. There are different words used in this sport. What sport is it? Remember, the words can run up, down, backward, forward, and diagonally. Challenge yourself!

```
R  B  U  N  T  X  Z  S  T  R  I  K  E  X  R  X
S  H  H  P  N  M  B  F  F  Q  W  A  R  P  B  Q
L  B  R  O  R  R  E  I  N  D  G  R  A  R  H  D
C  L  A  E  T  S  D  P  I  Y  E  O  R  T  K  R
P  O  W  G  I  I  O  A  B  D  R  T  A  G  C  S
L  Y  G  A  B  T  M  U  N  F  C  G  O  I  D  G
A  R  P  R  L  O  C  U  O  U  T  G  A  L  P  L
T  E  L  E  N  K  O  U  T  S  A  W  E  D  L  O
E  T  U  D  S  R  U  Y  I  R  C  I  T  O  A  V
B  T  O  R  G  D  N  M  N  T  F  Q  R  U  Y  E
C  A  F  J  A  Y  T  O  N  N  A  R  I  B  E  X
Y  B  E  C  R  O  F  T  I  Z  Q  R  P  L  R  B
Y  C  L  E  A  N  U  P  N  S  E  E  L  E  S  A
K  R  E  H  C  T  I  P  G  B  A  S  E  G  P  S
C  S  A  C  R  I  F  I  C  E  B  A  T  I  N  E
N  L  E  A  D  O  F  F  Z  S  R  U  N  S  S  N
```

Leadoff	Grounder	Walk	Infield	Triple	Inning
Steal	Strike	Out	Sacrifice	Pitcher	RBI	Foul
Bag	Bunt	Force	Battery	Error	Cleanup	Double
Count	Runs	Base	Diamond	Cut	Glove	Plate

What sport is this? _____

From *PE-4-ME* by Cathie Summerford, 2000, Champaign, IL: Human Kinetics.

Wow . . . Double Trouble!

In many sports, there are terms that may apply in one sport and also in another. For example, in the sport of fishing, the gear used is called "tackle." In football, a "tackle" is a member of the team.

   Check out the sports below. Each of the sports on the left shares a term with a sport on the right. Look at the definitions, and fill in their common word on the line in the middle. Have fun!

● ●

1. Football:
   A member of the team

   _____

1. Fishing:
   What the gear is called

2. Auto racing:
   A person who operates the car

   _____

2. Golf:
   A type of club

3. Football:
   A mark across the field

   _____

3. Fishing:
   The string or cord used on a fishing pole

4. Boxing:
   A type of swing, hit, or blow

   _____

4. Fishing:
   What catches the fish and is sharp

5. Shooting:
   One shot

   _____

5. Boxing:
   One period of a match

6. Billiards:
   Another name for the game

   _____

6. Swimming:
   The facility you swim in

7. Yachting:
   A trophy

   _____

7. Golf:
   The ball falls into it

8. Wrestling:
   Your objective when wrestling

   _____

8. Bowling:
   The object you try to knock down

9. Bowling:
   When you knock down all ten bowling pins at once

   _____

9. Baseball:
   Three of these count you out

10. Tennis:
    It divides the court and the ball needs to go over it

   _____

10. Fishing:
    A device used to catch fish

From *PE-4-ME* by Cathie Summerford, 2000, Champaign, IL: Human Kinetics.

Name _____ Date _____ Period ____

Fun Stuff #7

PE-4-ME Radical Wellness Program

Muscle Magic

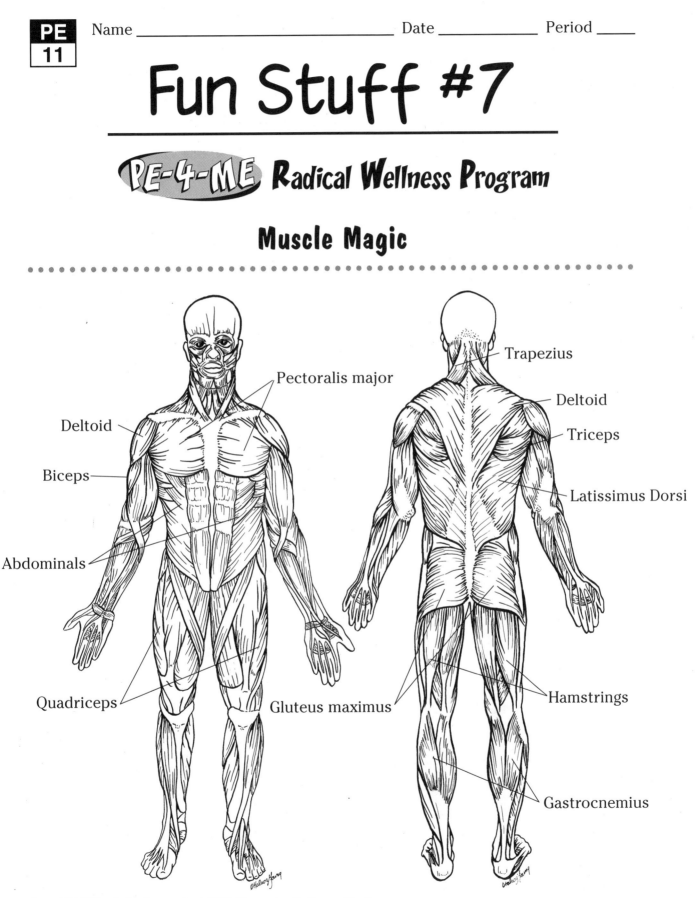

Trapezius

Pectoralis major

Deltoid

Deltoid

Triceps

Biceps

Latissimus Dorsi

Abdominals

Quadriceps

Hamstrings

Gluteus maximus

Gastrocnemius

From *PE-4-ME* by Cathie Summerford, 2000, Champaign, IL: Human Kinetics.

Muscle Word-Search

```
H P O P O L M B V V C A E U Y H Y Z V O R
J K T T E Q A S X C H J K S T R O N G P I
H A M S T R I N G S L U A R T P Q P D O K
C B Y M L K P X Z V J I O E R T V N B K A
P D G H J S L E U I O N V X A L G N I H Z
L O A U T R F U C C J I T Y P Z A K C G B
J M S D F I P K M T X Z C U E O S P E W Q
H I F G A Z X V Y U O M K S Z U T M P W M
S N X V G A U N M K L R P U I R R H S A H
K A Z R Y G B N Q M J Z A U U E O V C Z N
X L H S U R E I M U S D K L S H C U P R E
A S C R D E F G H I A J K L I M N O P Q R
Z Y X A W V U T S R Q D P O N S E M L K J
L A T I S S I M U S D O R S I L M I Y K L
S W D E L T O I D W R Z A I H Y I A J C X
G T X Z W A T E R B O D Y V C H U Q J K B
E X E I R C I S E R U N V Y S E S H I O C
Q I M U F O R C E V Y T R I C E P S G O R
J O G S H U M E R U S C L O C K F S T H E
G L U T E U S M A X I M U S K M O S N O W
```

❑ Pectoralis major   ❑ Quadriceps   ❑ Hamstrings

❑ Triceps   ❑ Biceps   ❑ Abdominals   ❑ Deltoid   ❑ Trapezius

❑ Latissimus dorsi   ❑ Gastrocnemius   ❑ Gluteus maximus

From *PE-4-ME* by Cathie Summerford, 2000, Champaign, IL: Human Kinetics.

Name _____ Date _____ Period _____

Fun Stuff #8

PE-4-ME Radical Wellness Program

Sports Fun Puzzle

Locate and circle sports words in the letter maze. Remember, the words are written forward, backward, vertically, horizontally, and diagonally. There are some surprise words…see if you can find them!

```
Z  G  N  I  L  C  Y  C  X  L  L  R  U  G  B  Y  M  M  P  A  Q
D  B  A  D  M  I  N  T  O  N  C  R  E  C  C  O  S  X  O  P  P
I  J  J  K  S  A  R  T  D  D  F  E  N  C  I  N  G  C  C  M  R
V  S  L  D  L  E  I  F  D  N  A  K  C  A  R  T  Y  T  O  S  O
I  C  L  L  A  B  E  S  A  B  O  X  I  N  G  G  E  U  G  W  W
N  I  A  L  A  C  R  O  S  S  E  D  N  I  N  N  K  M  N  I  I
G  T  B  A  A  B  G  N  I  L  I  A  S  I  N  A  C  B  I  M  N
O  S  T  B  R  B  Y  N  O  V  I  D  I  I  R  R  O  L  L  M  G
O  A  E  T  K  C  D  E  I  I  I  K  S  A  E  C  H  I  T  I  X
U  N  K  O  A  K  H  N  L  L  S  I  T  C  R  A  E  N  S  N  F
B  M  S  O  K  A  G  E  A  L  W  E  C  S  O  C  C  G  E  G  I
C  Y  A  F  G  O  L  F  R  H  O  O  E  W  O  B  I  O  R  A  E
K  G  B  H  S  A  U  Q  S  Y  S  V  B  A  R  C  H  O  W  E  L
Q  H  O  C  K  E  Y  Z  Z  U  S  K  A  T  I  N  G  O  U  O  D
```

❑ Soccer	❑ Diving	❑ Track and field	❑ Gymnastics
❑ Volleyball	❑ Football	❑ Golf	❑ Badminton
❑ Lacrosse	❑ Cycling	❑ Bowling	❑ Field
❑ Squash	❑ Rugby	❑ Swimming	❑ Skating
❑ Basketball	❑ Rowing	❑ Skiing	❑ Fencing
❑ Archery	❑ Baseball	❑ Tennis	
❑ Ice hockey	❑ Handball	❑ Hockey	

From *PE-4-ME* by Cathie Summerford, 2000, Champaign, IL: Human Kinetics.

Sports Name Game

What sport matches with the following terms?

_____	rings, vaulting, parallel bars
_____	boat, ski, wake, water
_____	fletching, nock, shaft, range
_____	blade, rink, face-off, check
_____	skates, knee pads, helmet
_____	cross, goalie, rake, crease
_____	binding, edges, powder, mogul
_____	butterfly, backstroke, breaststroke, relay
_____	choke, fly, bunt, rundown
_____	wood, iron, putter, driver
_____	tanks, snorkel, mask, fins
_____	divot, rough, birdie, eagle
_____	release, strike, hook, spare
_____	huddle, option, safety, offside
_____	gears, wheels, brakes, pedal
_____	dribble, screen, layup, blind side
_____	birdie, net, racquet, score
_____	dig, spike, setter, dink

Diving	Waterskiing	Tennis
Volleyball	Baseball	Badminton
Lacrosse	Handball	Gymnastics
Squash	Track and field	Fencing
Basketball	Golf	In-line skating
Archery	Bowling	Cycling
Ice hockey	Swimming	
Football	Skiing	

From *PE-4-ME* by Cathie Summerford, 2000, Champaign, IL: Human Kinetics.

Name _____ Date _____ Period _____

Fun Stuff #9

PE-4-ME Radical Wellness Program

Basketball Hidden Picture

Can you find the measuring cup, seal, golf club, pitcher, cap, worm, banana, sailboat, teapot, fish, and carrot in this hidden picture?

• •

From *PE-4-ME* by Cathie Summerford, 2000, Champaign, IL: Human Kinetics. Copyright © 1993, Highlights for Children, Inc., Columbus, OH. Reprinted by permission.

Math Factors Fruit

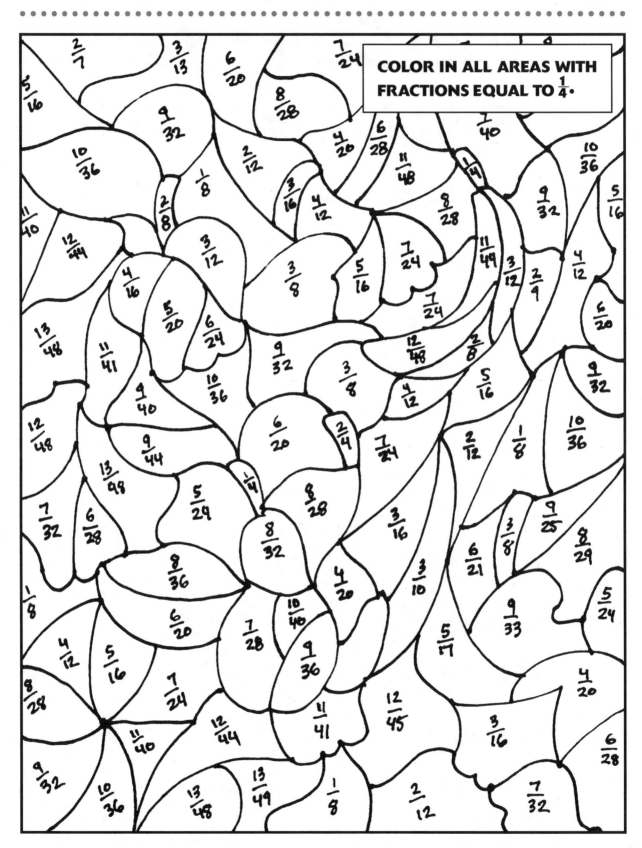

COLOR IN ALL AREAS WITH FRACTIONS EQUAL TO $\frac{1}{4}$.

From *PE-4-ME* by Cathie Summerford, 2000, Champaign, IL: Human Kinetics. Printed by permission of Meghann Bell.

Name _____ Date _____ Period _____

Fun Stuff #10

 **Radical Wellness Program**

Freaky Football Find

In football, there are different player positions. Try to find the positions in the word maze below. Remember, the words can go backward, forward, up, down, and diagonally. Good luck!

● ●

```
Y  A  R  D  A  G  E  B  C  S  A  F  E  T  Y  O
X  J  K  I  O  P  P  O  U  Y  M  F  U  N  L  P
L  K  I  C  K  E  R  T  D  N  E  K  N  D  N  P
T  D  Z  X  L  Y  E  R  I  W  C  Y  B  C  A  M
O  L  I  N  E  M  A  N  T  A  K  T  P  T  O  P
U  R  L  P  L  U  G  N  B  L  I  U  B  I  N  E
C  E  X  Q  G  A  U  F  T  L  N  N  Z  G  I  N
H  V  B  G  U  Q  L  U  P  T  E  R  O  H  O  A
D  I  N  R  H  A  N  S  E  M  F  E  I  T  D  L
O  E  D  U  H  N  R  R  E  N  O  T  K  E  R  T
W  C  P  L  A  C  E  T  E  E  K  N  O  N  A  Y
N  E  A  D  E  F  A  N  E  S  E  E  O  D  U  C
V  R  C  D  B  C  E  U  S  R  N  C  A  N  G  V
X  R  H  Z  K  N  W  K  C  A  B  L  L  U  F  D
S  A  T  L  J  M  Y  G  N  I  W  A  S  E  O  Q
S  O  E  D  E  F  E  N  S  E  S  O  C  N  T  R
T  Y  U  O  C  H  R  I  L  E  P  L  E  K  K  S
U  P  W  S  W  O  F  F  S  I  D  E  S  X  N  O
```

❏ Offsides ❏ Fullback ❏ Defense ❏ Halfback ❏ Punter ❏ Yardage
❏ Receiver ❏ Tight end ❏ Penalty ❏ Kicker ❏ Center ❏ End ❏ Guard
❏ Lineman ❏ Quarterback ❏ Tackle ❏ Touchdown ❏ Wing ❏ Safety

From *PE-4-ME* by Cathie Summerford, 2000, Champaign, IL: Human Kinetics.

Soccer City

Listed below are common words used in soccer. Fill in the blanks below with the correct term.

• •

Trapping	Fun	Training
Number	Goalkeeper	Rules
Grass	Kick	Everyone
Condition	Professional	Feet
Heading	Fast	Small
Dribbling	Ball	Net

If you don't have _____ to play on, it is difficult to play soccer.

In soccer, some players can run very _____ .

The World Cup soccer players are continually practicing and _____.

To keep the ball from entering the _____, one needs to stop it.

The most common way to move the ball in soccer is to use your _____ .

To get the soccer ball in the air, one needs to _____ it.

Some people are _____ soccer players, while others are amateurs.

A few skills in soccer are _____, _____, and _____ .

Sarah's dad is a referee. He makes sure both teams are following the _____.

The round object used in soccer is called a soccer _____.

If you play a lot of soccer, you should be in top _____ .

The _____ of players in a soccer game is eleven.

Susan plays the _____ position.

Jon enjoys playing soccer, because it's so much _____.

Most soccer fields are not _____, they are large.

Soccer is a great game for _____.

From *PE-4-ME* by Cathie Summerford, 2000, Champaign, IL: Human Kinetics.

Fun Stuff #11

 **Radical Wellness Program**

Skin Facts: Simple Steps to Protect Your Skin

Ten years ago, it was very unusual for doctors to see a patient under 40 with melanoma skin cancer. Today, over 25% of melanoma patients are under 40.

Your skin performs many vital functions, yet it's often taken for granted. It's up to you to take a few simple steps to protect your skin and to detect problems early, when they are most treatable.

Most skin growths or conditions are harmless, but any new growth or sore that does not heal is reason to see the doctor. Get into the habit of carefully checking your skin at least once a month.

Skin Cancer Prevention

Overexposure to the sun is a major factor in skin cancer and aging. You can still enjoy the sun and stay outdoors by exercising a few precautions:

Use sunscreen

Wear hats and sunglasses

Skin Myths and Facts

Myth: In order for sunlight to cause skin cancer, you must get a sunburn.

Fact: People who sunburn are more likely to get skin cancer, but tanning damages the skin whether a sunburn occurs or not.

Myth: The skin repairs itself after a sunburn or after tanning if you allow it to "rest" between sun exposures.

Fact: Sun damage accumulates with each successive exposure to the sun. The damage may not be apparent for 20 or 30 years, though.

Myth: Tanned skin is healthy skin.

Fact: A tan is really a sign of skin injury. Permanent damage will show up.

From *PE-4-ME* by Cathie Summerford, 2000, Champaign, IL: Human Kinetics.

Safety First

In any activity, you should think of safety first. Hidden in this puzzle are seven safety words. Look across, up, down, backward, and diagonally. Then complete each sentence with one of the words you found. The word *dash* appears nine times—can you find them all?

```
J  L  L  O  P  C  V  A  D  E  E
S  H  A  T  D  I  T  H  T  O  K
D  A  S  H  A  N  O  W  R  L  T
P  E  D  E  S  T  R  I  A  N  S
C  R  A  R  H  E  A  W  F  A  I
A  T  R  S  T  R  S  O  F  V  H
R  O  A  Q  D  S  W  D  I  S  T
E  D  P  A  O  E  V  A  C  H  O
F  R  S  R  T  C  A  S  T  H  B
U  H  C  B  H  T  S  H  E  S  G
L  S  I  J  S  I  L  S  M  A  H
L  A  Q  D  A  O  H  S  A  D  X
Y  D  H  Y  D  N  X  D  S  S  V
R  Z  B  L  F  S  R  T  H  B  C
```

When you are at a corner, look for vehicles and cross _____.

Always push the button and follow the directions of "Walk/Don't walk" signs found at many _____.

After looking _____ ways, step cautiously before crossing.

Don't use a crosswalk for a 100-yard _____. It's not a place to race.

You and your friends, as _____, must obey traffic signals the same as drivers.

Remember that a _____ cannot stop vehicles from hitting you.

Obey _____ signals if you are walking, riding a bike, or skateboarding.

❑ Both   ❑ Dash   ❑ Carefully

❑ Intersections   ❑ Pedestrians   ❑ Traffic   ❑ Crosswalk

From *PE-4-ME* by Cathie Summerford, 2000, Champaign, IL: Human Kinetics.

Name _____ Date _____ Period ____

Fun Stuff #12

 Radical Wellness Program

Chef Hidden Picture

Can you find the mouse, lollipop, fork, bell, ring, pear, toothbrush, candle, rabbit, flower, top hat, and bird's head in the hidden picture?

• •

From *PE-4-ME* by Cathie Summerford, 2000, Champaign, IL: Human Kinetics. Copyright © 1994, Highlights for Children, Inc., Columbus, OH. Reprinted by permission.

Math Fractions Running

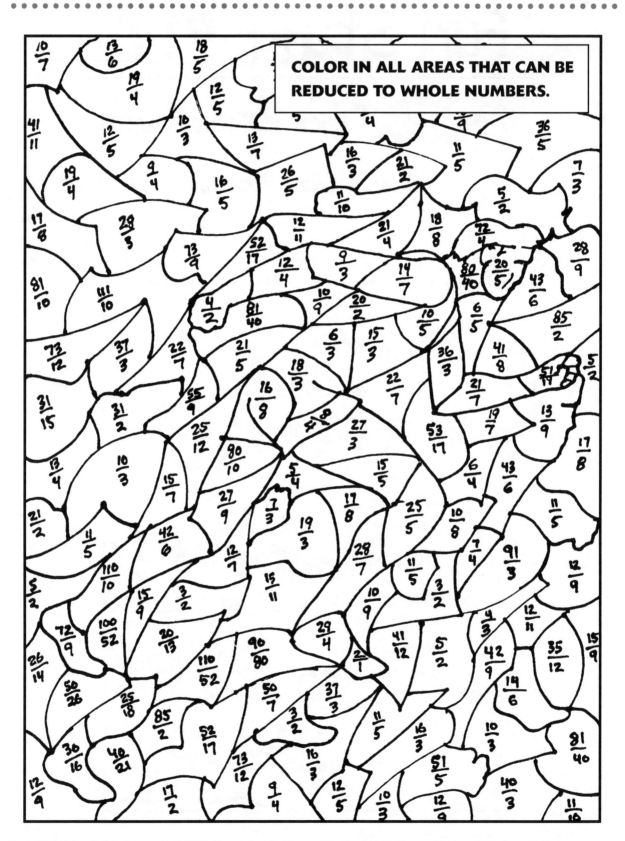

From *PE-4-ME* by Cathie Summerford, 2000, Champaign, IL: Human Kinetics. Printed by permission of Meghann Bell.

Fun Stuff #13

 **Radical Wellness Program**

Brain and Body Fitness

Fitness, and so much more!

Fitness is the ability to feel better, think better, move better, and generally do better on a daily basis.

When you're "fit," you have a brain and a body that say "YES!"

On the following chart, check off the activities that qualify you to be a "mover and shaker" or a "couch potato."

••

Activities	Mover and shaker	Couch potato
Playing video games	❏	❏
Dancing with friends	❏	❏
Playing soccer	❏	❏
Watching TV	❏	❏
Planting a garden	❏	❏
Riding a bicycle	❏	❏
Helping vacuum the house	❏	❏
Lying in bed eating potato chips	❏	❏
Lying in bed eating too much	❏	❏
Riding a bus instead of riding your bike	❏	❏
Walking to school instead of riding in a car	❏	❏
Jogging	❏	❏
Sleeping all day	❏	❏

Are you more of a "mover and shaker" or a "couch potato"?

From *PE-4-ME* by Cathie Summerford, 2000, Champaign, IL: Human Kinetics.

Test yourself to see what kind of shape you're in:

PLUSES	Yes	No
I wake up refreshed.	+2	0
I exercise vigorously (running, fast biking, etc.) three times a week.	+2	0
I get some moderate exercise (slow biking, walking, etc.) each week.	+2	0
My pulse rate is normal at rest (no more than 72 beats per minute).	+2	0
I'm active during the day (walking to the store, using stairs, etc.).	+2	0

Total pluses: _____

MINUSES		
I eat too much.	-2	0
I weigh more than I should.	-2	0
My muscles ache when I climb stairs.	-2	0
I don't sleep well at night.	-2	0
My heart pounds rapidly after I exert myself.	-2	0

Total minuses: _____

Net fitness score: _____

Any score less than 10 means that you're not as fit as you could be!

From *PE-4-ME* by Cathie Summerford, 2000, Champaign, IL: Human Kinetics.

Name _____ Date _____ Period _____

Fun Stuff #14

PE-4-ME Radical Wellness Program

Moving for Learning

Brainy info: How movement promotes learning.

• •

Movement:

- supplies more oxygen to the brain.

- boosts the number of brain cells in the brain (hippocampus).

- rewards pleasure center in the brain (thalamus).

- increases neural activity in the brain.

- increases dopamine and serotonin (neurotransmitters) levels in the brain.

- improves memory (kids learn in multiple pathways).

- boosts ability of neurons to communicate with each other.

- enhances memory (especially cardiovascular exercise).

- increases arts and drama test scores in some studies.

- projects neural pathways from cerebellum to cortex.

- reduces stress.

- promotes sound body and sound mind.

From *PE-4-ME* by Cathie Summerford, 2000, Champaign, IL: Human Kinetics.

Name _____ Date _____ Period ____

Fun Stuff #15

PE-4-ME Radical Wellness Program

Basketball Boogie Word Find

Find the basketball terms in the puzzle. Remember, the words can go forward, backward, up, down, and diagonally.

. . . .

```
L C H E E R L E A D E R S X M I R P
V P O Q W S S A S T J U O M M N R S
E S E A B O U N C E P A S S B U Y L
D H U S K C H I F A L N O B I G O C
R T R A V E L I N G E E B O B T E E
I N C T O V I P Z D Z E K M A O N E
B O T R K R B Q R B A R A N H H E L
B F I E T O L A Y I N C K I K S T B
L F N T T E O C S I N S S H O T X A
I E Y N Q B I H R E P M U J E E L S
N N D E K R A Q P Y L I L W P S M K
G S R C T Y U S R E V I R D C N S E
L E A N T D E F E N S E N Y T W S T
L B W S P E N S L B I C K E W Y A X
P G R N I T W P D R A U G T L I P Z
O X O D N U O B E R C L C N X M T S
O P F R E E T H R O W N L C B C S S
H O C K L N X C N T Y P O P O P E R
C N E T H A N G S F R O M T A O H H
B T R Y T O S C O R E X M L A S C R
C G E P T R A K N L O S M K N T S L
K D C S U P E R F A N S X L M N M P
```

Basket   Hoop   Dribbling   Lay in   Jumper   Hook   Bounce pass
Chest pass   Drive   Post   Forward   Free throw   Offense   Pivot
Traveling   Set shot   Score   Screen   Rebound   Super fans   Rim
Cheerleaders   Guard   Defense   Center   Baseline   Backboard

From *PE-4-ME* by Cathie Summerford, 2000, Champaign, IL: Human Kinetics.

And the Rest Is History . . .

Create a title and finish the story about the exciting volleyball game.

• •

Title _____

The Johnson family watched the game nervously. The only sound in the gymnasium was the continuous strike of the girls' hands on the volleyball. Their daughter, Nicole, the star of the Eagle team, had been instrumental in engineering her team's comeback. They had been trailing at one time by two games, but the Eagles fought back. They won two games and were now tied. During this fifth game, the Eagles were down by five points, but the girls now had the ball. It would be a miracle if they could pull off a victory.

_____

_____

_____

_____

_____

_____

_____

_____

_____

_____

_____

_____

_____

_____

_____

_____

_____

_____

_____ The end.

From *PE-4-ME* by Cathie Summerford, 2000, Champaign, IL: Human Kinetics.

Fitness Fuel #1

PE-4-ME Radical Wellness Program

Calorie Graph

Energy keeps our bodies going. A calorie is a measure of energy. Some bodies use more energy than others. And some activities take more energy than others.

• •

Ashley weighs 150 pounds. Meghan weighs 100 pounds. Read the chart below to find out how many calories each girl uses while doing the same activities. Then complete the double bar graph.

Calories used in 10 minutes

Activity	Meghan	Ashley
walking	27 calories	40 calories
skating	36 calories	54 calories
bicycling	54 calories	81 calories
canoeing	46 calories	70 calories

	Walking	**Skating**	**Bicycling**	**Canoeing**
90				
80				
70				
60				
50				
40				
30				
20				
10				
0				
	Meghan/Ashley	**Meghan/Ashley**	**Meghan/Ashley**	**Meghan/Ashley**

From *PE-4-ME* by Cathie Summerford, 2000, Champaign, IL: Human Kinetics.

Answer the questions by reading the graph on the previous page.

Ashley uses the most calories doing which activity?

_____

Meghan uses the least calories doing which activity?

_____

Which activity shows the greatest difference in calories used by Meghan and Ashley?

_____

_____

_____

From *PE-4-ME* by Cathie Summerford, 2000, Champaign, IL: Human Kinetics.

Fitness Fuel #2

PE-4-ME Radical Wellness Program

Nutrition Puzzle

There are different nutritional words in this puzzle. Find and circle the following words. Remember, the words can run up, down, backward, forward, and diagonally. Challenge yourself!

• •

```
X  M  U  N  C  H  I  E  S  K  L  M  P  I  U  U  A  Z  Q  I
W  O  K  F  U  R  S  U  G  A  R  S  M  V  C  P  K  A  B  E
P  P  L  N  Q  U  A  M  I  S  G  D  G  H  W  L  A  M  D  T
L  C  M  A  I  N  T  A  I  N  L  K  A  X  Z  E  I  U  A  W
S  U  S  L  I  A  U  W  U  L  N  G  S  I  I  N  I  I  O  N
N  S  Z  A  E  R  R  P  L  M  I  W  O  S  L  T  U  G  N  O
I  A  E  Y  U  I  A  G  C  V  A  R  I  E  T  Y  P  M  H  I
M  I  E  N  O  S  T  K  U  R  S  E  C  X  A  W  V  C  I  T
A  S  X  E  T  J  E  M  N  F  O  H  E  E  Y  O  I  P  N  A
T  U  W  N  B  I  D  I  E  T  O  M  K  R  A  W  C  R  U  R
I  O  P  O  F  D  F  F  T  O  K  O  N  C  T  G  K  J  T  E
V  S  S  E  L  B  A  T  E  G  E  V  D  I  N  B  R  F  R  D
J  K  F  R  U  I  T  S  K  L  N  B  W  S  O  N  B  E  I  O
L  P  C  N  B  K  I  R  E  U  S  F  L  E  T  Z  X  I  T  M
N  V  I  E  W  L  S  X  C  U  R  A  W  P  A  N  M  E  I  O
L  G  F  F  U  R  S  S  N  Y  H  T  L  A  E  H  P  O  O  S
H  D  I  E  T  A  R  Y  G  U  I  D  E  L  I  N  E  S  N  V
```

Eat   Maintain   Fat   Plenty   Grain   Exercise   Vitamins   Variety
Healthy   Diet   Nutrition   Vegetables   Sugars   Dietary guidelines
Foods   Weight   Saturated fat   Fruits   Moderation   Daily

From *PE-4-ME* by Cathie Summerford, 2000, Champaign, IL: Human Kinetics.

Name _____ Date _____ Period _____

Fitness Fuel #3

PE-4-ME Radical Wellness Program

Energy Expenditure Info

• •

Energy Expenditure by a 150-Pound Person in Various Activities

Activity	Calories used per hour	Activity	Calories used per hour
Rest and light activity	*50–200*	*Vigorous activity*	*over 350*
Lying down or sleeping	80	Table tennis	360
Sitting	100	Ditch digging (hand shovel)	400
Driving a car	120	Ice skating (10 mph)	400
Standing	140	Woodchopping or sawing	400
Domestic work	180	Tennis	420
Moderate activity	*200–350*	Water skiing	480
Bicycling (5 1/2 mph)	210	Hill climbing (100 feet per hour)	490
Walking (2 1/2 mph)	210	Skiing (10 mph)	600
Gardening	220	Cycling (13 mph)	900
Canoeing	230	Running (10 mph)	900
Golf	250		
Lawn mowing (power mower)	250		
Bowling	270		
Rowing a boat (2 1/2 mph)	300		
Swimming (1/4 mph)	300		
Walking (3 1/4 mph)	300		
Badminton	350		
Horseback riding (trotting)	350		
Square dancing	350		
Volleyball	350		
Rollerskating	350		

Source: President's Council on Physical Fitness and Sports, "Exercise and Weight Control," (Washington, DC: U.S. Government Printing Office, 1979).

From *PE-4-ME* by Cathie Summerford, 2000, Champaign, IL: Human Kinetics.

PE-4-ME Radical Wellness Program

Let's Do Lunch!

· ·

_____'s Place Menu

Sandwiches	Salads	Dinners	Desserts	Beverages

As the owner, chef, and server of your brand new restaurant, answer these questions. What is the name of your restaurant?

_____

Describe the menu at your restaurant. What kind of foods would you serve? Fill in the menu.

Describe at least four things that you as owner could do to make sure your customers get nutritious food.

_____

_____

_____

If you were to order something from your restaurant, what would it be and why?

_____

_____

_____

From *PE-4-ME* by Cathie Summerford, 2000, Champaign, IL: Human Kinetics.

Name _____ Date _____ Period _____

Fitness Fuel #4

 Radical Wellness Program

Healthy Hamburger . . . Is It Possible?

Can a hamburger be heart-healthy? To find out, draw a giant burger below. Answer the following questions as you create your masterpiece:

• •

Some hamburger sauces are full of unhealthy fat. What fats or oils could you use? Which are heart-healthy? Why?

_____

_____

_____

What are your favorite burger toppings? Which are heart-healthy? Why?

_____

_____

_____

A healthy burger includes items from the food guide pyramid. What are these groups? What hamburger ingredients belong to each group?

_____

_____

_____

How can you make your hamburger even more healthful?

_____

_____

_____

The food you eat is only half of the fitness balance. What is the other half? How can you develop it?

_____

_____

_____

From *PE-4-ME* by Cathie Summerford, 2000, Champaign, IL: Human Kinetics.

Fitness Fuel #5

 **PE-4-ME Radical Wellness Program**

Alien Label Connection

Aliens have landed at the local grocery store. After finding humans too bland, they have decided to buy some nice heart-healthy human cereals. But how will they find which ones are the most nutritious? Help your intergalactic friends read the food labels to answer these questions!

Study the label below. Then compare it to two other cereal labels to see which is best for your heart.

• •

1. You pour a bowl of cereal, then check to see how much is in your bowl. There are 2 cups. How many servings is that? _____

2. How much fat is in your 2 cups? _____

3. Is this cereal a good source of vitamin C? _____

4. The ingredients list is in order—most of the cereal is made of the first item, less of the second, and less yet of the third. What's the main ingredient? _____

   Is it heart-wise? _____

5. Fat often comes in oil, shortening, butter, or lard. Does this cereal contain any extra fat? _____

6. Is this a good cereal for your heart-conscious alien friends? _____

Extraterrestrial Cereal

NUTRITION INFORMATION PER SERVING

Serving size	1 cup
Servings per container	12
Calories	110
Protein	3 grams
Carbohydrate	26 grams
Fat	1 gram
Sodium	220 milligrams

PERCENTAGE OF U.S. RECOMMENDED DAILY ALLOWANCES (U.S. RDA)

Protein	4%	Vitamin D	10%
Vitamin A	25%	Vitamin B6	25%
Vitamin C	*	Folic Acid	25%
Thiamine	25%	Vitamin B12	25%
Riboflavin	25%	Phosphorus	25%
Niacin	5%	Magnesium	10%
Calcium	*	Zinc	10%
Iron	25%	Copper	10%

* contains less than 2% of the U.S. RDA of these nutrients

Ingredients: Whole wheat, wheat bran, sugar, raisins, almonds, natural flavoring, salt, corn syrup, coconut oil, and artificial flavor. BHA added to preserve freshness.

From *PE-4-ME* by Cathie Summerford, 2000, Champaign, IL: Human Kinetics.

It's time to investigate two other cereals.

	Extraterrestrial Cereal 2	Extraterrestrial Cereal 3
Serving size		
Fat per serving		
Extra fat or oil?		
Type of fat		
First ingredient		
Cholesterol-free?		
Heart-healthy?		

From *PE-4-ME* by Cathie Summerford, 2000, Champaign, IL: Human Kinetics.

Name _____ Date _____ Period ____

Fitness Fuel #6

 **Radical Wellness Program**

Eating What's Fit

Directions: What is your sports nutrition knowledge? Answer the following True/False statements by circling *T* for True or *F* for False. Give it your best shot! Who knows? You just may be more proficient at nutrition than you think!

● ●

T F 1. Protein is an athlete's most immediate source of energy from food.

T F 2. Protein cannot be stored in the body.

T F 3. If a person exercises regularly, he or she will become hungry more often.

T F 4. Drinking water during exercise is dangerous.

T F 5. It is possible for an athlete to lose five pounds of fluid during a single competition.

T F 6. Vitamin supplements are a necessary addition to any athlete's training diet.

T F 7. An athlete can get all of the nutrients he or she needs from a well-balanced diet.

T F 8. An athlete should always enter competitions with an empty stomach.

T F 9. Fat is stored in the muscles.

T F 10. Certain drugs improve athletic performance.

T F 11. Sugar is required to supply the extra energy needed by athletes.

T F 12. Athletes need more protein in their diets than nonathletes need.

T F 13. An athlete should not eat a vegetarian diet.

T F 14. A person shouldn't try a crash weight-loss diet during periods of increased physical activity.

T F 15. Salt tablets are one of the best ways to replace salt lost in sweat.

T F 16. Commercially prepared thirst-quenching beverages are the best to drink during exercise.

T F 17. Vitamins are found in almost every food.

T F 18. An athlete needs more of some minerals than a nonathlete needs.

T F 19. With regular physical exercise, food passes through the system at a faster rate.

T F 20. We burn more calories when exercising in hot weather than in cool weather.

From *PE-4-ME* by Cathie Summerford, 2000, Champaign, IL: Human Kinetics. Adapted from Butterick Publishing, A Division of American Can Company, 1979.

226

Name _____ Date _____ Period _____

Fitness Fuel #7

PE-4-ME Radical Wellness Program

Balancing Act

Directions: Fill in the numbers of the words or phrases that best complete each statement below. Answers 1-6 apply to the first blank in each sentence and 7-12 to the second blank.

• •

1. digest   2. muscle   3. mineral   4. dehydration
5. carbohydrates   6. calories   7. eat bananas
8. drink plenty of water   9. eat second helpings of healthy food
10. eat almonds   11. eat plain spaghetti   12. eat less fats and proteins

_____ are the nutrients burned first during exercise. An athlete's diet should be made up of about 60% of this nutrient. Starchy foods are high in this nutrient, which is why some athletes like to _____.

Magnesium, a mineral, helps to control _____ contractions and is lost through sweat. Meats, nuts, and grains are good sources of magnesium. To replace magnesium, an athlete might _____.

Before a game or race, it is important for an athlete to eat foods that are easy to _____ . Therefore, just before a race, an athlete might _____.

Fluid lost through sweating during hard physical exercise can lead to _____. To avoid this, it's important for the athlete to _____.

Potassium, a _____ found in fruits and vegetables, is released to carry heat from working muscles into the bloodstream and out of the body through the sweat and urine. Potassium shortages can cause fatigue and irritation. That's why many athletes _____.

_____ (food energy units) are needed in greater quantity by the athlete in training to maintain weight and total fitness. To make sure that he or she meets daily energy requirements, and athlete might _____.

From *PE-4-ME* by Cathie Summerford, 2000, Champaign, IL: Human Kinetics. Adapted from Butterick Publishing, A Division of American Can Company, 1979.

Fitness Fuel #8

PE-4-ME Radical Wellness Program

All Systems Go!

Directions: Ryan, a track sprinter, watches what he eats while training. His typical morning food and activity plan is filled below. Using Ryan's chart as an example, record your food intake and activities for one day. Include the time spent in each activity and the amount of food you eat, as well as the food group it comes from. At the end of the day, total the number of servings you ate from each food group and compare your totals to the number recommended for your age group.

● ●

Ryan's food and activity plan

Time	Activity	Foods eaten	Fruits	Vegetables	Breads/Cereals	Meats	Dairy
6:00	Run 30 min						
7:15	Breakfast	1 glass orange juice	1				
		1 cup oatmeal			1		
		1 cup milk					1
		1 slice toast			1		
7:40	Bicycling 2 miles @ 5.5 mph						
10:00		1 apple	1				
Total servings			2		2		1

My food and activity plan

Time	Activity	Foods eaten	Fruits	Vegetables	Breads/Cereals	Meats	Dairy
Total servings							

From *PE-4-ME* by Cathie Summerford, 2000, Champaign, IL: Human Kinetics. Adapted from Butterick Publishing, A Division of American Can Company, 1979.

228

Questions

Did you eat enough servings from each of the food groups? If not, what foods could you add to your food intake to meet the requirements for your age?

_____

_____

_____

_____

_____

What foods did you eat that were not in any of the food groups? Are these foods good for your fitness program? Why or why not?

_____

_____

_____

_____

_____

Did you go over any of the recommended food groups?

_____

_____

_____

_____

_____

How do you plan to adjust your food intake for better fitness?

_____

_____

_____

_____

_____

From *PE-4-ME* by Cathie Summerford, 2000, Champaign, IL: Human Kinetics. Adapted from Butterick Publishing, A Division of American Can Company, 1979.

Name _____ Date _____ Period _____

Fitness Fuel #9

 Radical Wellness Program

The "Wild and Crazy" *Chef de Haute* Cuisine

Directions: This recipe is a delicious and easy way to add good nutrients to your fitness program. Try the basic recipe and some of the suggested variations. Can you think of other variations? Complete part 2 on the bottom of the page.

Part 1: Wild and Crazy Wonder Shake (serves one)

	Calories	Protein	Fat	Carbohydrates
1 cup milk	150	8 g	8 g	12 g
1 banana	127	2 g	0 g	34 g
2/3 cup strawberries	37	0 g	0 g	8 g
1 cup nonfat yogurt	120	11 g	0 g	19 g
1 tablespoon honey or sugar	64	0 g	0 g	17 g
TOTALS	498	21 g	8 g	90 g

Blender: Chill fruit and milk. Place fruit in blender with 1/2 cup milk. Blend until fruit is very fine. Add remaining milk and other ingredients. Blend until smooth and creamy, 45-60 seconds. Serve immediately.

Electric mixer: Mash fruit. Mix in yogurt and honey. Gradually add milk. Beat until frothy. Serve chilled.

Variations: The shake can be a complete meal if you include a food from each of the food groups. Add or substitute one or two of the following ingredients: 1 cup nonfat ice cream; 1 cup orange juice; 2 tablespoons peanut butter; 2 tablespoons wheat germ

From *PE-4-ME* by Cathie Summerford, 2000, Champaign, IL: Human Kinetics. Adapted from Butterick Publishing, A Division of American Can Company, 1979.

Write your recipe below and fill in the quantity of each nutrient provided by your shake.

Shake name: _____

Ingredients	Calories	Protein	Fat	Carbohydrates
TOTALS				

Part 2: Pregame shake

Experts say that the meal before a game should be (1) easy to digest, (2) high in carbs and low in sugar, (3) low in protein, (4) low in fat, and (5) equal in volume to at least three glasses of fluid. How can you alter your shake?

_____

_____

_____

_____

From *PE-4-ME* by Cathie Summerford, 2000, Champaign, IL: Human Kinetics. Adapted from Butterick Publishing, A Division of American Can Company, 1979.

Fitness Fuel #10

 **PE-4-ME** **Radical Wellness Program**

Dying of Thirst?

Directions: Compare the nutritional value of a typical thirst-quenching drink and orange juice. Answer the questions below to compare the two thirst quenchers.

● ●

<table>
<tr><td>

THIRST-ADE

NUTRITION INFORMATION PER SERVING

Serving size .... 1 fluid ounce

Servings per container 4

Calories 64

Carbohydrates .... 16 grams

Protein 0

Fat 0

Sodium .... 130 milligrams

PERCENTAGE OF U.S. RECOMMENDED
DAILY ALLOWANCES (U.S. RDA)

Contains less than 2% of the U.S. RDA of protein, vitamin A, vitamin C, thiamine, riboflavin, niacin, calcium, and iron.

Ingredients: Water, glucose, sucrose, citric acid, salt, sodium phosphate, sodium citrate, potassium citrate, natural and artificial flavors, ester gum, and artificial color (contains FD & C Yellow No. 5).

</td><td>

ORANGE JUICE

NUTRITION INFORMATION PER SERVING

Serving size .... 8 fluid ounces

Servings per container 4

Calories 110

Carbohydrates .... 27 grams

Protein 0

Fat 0

Sodium 0

Potassium .... 480 milligrams

Contains 160% of vitamin C intake based on a 2,000 calorie diet.

PERCENTAGE OF U.S. RECOMMENDED
DAILY ALLOWANCES (U.S. RDA)

Contains less than 2% of the U.S. RDA of protein, vitamin A, calcium, and iron.

Ingredients: 100% orange juice

</td></tr>
</table>

Questions:

How are the two products different? How are they alike?

_____

Which product is more nutritious? Why?

_____

Which product would make a better pregame drink? Why?

_____

What could you add to plain orange juice to make it better to drink during exercise?

_____

From *PE-4-ME* by Cathie Summerford, 2000, Champaign, IL: Human Kinetics. Adapted from Butterick Publishing, A Division of American Can Company, 1979.

Name _____ Date _____ Period _____

Fitness Fuel #11

PE-4-ME Radical Wellness Program

Scrambled Words, Not Eggs

Directions: This word game will help you to understand important fitness vocabulary. Read the definitions in the left-hand column, then unscramble the words in the right-hand column. The words used in the puzzle are:

• •

DEHYDRATION   HYPERTENSION   HEAT EXHAUSTION
CARBOHYDRATES   ANEMIA   EVAPORATION   GLYCOGEN
AMPHETAMINES   HITTING THE WALL   CARBOHYDRATE LOADING

Carbohydrates are stored in the muscles in this form.   COYGNELG

Many athletes have a greater volume of blood than nonathletes
and may need more iron. Iron shortages can lead to this condition.   IAMANE

Another word for sweating; this process helps to cool the body
during exercise.   NOITPAROVAE

An expression athletes use to describe what happens when
muscles run out of stored carbohydrates and movements
become extremely painful.   TINHITG ETH LAWL

Taken by some athletes, these stimulants can be habit-forming,
and their use has been associated with heatstroke.   METAIENPSAHM

The quickest source of energy for the muscles.   ROBYRACHETDSA

A condition caused by severe losses of fluids through sweat.   NTRDYHADIEO

Before beginning an exercise program, one should visit a
doctor for a complete physical exam to detect problems
such as this illness.   NROHPETYESIN

A dietary practice calling for very high intake
of one nutrient, used to increase muscle endurance.   BOYRARHCETDA GLAOIDN

Too much salt draws fluid out of the body and
contributes to this hot-weather phenomenon.   EHAT XASTENUOHI

From *PE-4-ME* by Cathie Summerford, 2000, Champaign, IL: Human Kinetics. Adapted from Butterick Publishing, A Division of American Can Company, 1979.

Name _____ Date _____ Period ____

Fitness Fuel #12

 **Radical Wellness Program**

Interview an Athlete

Directions: It's time to interview an athlete. The athlete can be a professional, in college or high school, someone in your family, or one of your friends. All of us are athletes in one form or another. Use these questions to gather information.

• •

Name of person you interviewed

_____

Interview Questions

Do you watch what you eat, or do you eat anything you feel like?

_____

Do you prepare your own meals or snacks? Why or why not?

_____

_____

How much water do you drink a day? How does this vary for hot and cool weather?

_____

_____

Approximately how many calories do you eat a day? How do you keep track of them?

_____

_____

Do you try to decrease your fat intake? Your sugar intake? Your salt intake? Please explain.

_____

_____

Do you think a well-balanced diet affects performance in sports?

_____

Do you take vitamin supplements? Why or why not?

_____

From *PE-4-ME* by Cathie Summerford, 2000, Champaign, IL: Human Kinetics. Adapted from Butterick Publishing, A Division of American Can Company, 1979.

FF 4

Name _____ Date _____ Period _____

Fitness Fuel #13

PE-4-ME **Radical Wellness Program**

Our Bodies . . . Mean Machines

• •

List five benefits a person might expect to gain from a fitness program.

1. _____
2. _____
3. _____
4. _____
5. _____

List five myths about training diets and explain the danger of each.

For example: Myth—Never drink water during a game. Danger—The danger is dehydration.

Myth

1. _____
2. _____
3. _____
4. _____
5. _____

Danger

1. _____
2. _____
3. _____
4. _____
5. _____

From *PE-4-ME* by Cathie Summerford, 2000, Champaign, IL: Human Kinetics. Adapted from Butterick Publishing, A Division of American Can Company, 1979.

Name _____ Date _____ Period ____

Fitness Fuel #14

 Radical Wellness Program

Answer Sheet
for Fitness Fuel sheets #7, #8, and #11

Fitness Fuel #7:   F, T, F, F, T, F, T, T, F, F, F, F, F, T, F, F, T, T, T, T

Fitness Fuel #8:   5, 11; 2, 10; 1, 12; 4, 8; 3, 7; 6, 9

Fitness Fuel #11:

Thirst-Ade has more water, sugar, sodium, additives, and artificial ingredients than orange juice. The drinks have the same volume.

Orange juice: it contains higher percentages of the RDA for Vitamin C.

Orange juice: it is higher in carbohydrates and lower in sugar and sodium. Orange juice also contains potassium, which is depleted during exercise.

Water could be added to increase the fluid volume to three glasses.

From *PE-4-ME* by Cathie Summerford, 2000, Champaign, IL: Human Kinetics.

Name _____ Date _____ Period _____

Fitness Fuel #15

PE-4-ME Radical Wellness Program

You Choose!

Build your pyramid as strong as you can. Trade extras for food-group foods. Keep moving, keep fit—get at least 60 minutes of physical activity every day.

From *PE-4-ME* by Cathie Summerford, 2000, Champaign, IL: Human Kinetics. Originally published in *Exercise Your Options* by the Dairy Council of California, 1995, Sacramento, CA. United States Departments of Agriculture and Health and Human Services. See Howley and Frank's *Health Fitness Instructor's Guidebook*, p. 160, for an example.

Name _____ Date _____ Period _____

Fitness Fuel #16

 Radical Wellness Program

Food Record!

Once again, it's time to list everything you eat and drink in one day. Be sure to include the amounts. Later, you'll indicate the number of servings you had in each food group.

Foods (include the amounts you ate)	Milk and milk products	Meats, beans, and nuts	Vegetables	Fruits	Bread and grains	Extras
Example: two slices of cheese pizza						
Before school						
At school						
After school						
Dinner						
After dinner						
TOTAL SERVINGS:						

From *PE-4-ME* by Cathie Summerford, 2000, Champaign, IL: Human Kinetics. Originally published in *Exercise Your Options* by the Dairy Council of California, 1995, Sacramento, CA.

Name _____ Date _____ Period ____

Fitness Fuel #17

 Radical Wellness Program

Building My Pyramid

Fill in your pyramid using the "Total Servings" numbers at the bottom of your food record on the previous page.

• •

Milk and milk products: I need *4* servings.

   I had ___ servings.

   I still need ___ servings.

Meats, beans, and nuts: I need *2* servings.

   I had ___ servings.

   I still need ___ servings.

Vegetables: I need ___ servings.

   I had ___ servings.

   I still need ___ servings.

Fruits: I need ___ servings.

   I had ___ servings.

   I still need ___ servings.

Breads and grains: I need ___ servings.

   I had ___ servings.

   I still need ___ servings.

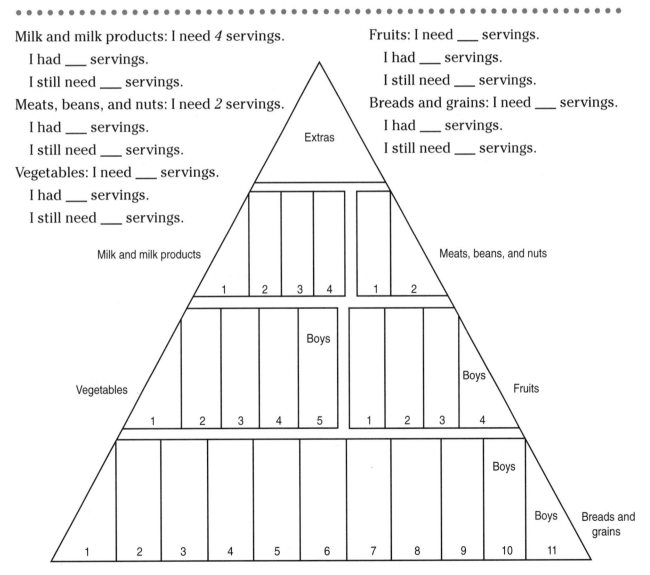

From *PE-4-ME* by Cathie Summerford, 2000, Champaign, IL: Human Kinetics. Originally published in *Exercise Your Options* by the Dairy Council of California, 1995, Sacramento, CA.

Just as each of us is unique, the foods that fill our pyramids are also unique. Everyone's pyramid probably contains a different number of servings of different kinds of foods.

Although our pyramids are different, we can all try to build strong pyramids. Building your pyramid may not happen all at once—especially if you have several missing pieces.

But even small changes can strengthen your pyramid and make a big difference to you.

Before considering your options, answer these questions:

1. Do I eat more extras than food-group foods?   YES   NO

2. Is there any food group in which I have no servings?   YES   NO

If so, which group or groups?

_____

_____

_____

_____

_____

3. In which group(s) do I need more servings to "build" my pyramid?

_____

_____

_____

_____

_____

_____

_____

_____

From *PE-4-ME* by Cathie Summerford, 2000, Champaign, IL: Human Kinetics. Originally published in *Exercise Your Options* by the Dairy Council of California, 1995, Sacramento, CA.

Name _____ Date _____ Period _____

Fitness Fuel #18

PE-4-ME Radical Wellness Program

How Much Is a Serving?

Two rules to remember: Most foods you eat count as one serving—glass of milk; piece of meat, chicken, or fish (about the size of a deck of cards); piece of fruit like an apple, orange, or banana; 1/2 cup of cooked vegetables; slice of bread; bowl of cereal; 1/2 cup of rice or pasta—except when foods are combined with other foods, they often count as 1/2 or 2 servings.

- Meat toppings or fillings in a taco, burrito, or pizza equal 1/2 serving (meats, beans, and nuts).
- Lettuce and tomato on a taco or in a sandwich equal 1/2 serving (vegetables).
- Cheese in a mixed food equals 1/2 serving (milk and milk products).
- Tomato sauce equals 1/2 serving (vegetables).
- Two pieces of bread for a sandwich equals two servings (bread and grains).
- Milk on cereal equals 1/2 serving (milk and milk products).
- Any sandwich filling equals 1/2 serving (meats, beans, and nuts).

● ●

Milk and Milk Products
4 servings

Milk or chocolate milk	Pudding, custard, or flan	*Extras*
Low-fat or nonfat yogurt	Cheese	Cream cheese or sour cream
Cottage cheese	Ice cream or milkshake	Whipped cream
Ice milk or frozen yogurt		Butter or margarine
Hot chocolate		

Meats, Beans, and Nuts (Protein)
2 servings

Dry beans (pinto, lima, red, white)	Hamburger	Nuts or seeds
Fish or shrimp	Beef steak	Sausage, pepperoni, or
Refried beans	Pork chop	chorizo
Tofu	Ham	*Extras*
Chili	Tuna or chicken salad	Bacon
Eggs	Hot dog or corn dog	Beef jerky
Chicken or turkey	Peanut butter	Gravy

From *PE-4-ME* by Cathie Summerford, 2000, Champaign, IL: Human Kinetics. Originally published in *Exercise Your Options* by the Dairy Council of California, 1995, Sacramento, CA.

Vegetables (Vitamin A)
4 servings (girls); 5 servings (boys)

Fresh, frozen, or canned vegetables
Bok choy
Broccoli
Cactus
Carrots
Cauliflower
Green beans
Mushrooms
Okra

Peas
Potatoes
Spinach
Squash
Sweet potatoes or yams
Tomatoes
Vegetable juice
Vegetable soup
Salsa
Lettuce or salad

Tomato sauce or pizza sauce
Avocado
Hash browns
Potato salad
Extras
Fast food french fries
Pickles, olives, or relish
Potato or corn chips

Fruits (Vitamin C)
3 servings (girls); 4 servings (boys)

Fresh, frozen, or canned fruits
Apples
Apricots
Bananas
Cantaloupe
Grapefruit
Grapes
Kiwi

Oranges
Papaya
Peaches
Pears
Pineapples
Strawberries
Watermelon
100% fruit juice

Mixed fruit
Raisins or dried fruit
Creamy fruit salad
Extras
Jam or jelly
Fruit rolls or fruit snacks
Fruit drink or punch
Fruit gelatin

Breads and Grains (B vitamins)
9 servings (girls); 11 servings (boys)

Bread (whole wheat or white)
Rolls
Rice or grits
Spaghetti, macaroni, or other noodles
Oatmeal
Cereal
Rice sticks
Crackers

Tortillas (flour or corn)
Pizza crust
Hamburger or hot dog buns
Pancakes or waffles
French toast
Cornbread or biscuits
Mexican sweet bread
Muffins

Granola
Pasta salad
Extras
Pretzels or popcorn
Granola bars
Cookies, cakes, or pie
Toaster pastry
Donuts or pastry

Extras

Soft drinks
Syrup, honey, sugar
Mustard or ketchup
Candy
Salad dressing or mayonnaise

From *PE-4-ME* by Cathie Summerford, 2000, Champaign, IL: Human Kinetics. Originally published in *Exercise Your Options* by the Dairy Council of California, 1995, Sacramento, CA.

Fitness Fuel #19

 Radical Wellness Program

Where's the Fat?

Trading *Extras* for food-group foods provides you with more of the nutrients you need, but there's another bonus—trading *Extras* can lower the amount of fat you consume! That's right. Most of the fat we eat comes from *Extras*. So "trading in" an *Extra* food for a food-group food can really make a difference!

The Food List on pages 241-242 can also help you lower the fat in your good choices. In each group, the foods are listed according to fat content—the foods at the top of the list have less fat per serving than foods at the bottom.

So, where's the fat? In the *Extras* at the **top** of the pyramid and in the food groups at the **bottom** of each list!

The Options I Choose

Now you know what you *could* do to help build your pyramid, so what are you really going to do?

• •

Choose two or three things that you will do to improve your food choices. Remember, you can TRADE *Extras* and you can ADD servings.

1. I will _____

   (when?) _____

2. I will _____

   (when?) _____

3. I will _____

   (when?) _____

From *PE-4-ME* by Cathie Summerford, 2000, Champaign, IL: Human Kinetics. Originally published in *Exercise Your Options* by the Dairy Council of California, 1995, Sacramento, CA.

Name _____ Date _____ Period _____

NO ZONE #1

PE-4-ME Radical Wellness Program

Substance and Safety Survey

Directions: Answer the following survey questions the best that you can. Remember, you can go out to the Information Superhighway (that is, the Internet), the library, or any reliable source to answer the questions. Good luck!

• •

1. Smoking can cause
   a. heart disease.
   b. lung cancer.
   c. yellow fingers.
   d. all of the above.

2. Why is alcohol especially harmful to children?
   a. The alcohol ferments more quickly in smaller bodies.
   b. Children are more active.
   c. Children's bodies are still growing.
   d. Alcohol isn't especially harmful to children.

3. Chewing tobacco
   a. decreases the blood pressure.
   b. can cause cancer of the mouth.
   c. is harmful only if swallowed.
   d. has no effect on the oxygen level in your body.

4. Which of the following statements about steroids is true?
   a. They can cause boys to grow enlarged breasts.
   b. They can cause increased performance while requiring little training.
   c. Moody people who take them become more calm and stable.
   d. They are commonly smoked.

5. List two effects of alcoholism

   _____   _____

From *PE-4-ME* by Cathie Summerford, 2000, Champaign, IL: Human Kinetics.

6. If an advertisement suggests that "everyone" is drinking a certain beverage, what technique is the advertisement using?

    a. plain folks

    b. card stacking

    c. testimonial

    d. bandwagon

7. Which of the following is a common effect of cocaine?

    a. a lowering of the heart rate

    b. a pleasant feeling lasting for hours

    c. a short but intense high

    d. all of the above

8. How long do the chemicals in marijuana remain in the body?

    a. several days

    b. up to a month

    c. forever

    d. several hours

9. If you are being pressured by a group of friends to take a drink, and you find it hard to get a word in to suggest any alternatives, then the best thing to do is to

    a. single out one of your friends to talk with.

    b. take the drink.

    c. raise your voice until you get the group's attention.

    d. not say anything.

10. Name two kinds of consequences of using drugs

    _____

    _____

11. Suppose that you're taking a walk with your friend. All of a sudden you notice that your friend is lighting a marijuana joint and passing it to you. You don't want to take it because you don't think it's good for you, and your family doesn't allow you to use drugs. Your friend really wants you to smoke it, though. You want to keep your friend, you want to have fun, but you don't want to get into trouble. How sure are you that you could handle this situation?

    a. I would have a lot of trouble handling this situation.

    b. I'm not so sure that I could handle this situation.

    c. I'm pretty sure that I could handle this situation.

    d. I'm very sure that I could handle this situation.

From *PE-4-ME* by Cathie Summerford, 2000, Champaign, IL: Human Kinetics.

What exactly would you say to your friend? Be as specific as you can:

_____

_____

_____

_____

_____

_____

_____

_____

12. What are two ways that using drugs could affect your appearance?

_____

_____

13. What does it mean when we say that someone is dependent on a drug?

_____

_____

14. Name two drugs on which a person could become chemically dependent.

_____

_____

15. Following are the five steps of making friends, but they're in the wrong order. Put them in the correct order.
    a. Suggest something to do.
    b. Break the ice.
    c. Greet the person.
    d. Relax.
    e. Pick a good time.

16. Which of the following statements about living with alcoholic parents is false?
    a. Children don't cause alcoholism in someone else.
    b. Children can't cure their parents' alcoholism.
    c. Sometimes children can control their parents' alcoholism.
    d. The best thing that children of alcoholic parents can do is to take good care of themselves.

From *PE-4-ME* by Cathie Summerford, 2000, Champaign, IL: Human Kinetics.

17. Give two reasons why so many automobile accidents are caused by people who have been drinking too much.

_____

_____

18. If you're in a group, and everyone else wants to do something you think is unsafe, what are two good things you could do?

_____

_____

Write a short story about someone who could have made a very bad decision, but used refusal skills and made the right choice. What did they do? What were the consequences? Did they use strong refusal skills?

_____

_____

_____

_____

_____

_____

_____

Refusal Skills

Step	Reason	Key phrase
1. Ask questions.	To determine if a situation is likely to be trouble	e.g., "What are you doing after school?" or "Why do you want to do that?"
2. Name the trouble.	To make your friend think more seriously about the trouble	"That's a drug; that's not a good idea."
3. Identify the consequences.	To identify different kinds of consequences—legal, school, family, health, and personal consequences (e.g., moral or religious feelings)	"If I do that, I could be suspended from school," or "If I do that, my parents will ground me forever."
4. Suggest an alternative.	To let your friend know that the activity is being rejected, not the person	"Instead, why don't we go see a movie?" or "Instead, why don't we ride our bicycles?"
5. Don't use pressure if your friend doesn't agree.	To help the person using the skill to stay in control; to let your friend know that you are serious; to make the alternative sound fun or challenging; to give an opportunity for your friend to reconsider	"If you change your mind, call me at home," or "If you change your mind, I am here for you."

Answers: 16-c; 15-edcba; 9-a; 8-b; 7-c; 6-d; 4-a; 3-b; 2-c; 1-d

From *PE-4-ME* by Cathie Summerford, 2000, Champaign, IL: Human Kinetics.

NO ZONE #2

PE-4-ME Radical Wellness Program

Dear Ms. Advice

How would you answer a letter to Dear Ms. Advice?

• •

Dear Ms. Advice,

Every time I open up a magazine, I can't help but notice all of the cigarette ads in it. I can't believe how everyone in the ads looks so happy, cute, thin, and popular, like they are having tons of fun. I've never wanted to smoke, but they sure look cool with all of their friends. What should I do?

Signed,

Popularity Desired

Dear Popularity Desired,

_____

_____

_____

_____

Do you have a question you would like to ask Ms. Advice? There is space below to write your question. After you write your question, find someone you are comfortable with, such as a family member, friend, or teacher. Ask that person to be Ms. Advice.

Dear Ms. Advice,

_____

_____

_____

_____

From *PE-4-ME* by Cathie Summerford, 2000, Champaign, IL: Human Kinetics.

Name _____ Date _____ Period _____

NO ZONE #3

Tobacco Quiz

Take this quiz to find out your tobacco score. For each statement, circle either *T* or *F*. Challenge yourself. The answers are on the back side of this page—try not to peek. After you find out your score, test your friends and family.

• •

T F   1. Twenty-five out of 100 high school seniors chew tobacco every day.

T F   2. It is safe to smoke a pipe or cigars instead of cigarettes.

T F   3. If you don't smoke much, it won't affect you.

T F   4. Chew (chewing tobacco) must be safe, because athletes use it.

T F   5. A little bit of snuff or chewing tobacco now and then won't get you hooked.

T F   6. Although smoking tobacco is not safe, dipping or chewing tobacco is safe.

T F   7. No one ever died from using chew.

T F   8. About half of all high school seniors smoke cigarettes every day.

T F   9. Tobacco can be sold legally to anyone of any age.

T F   10. If you smoke low-tar, low-nicotine cigarettes, smoking can't hurt you.

T F   11. You are not hurting anybody else if you smoke.

T F   12. It's easy to quit chewing or smoking tobacco.

T F   13. My friends use chew, and it's not hurting them.

T F   14. Not very many people die from smoking cigarettes.

T F   15. Quitting tobacco use won't make a person any healthier.

From *PE-4-ME* by Cathie Summerford, 2000, Champaign, IL: Human Kinetics.

Tobacco Facts

Answers to Tobacco Quiz

1. False. Very few people chew tobacco. Only 3 out of 100 high school seniors in America chew tobacco every day.

2. False. Smoking tobacco in any form increases your chances of getting cancer and heart disease.

3. False. Smoking damages your lungs with every puff. It makes your hands shake, your heart work harder, and turns your teeth yellow. The more you use tobacco, the greater your chances are for heart disease.

4. False. Chew can lead to mouth cancer, tooth loss, and gum decay. Many athletes are deciding not to use tobacco of any kind.

5. False. It is easy to become addicted to chewing tobacco. It contains lots of nicotine, just like cigarettes do, and quitting is very difficult.

6. False. Dipping and chewing tobacco are not safe. In fact snuff, a form of chew, contains 10 times as much of a cancer-causing agent as cigarettes.

7. False. Many people have died from cancer that was caused by chewing tobacco. A high school track star died at an early age because he used chew, which caused cancer of the mouth.

8. False. Smoking cigarettes has become unpopular! Only 19 out of 100 high school seniors in America smoke cigarettes every day.

9. False. In most states, it's against the law to sell tobacco to minors.

10. False. Even in low-tar, low-nicotine cigarettes, every puff contains toxins like lead, ammonia, formaldehyde, and poisonous gases like carbon monoxide.

11. False. Cigarette smoke can affect everyone around you, making their eyes water, their allergies act up, and their clothes smell for hours. Researchers are concerned that exposure to cigarette smoke increases the risk of lung cancer among nonsmokers.

12. False. It's hard to quit! Most people don't succeed in quitting their tobacco habit the first time they try.

13. False. If your friends use chew regularly, ask them to show you the spot in their mouths where they hold the tobacco. You'll probably see white patches or sores.

14. False. One out of every six people who die in America, die because of their cigarette smoking.

15. False. The minute a smoker or chewer stops using tobacco, the body goes to work healing itself. The healing begins when the tobacco use ends.

From *PE-4-ME* by Cathie Summerford, 2000, Champaign, IL: Human Kinetics.

Name _____ Date _____ Period _____

NO ZONE #4

PE-4-ME Radical Wellness Program

Poster Power

Make a poster that "Tells it like it is" about alcohol. You can make a poster that shows what alcohol really does to you, or you can make a poster that shows people having fun and being popular, cool, sporty, and other things because they *don't* drink alcohol. Use the back side of this page to make your poster. Use markers, pens, crayons—anything you like! Draw a sketch of your poster ideas in the space below. Have fun expressing yourself!

• •

From *PE-4-ME* by Cathie Summerford, 2000, Champaign, IL: Human Kinetics.

NO ZONE #5

 **Radical Wellness Program**

"Random Acts of Kindness" Survey

You, Me, and Our School

In this project, you will survey a friend, a family member, or a teacher and ask them about violence (or the lack of it) in our school.

• •

Person Interviewed

_____

Do you think there are people that bully other people in our school?

_____

Why do you think some people feel like they have to pick on other people?

_____

Have you ever been threatened at school?

_____

If you have been threatened, please explain.

_____

Has anyone ever offered you drugs, tobacco, or alcohol at school? Please explain.

_____

What do you think a "random act of kindness" would be?

_____

Has anyone at school ever been especially kind to you that you did not know? If so,

_____

Do you think our school should have a "Random Acts of Kindness" Day? How about a Week? Or a Year? Please explain.

_____

_____

Say No to Violence

From *PE-4-ME* by Cathie Summerford, 2000, Champaign, IL: Human Kinetics.

NO ZONE #6

 **Radical Wellness Program**

Protecting Yourself

The following tips could help prevent anyone from being a victim of an attack:

- Be aware of your surroundings, including who is in front of you and who is behind you.
- Don't walk alone, especially if you are upset or distracted.
- Walk on busy, well-lit streets.
- Walk near the curb, avoiding construction sites and parks after dark.
- If you feel threatened, cross the street, change direction, or run to a safe place.
- Always have money for a phone call.
- Have your house key, if needed, ready in your hand when you reach your house.
- Conceal your money.
- Carry a whistle or "screamer," or shout to attract attention if you are threatened.
- Do not invite a stranger to your house without permission.
- Harassment (persistent disturbance, torment, or pestering) is often a prelude to an assault.
- Don't answer back if someone harasses you.
- Don't wear a headset when out and about.
- Stand more than an arm's length (the length of an adult's arm, plus a few feet) away from anyone asking for directions.
- Notice details about any suspicious cars or people.
- NEVER get in a car with someone you don't know well enough to trust.
- Police officers and other uniformed personnel should always have identification, and don't be afraid to ask for it.
- Trust your instincts: if a person or situation makes you uncomfortable, that's reason enough to make a scene or to get away.

From *PE-4-ME* by Cathie Summerford, 2000, Champaign, IL: Human Kinetics.

References

Castruita, R.M. 1998. *From the County Superintendent.* Notes from Research, San Diego County Office of Education (Vol. 6, No. 2). San Diego, CA.

Covey, S.R. 1989. *The Seven Habits of Highly Effective People.* New York: Simon & Schuster.

Dennison, P.E. and G.E. Dennison. 1994. *Brain Gym.* Ventura, CA: Edu-Kinesthetics.

Hannaford, C., ed. 1995. *Smart Moves: Why Learning Is Not All in Your Head.* Arlington, VA: Great Ocean Publishers.

Howard, P.J. 1994. *The Owner's Manual for the Brain: Everyday Applications From Mind-Brain Research.* Austin, TX: Leornian Press.

Jensen, E., ed. 1998. *Teaching With the Brain in Mind.* Alexandria, VA: Association for Supervision and Curriculum Development.

Jensen, E. 1997. *Special Report #4: Movement and Learning.* San Diego, CA: Turning Point Publishing.

Jensen, E., ed. 1995. *Brain-Based Learning and Teaching.* Del Mar, CA: Turning Point Publishing.

Jensen, E., ed. 1995. *Super Teaching: Over 1,000 Practical Teaching Strategies*, 3rd ed. San Diego, CA: The Brain Store.

Faculty of the New City School, The. 1998. *Celebrating Multiple Intelligences: Teaching for Success.* St. Louis, MO.

Kirkpatrick, Beth and Burton Birnbaum. 1997. *Lessons From the Heart: Individualizing Physical Education With Heart Rate Monitors.* Champaign, IL: Human Kinetics.

Pert, C.B. 1997. *Molecules of Emotion: Why You Feel the Way You Feel.* New York, NY: Scribner.

President's Council on Physical Fitness and Sports. 1979. *Exercise and Weight Control.* Washington, DC: Government Printing Office.

Salk Institute for Biological Studies. 1999. Running boosts number of brain cells, according to new Salk study. *Recent News Releases* [Online] February 22. **http://www.salk.edu/NEWS/rungage.html** [October 22, 1999].

Sylwester, R. 1995. *A Celebration of Neurons: An Educator's Guide to the Human Brain.* Alexandria, VA: Association for Supervision and Curriculum Development.

U.S. Department of Health and Human Services. 1996. *A Report of the Surgeon General: Physical Activity and Health.* Washington, DC: Government Printing Office.